Contents

Preface

Study material

As you work through these units, you will need to refer to the following pieces of course material:

The set texts, viz.: Wordsworth, *Selected Poems*, ed. Walford Davies, Dent (Everyman's Library); Wordsworth, *The Prelude*, 1805 version, ed. Ernest de Selincourt, corrected edn. by Stephen Gill, Oxford University Press; Coleridge, *Selected Poems of Samuel Taylor Coleridge*, ed. James Reeves, Heinemann.

The critical anthology, *English Romantic Poets: Modern Essays in Criticism*, ed. M. H. Abrams, Oxford University Press, second edition: the sections entitled 'The Romantic Period', 'Wordsworth', and 'Coleridge'. (Referred to as 'Abrams'.)

The *Prose Booklet: Romantic Criticism* (the extracts from Wordsworth, Coleridge, Jeffrey and Hazlitt).

Spoken poetry on Cassette AC611 (read by Frances Horovitz and Gerard Benson). The poems of Wordsworth include 'There was a boy', 'The Solitary Reaper', 'Stepping Westward', 'Expostulation and Reply', 'The Tables Turned', 'Lucy Gray', 'Resolution and Independence', 'Strange fits of passion have I known', 'Three years she grew in sun and shower', 'She dwelt among the untrodden ways', 'A slumber did my spirit seal', lines 372–427 and 586–640 of *The Prelude*, Book I, 'Composed upon Westminster Bridge', 'To Toussaint L'Ouverture', 'Surprised by joy', and 'The world is too much with us'. Poems of Coleridge include 'This Lime-Tree Bower my Prison', 'Kubla Khan', 'The Pains of Sleep', 'Dejection: an Ode', 'Frost at Midnight', and 'Christabel', lines 1–68.

Radio Programmes 1–5, which go with these units: 'One Romanticism or Many?' (by Marilyn Butler), 'Ballads, Folksong and the Romantics' (by Thomas Crawford), 'The Radical 1790s' (by Kelvin Everest), 'Wordsworth and Memory' (by Christopher Salvesen), and 'The Overthrowing of the Mechanical Philosophy' (by Roger Sharrock).

Television Programme 2, 'The Romantic Poets in the Alps'.

How to use these units

We have designed the Wordsworth and Coleridge material with the following work-schedule in mind:

1 week's work *Introduction* and '*Lyrical Ballads*' (i.e. sections 1 and 2)

1 week's work *Coleridge as poet* (section 3)

2 weeks' work *Wordsworth's 'Prelude'* and *Imagination* (sections 4 and 5)

1 week's work *Dejection and Joy; Figures in a landscape; 'Housed in a dream, at distance from the Kind'; Wordsworth and Blake* (sections 6–9)

There is, however, no need to observe this work-pattern too strictly, so long as you study the material up to and including *Imagination* in the order in which it is presented.

The concluding four sections (*Dejection and Joy*, etc.) are, as you will see, more thematic in nature than the earlier ones and are intended to put Wordsworth and Coleridge in a wider perspective. They represent your first piece of comparative work, which will figure increasingly in the later stages of the course and in the examination.

4

THE OPEN UNIVERSITY
Arts: A Third Level Course
Units 4–8

Romantic Poetry

Wordsworth and Coleridge

Prepared for the Course Team by Simon Eliot, P.N. Furbank, Laurence Lerner,
Graham Martin, Brian Stone and Dennis Walder

The Open University Press

Cover: Engraving by Thomas Bewick (1753–1828), from Thomas and John Bewick,
Bewick Gleanings, Being Impressions from copperplates and wood block
engravings in the Bewick workshop, *Part I, Newcastle upon Tyne, Andrew Reid,*
1886. (Reprinted in 1800 Woodcuts by Thomas Bewick and His School, *Dover,*
1962)

The Open University Press
Walton Hall, Milton Keynes
MK7 6AA

First published 1984

Designed by the Graphic Design Group of the Open University.

Printed in Great Britain by Albert Gait Ltd., Castle Press, Grimsby.

ISBN 0 335 11227 7

This text forms part of an Open University course. The complete list of units in the course
appears at the end of this text.

For general availability of supporting material referred to in this text, please write to Open
University Educational Enterprises Limited, 12 Cofferidge Close, Stony Stratford, Milton
Keynes, MK11 1BY, Great Britain.

Further information on Open University courses may be obtained from the Admissions
Office, The Open University, PO Box 48, Walton Hall, Milton Keynes, MK7 6AB.

1.1

1 Introduction

(By PNF)

There is fairly general agreement that the joint arrival of Wordsworth and Coleridge on the poetic scene was a major event in our literature and culture. And it is convenient to date this arrival as 1798, the year in which they published their joint production *Lyrical Ballads*, or 1800, the year in which there appeared a much enlarged version of *Lyrical Ballads*, together with a long and controversial Preface. Shall we say that in 1798 or in 1800 Wordsworth and Coleridge 'began the Romantic Movement'? This would be extremely foolhardy, for about twenty different reasons. For one thing, are we sure there *was* a 'Romantic Movement', and if so, how did it manage to accommodate two such extraordinarily different poets as Wordsworth and Coleridge, let alone Byron who was contemptuous of Wordsworth? Or again, was there anything especially innovatory or revolutionary in *Lyrical Ballads*? And further, what shall we do about Blake, who published *Songs of Innocence* in 1789, nine years before the 'Movement' supposedly started? All these issues were raised by Marilyn Butler in Radio Programme 1, and we shall have to come back to them. For the moment I shall ignore them and shall continue about the 'major event', the arrival of Wordsworth and Coleridge. What can be said about it, again more or less beyond dispute, is that, chronologically speaking, it was the beginning of one of the greatest ages of English poetry (and not just of poetry, for it was the period of the novels of Jane Austen, Scott and Peacock, and the prose of Hazlitt, Lamb and Cobbett).

Another fact which may safely be asserted is that Wordsworth and Coleridge were profoundly affected by the French Revolution of 1789, the Revolutionary Terror of 1793–94, and the counter-revolution in Britain. And a further fact of a different kind is that the leading writers of this period were intensely aware of one another, and that *friendship* played a more important role in English literature then than ever before (and perhaps ever since). One needs to remember that in seventeenth- or eighteenth-century England you could scarcely hope to get on in the world without the aid of influence and of your 'friends', and this must inevitably have done much to poison the idea of friendship. Thus the famous friendships of Wordsworth and Coleridge and their associates, of Byron and Shelley, and of Keats and his circle have great historical significance. What had been born, you might almost say (of course, I am exaggerating), was the idea of free and disinterested intellectual friendship among equals. (Something not dissimilar was happening elsewhere and in the other arts also: Schubert's music was produced essentially for friends—for a circle of friends brought together by sheer love of music.) The fruits of this fact were manifold, and perhaps the most visible of all is that these writers wrote great poetry to one another and about one another. This is a point I want to come on to.

The growth of a friendship

But let me first briefly sketch the process by which Wordsworth and Coleridge came together in friendship. As a preliminary, will you now read pp. xiv–xvii of Walford Davies's introduction to your set text, Wordsworth's *Selected Poems*?

As Walford Davies shows, despite his family disasters William seems to have enjoyed an exceedingly happy boyhood and youth. (Indeed in 1812 he described himself as 'one of the happiest of men', saying that no-one had ever completely understood his poems, not even Coleridge—'He is not happy enough.') He was a vigorous, obstinate, self-reliant character, accustomed (from his schooldays on) to a hardy and frugal existence, and to some extent moulded by the Cumberland farming and labouring community, traditionally very independent in their attitude and not much overshadowed by 'great' houses and 'gentry' ways. (Conceivably Wordsworth's father had been too independent-minded for the Earl of Lonsdale.) In appearance he was lank and rather ugly, with a solemn expression disturbed by curious twitching around the lips. He had a great capacity for friendship, and as a boy, in several instances, became the boon companion of middle-aged men (one, an itinerant pedlar, figured a good deal in his verse). Equally, he had a great, perhaps even greater, capacity for solitude. From an early age he and his sister Dorothy were fanatical walkers, both in company and alone, and had a passion for natural things and scenes. This latter was evidently strengthened by the untimely death of their parents, and we receive a strong impression from Wordsworth's poetic dealings with landscape that for him natural forms like mountains represented maternal and paternal presences. One other curiosity of his psychology, again of importance to his verse, was that from childhood he was subject to trance-like states in which the outer world seemed to drop away from him and lose reality—so that he would have to clutch at some nearby object to remind him of material actuality.

As Walford Davies mentions, Cambridge University never meant much to Wordsworth, save as the place once inhabited by the poets Spenser and Milton. He did little work there, though reading sporadically for his own amusement. Here comes in a further trait: he had, at any rate by his own account, a great capacity for idleness—for which a more respectable name might be 'lying fallow' or (a phrase of his own in 'Expostulation and Reply') 'wise passiveness'.

The greatest event of his Cambridge years was that in 1790, during his last summer vacation, he and a friend made a walking expedition right across France and over the Alps into Italy. It was an extraordinary moment to be visiting France, not much more than a year after the outbreak of the French Revolution, and he and his friends—though as yet quite unpolitical in their interests—were swept up into the enthusiasm. As he wrote later in *The Prelude* (1850 version),

> . . . Europe at that time was thrilled with joy,
> France standing on the top of golden hours,
> And human nature seeming born again.

The experience was unforgettable; and next year, having graduated and possessing no particular plans for a career (he resisted family pressure on him to join the church), he gravitated back to France, where he now spent something over a year, mostly in the vicinity of Orleans and Blois. As a result, and partly through the friendly influence of a French army officer Michel Beaupuy, he became an ardent republican, even at one point seriously considering becoming an active revolutionary and throwing in his lot with the Girondist (moderate) party. He also at this time had an affair with a young Frenchwoman, Annette Vallon, daughter of a monarchist household, and had a daughter by her. He returned to England, leaving his mistress behind, in December 1792, a few weeks before the execution of Louis XVI.

He was by now a dedicated poet and, encouraged by friends, had given up thought of any other career. In 1791 he published two volumes of verse, *Descriptive Sketches* and *An Evening Walk*, conceived and partly written in France, and these attracted a certain amount of attention. Various friends gave him house-room and a little financial support, and early in 1795 he inherited £900 from a friend; and this enabled Dorothy and himself to realize a long-cherished dream of living together, and in September 1795 they settled at Racedown near the Dorset coast. Dorothy was intensely attached to William, indeed it would not put it too strongly to say that she was in love with him, and since they had temporarily taken guardianship of their friend Basil Montagu's young child, their *ménage* had many of the features of a marriage.

6

Wordsworth aged 35, drawing by Thomas Edridge, 1805. (Reproduced by permission of the Trustees, Dover Cottage, Grasmere)

One of the admirers of Wordsworth's *Descriptive Sketches* had been Samuel Taylor Coleridge. The two had various friends in common, moreover Wordsworth's younger brother Christopher had been in Coleridge's circle in Cambridge; so it followed rather naturally that, at about this period, an acquaintanceship sprang up between them. Will you now read pp. vii–xiv of James Reeves's introduction to the *Selected Poems of Coleridge*?

As you will have seen from Reeves's account, Coleridge's early youth had been an extraordinary mixture of the dazzling and the disastrous. The year 1796, with the fading of 'Pantisocratic' hopes, found him supporting himself as a Unitarian preacher and lecturer, meanwhile projecting a hundred different careers. His preaching was much admired, and indeed came naturally to him. (He once remarked to his friend Charles Lamb, 'Did you ever hear me preach, Charles?', to which Lamb, who stammered, replied, 'I nnn . . . ever heard you do anything else.' When in 1796 he launched a political-cum-literary journal *The Watchman*, the main reason why it so quickly failed was that Coleridge, in its pages, too incessantly *preached*, i.e. had no real *rapport* with his readers.) He was meanwhile acquiring a certain reputation as a poet, and his *Poems on Various Subjects*, published in April 1796, received favourable reviews. (The anonymous reviewer in the *Analytical Review*, June 1796, wrote that 'The general character of the composition is rather that of splendour than of simplicity; and the reader is left more strongly impressed with an idea of the strength of the writer's genius, than of the correctness of his taste.') By now he was married to Sarah Fricker and in need of a more settled home, and his friend and patron Thomas Poole, who lived in Nether Stowey in Somerset, came to their aid and installed the Coleridges in a cottage adjoining his own house.

Coleridge aged 23, from a crayon drawing by Robert Hancock, c. 1796. (Mansell Collection)

From here, in the following June (1797), Coleridge went on a first visit to the Wordsworths at Racedown. It was an immense success, both William and Dorothy being enchanted by Coleridge. 'His conversation teems with soul, mind and spirit,' Dorothy wrote to a friend (in an undated letter). 'Then he is so benevolent, so good-tempered and cheerful, and, like William, interests himself so much about very little trifles.' Within a matter of weeks after this, and again with the aid of the benevolent Thomas Poole, the Wordsworths had come to live at Alfoxden, in the vicinity of Nether Stowey, and the two families were visiting practically daily. It was in these circumstances that *Lyrical Ballads* was born.

Let us try to 'place' Wordsworth and Coleridge at this period. (There will be a more detailed 'placing' in Units 9–10.) First of all politically. England, where the French Revolution had at first been hailed with some enthusiasm, had since the days of the Terror entered into a phase of violent reaction and chauvinism; the country was at war with France, and Pitt's government had more than once suspended the Habeas Corpus Act, had conducted a witch-hunt for Jacobins (i.e. the followers of the French 'Jacobin Club', the most extreme of the French revolutionists), and had suppressed all the main radical societies. It was thus not surprising that, in Nether Stowey, both Wordsworth and Coleridge were rumoured to be dangerous Jacobins—the rumours even reaching the Government, which sent a spy to report on their activities. The reality was somewhat different. Neither was advocating revolution, let alone plotting it, though on the other hand they could still be fairly described as 'radicals'. This showed itself even in externals. Wordsworth wore his hair long and unpowdered, in radical style, and was careless and ungenteel in his dress. Coleridge flouted propriety by preaching in a blue coat and white waistcoat, instead of the conventional gown. Equally significant was the fact already mentioned, that they and their friends were confirmed pedestrians, doing most of their travelling by foot. This was a conscious challenge to *ancien régime*

8

values, which were symbolically associated with the 'cavalier' or horseman. Inwardly their political position was complicated and painful. Both had invested vast and generous enthusiasm in the Revolution; both had been bitterly chagrined at their country's declaring war on revolutionary France and were disgusted at the current suppression of freedoms. On the other hand, like many of their fellow-intellectuals, they had been shocked and thrown into moral bewilderment by the Terror. Wordsworth at the moment we are describing had just finished a tragedy, *The Borderers*, a powerful and agonized play, the theme of which was, according to a later Note, '. . . the awful truth, that, in the trials to which life subjects us, sin and crime are apt to start from their very opposite qualities'. The Note continues: 'During my long residence in France, while the Revolution was rapidly advancing to its extremes of wickedness, I had frequent opportunities of being an eye-witness of this process.' In reading this Note we must allow for the fact that it belongs to a much later period, when Wordsworth had become violently reactionary. Nevertheless the play itself gives us a vivid sense of his turmoil at this period, a turmoil evidently exacerbated by a sense of guilt at having abandoned Annette Vallon and his daughter by her. He was evidently on the verge of a serious break-down at this time; and his verse of the next few years, the work generally regarded as his greatest, can be seen from one point of view as an effort at finding rational grounds for *cheering himself up*. (I say this in no sense ironically, for he pursued the aim with great integrity, which explains the fact that readers all through the nineteenth century found Wordsworth their best support in cheering *themselves* up. For instance, it was by reading Wordsworth that the philosopher John Stuart Mill rescued himself from a nervous breakdown.)

Not much need be said here about the respective religious outlooks of Wordsworth and Coleridge. Wordsworth had been much influenced by the rationalism of William Godwin and was reputedly a 'semi-atheist' at this time, later moving (anyway in intention, but see page 136 below) towards a rather reactionary orthodoxy; Coleridge was a fervent Unitarian believer and eager theologian, but was before long to evolve a more transcendental brand of Christianity, which had much influence on the Oxford movement and nineteenth-century theology generally.

In character the two were in many ways opposites. Coleridge, though his career was to prove a tragic one, impresses one as in a way born for comedy. There were touches of a Dickensian hypocrite in him, and touches also of Dickens's Mr Micawber. A key to his character, perhaps, lies in a kind of playfulness. As a conversationalist, despite his sermonizing habits, he *played* with his listeners; and the best description of his amazing Notebooks is that they show a continuous and vertiginous play of mind, upon every possible topic. The point, and others I have mentioned, will become clearer if I quote some stanzas from a poem composed by Wordsworth in 1802, entitled 'Stanzas Written in my Pocket-Copy of Thomson's *Castle of Indolence*'. James Thomson's *The Castle of Indolence* (1748) was a fanciful poem written in imitation of Spenser, and in Spenserian stanzas (see Glossary); and Wordsworth, in imitating this imitation, pictures himself and Coleridge as inhabitants of a 'happy castle' (i.e. the Wordsworths' cottage in the Lakes). In serio-comic vein it depicts Wordsworth himself returning from roaming the countryside; he is pale and wan like a guilty or haunted man (in fact, of course, he has merely been writing poetry), and he lies for hours staring at the 'common grass' or sleeping 'like a naked Indian'. There follows a companion portrait of Coleridge:

> With him there often walked in friendly guise,
> Or lay upon the moss by brook or tree,
> A noticeable Man with large grey eyes,
> And a pale face that seemed undoubtedly
> As if a blooming face it ought to be;

Heavy his low-hung lip did oft appear,
Deprest by weight of musing Phantasy;
Profound his forehead was, though not severe;
Yet some did think that he had little business here:

Sweet heaven forfend! his was a lawful right;
Noisy he was, and gamesome as a boy;
His limbs would toss about him with delight,
Like branches when strong winds the trees annoy,
Nor lacked his calmer hours device or toy
To banish listlessness and irksome care;
He would have taught you how you might employ
Yourself; and many did to him repair, —
And certes not in vain; he had inventions rare.

Expedients, too, of simplest sort he tried:
Long blades of grass, plucked round him as he lay,
Made, to his ear attentively applied,
A pipe in which the wind would deftly play;
Glasses he had, that little things display,
The beetle panoplied in gems and gold,
A mailèd angel on a battle-day;
The mysteries that cups of flowers enfold,
And all the gorgeous sights which fairies do behold.

(*Poetical Works*, ed. Thomas Hutchinson/Ernest de Selincourt, page 85).

I find this, and the whole poem, most touching, as well as imaginatively shrewd; and, to me, equally touching is another poem, 'Extempore Effusion upon the Death of James Hogg', composed by Wordsworth thirty-three years later, when Coleridge, long estranged from him, was now dead, as was their mutual friend Charles Lamb, and when his own poetic powers were almost dried up.

. . . Nor has the rolling year twice measured,
From sign to sign,* its steadfast course,
Since every mortal power of Coleridge
Was frozen at its marvellous source;

The rapt One, of the godlike forehead,
The heaven-eyed creature sleeps in earth:
And Lamb, the frolic and the gentle,
Has vanished from his lonely hearth.

Like clouds that rake the mountain-summits,
Or waves that own no curbing hand,
How fast has brother followed brother
From sunshine to the sunless land!

(Will you look the whole poem up in your set text, pp. 213–14?)

It is very characteristic of Wordsworth to imagine his friends as powerful and untameable natural forces, rushing upon their own death. From this poem (as from William Hazlitt's memorable description of the Alfoxden household in 'My First Acquaintance with Poets'; see the Prose Booklet, pp. 40ff.) we gain the vividest sense of the extraordinary joy, energy and good feeling engendered by the two poets' friendship. For, the point is, their characters were not only opposite

* I.e. signs of the zodiac.

but complementary. Wordsworth, a very strong character, leaning towards harshness, supplied the solidity and stability that Coleridge always desperately needed; and this support seems to have been the indispensable condition for Coleridge's brief flowering as a poet. All Coleridge's few really fine and original poems belong to 1797 and the two or three years following. His 'Ancient Mariner' began as a joint effort between himself and the Wordsworths, on a day-and-night walk; and fittingly his very first truly characteristic poem, 'This Lime-Tree Bower my Prison', was a tribute to friendship, written at the time that the Wordsworths first arrived in Nether Stowey and were staying with Coleridge (Charles Lamb also being of the party) and before they had even moved into Alfoxden. Will you please look at this poem (page 18 in the set text) and listen to the cassette reading? The circumstances, as you will gather, were that Lamb and the Wordsworths had been sent off on a walk, to scenes minutely described to them by Coleridge, but he himself (suffering from a scalded foot) had been forced to stay behind, taking refuge in the lime-tree arbour in his friend Thomas Poole's garden.

Let us examine the poem a little. One is struck by how flexibly and effortlessly the whole thing is shaped: it is a long and involved train of thought, and there is a continuous rising up to the exalted and falling back into the conversational, and yet the whole seems to compose a single gesture of mind and feeling. But note that the poem has a 'plot'. Somewhere in the middle a crisis or change of direction occurs. Will you try to identify this, and jot down what this 'crisis', or turn in the argument, consists of?

Discussion

I was referring to the transition in line 43. The poet has been picturing more and more vividly and accurately the visual pleasures that his friend Lamb will be enjoying, though he himself is deprived of them, and has been urging Nature more and more fervently to provide Lamb with such pleasures ('richlier burn, ye clouds!'); and then suddenly, with a shock of pleasure, he realizes that he himself is *not* deprived of them. Imagination, combined with generosity on others' behalf, has enabled him to enjoy them just as much as if he had been physically present. Indeed, Imagination seems to have been working overtime, for whilst recreating the unseen hills, dell and waterfall, it has simultaneously been converting the poet's actual 'prison' into a most delightful entertainment, offering endless pleasure to the active mind. Granted sufficient Imagination, the poet does not even need to stir from his seat. The poem is thus a little inner drama, with a very definite and clear-cut plot, enacting a lesson about the Imagination—an experimental lesson.

For notice, finally, what the poet's imagination has most occupied itself upon, both in the distant scene and in the near-at-hand one: it is light—the play of light, the tricks that light plays (so that in the twilight the dark mass of the ivy makes the ash-trunks seem to grow lighter), and the way in which light can almost be said to be a creative power ('Live in the yellow light, ye distant groves!'). I mention this because Coleridge (as Wordsworth's 'Stanzas' remind one) was fascinated by optical phenomena—for instance by the familiar fact that, when one looks out of a lighted room, the image of the room imposes itself on the darkness outside, so that one cannot be sure what is image and what is reality. Such matters interested him because of their implication that the human mind is as much the creator of the world as it is a mere observer of it—a point which is discussed at length by Laurence Lerner in connection with Wordsworth, see pp. 84ff. And from here it is only one more brief step to a proposition of fundamental importance not only to Coleridge, but also to Blake, Wordsworth and Keats—viz. that the 'divine' or the 'holy' are not the antithesis of the 'human', and that one may say with equal truth that 'God' dwells in the external world and that 'He' dwells in the human breast and in Man's creative energies. It is a proposition or hypothesis that we shall keep coming across in this course under different disguises.

A colleague has pointed out to me a curious feature of this poem of Coleridge's, its constant repetition of words and phrases: 'roaring dell' (lines 9 and 10), 'ash' (lines 12 and 13), 'tremble' (line 15), 'gentle-hearted Charles' (lines 28, 68 and 75), etc. It strikes him as a weakness in the poem. What do you feel?

Discussion

I had not noticed the point myself previously, but having become aware of it, I am inclined to feel that the *three* 'gentle-hearted Charles' 's *are* a little clumsy— also perhaps having a touch of that unctuous or 'preaching' quality that sometimes came into Coleridge's voice. (Lamb himself protested vigorously to Coleridge: 'Substitute drunken dog, ragged-head, seld-shaven, odd-ey'd, stuttering, or any other epithet which truly and properly belongs to the Gentleman in question.') As for the other repetitions that I have mentioned, I would say that they serve a necessary function in the movement of the verse—providing, as it were, a prop or pillar to support the structure of that very long and over-arching sentence. One can think of them in cinematic terms. Coleridge has evidently (and characteristically) given his friends very strict instructions as to what visual experience *precisely* they should have in the dell; and his mental eye here focuses down, in distinct cinematic shots, from the dell itself to the ash-tree and then to the leaves on the ash-tree. As for the repetition of 'tremble', this needs no justification. It is essential to make Coleridge's point that the waterfall provides a *mimic* gale— another example of his imaginative response to all curious phenomena, and illusions, of *perception*.

2 'Lyrical Ballads'

'Lyrical Ballads' and its Preface
(By PNF and DW)

We come now to the *Lyrical Ballads*. Perhaps the first question that occurs is, why were they called by that title? Walford Davies's comment in the introduction to your Wordsworth set text (page xviii) is helpful: 'This is the paradox in the very title, *Lyrical Ballads*—with "lyrical" suggesting a *personal* interest in the emotions explored, and "ballads" indicating a measure of *dramatic* distancing.' Next, what impelled Wordsworth and Coleridge to write 'ballads'? The best way for you to form an opinion about this is by getting acquainted with one or two traditional ballads. There are (as suggested in Unit 1) two very large families of ballads: one, the medieval verse-tale, relating a tragedy of blood-revenge, infanticide or the like, and often supernatural in flavour; the other, the 'broadside' or broadsheet ballad, i.e. a ballad issued in printed form (on one side of a broad sheet of paper) and sung and sold in the street. Broadside ballads (a form which flourished well into the nineteenth century) were often comic or bawdy, and in general were more concerned with everyday (often urban) life than the medieval ballad.

This meagre statement about the two 'families' of ballads begs innumerable questions, but it may help just a little. Here is the medieval ballad 'Clerk Colven' (which, by the way, strikes us, as we hope it does you, as an amazing and haunting creation):

Clerk Colven

I

Clerk Colven, and his gay ladie,
    As they walk'd in yon garden green,
The belt about her middle jimp
    It cost Clerk Colven crowns fifteen.

II

'O hearken weel now, my good lord,
    O hearken weel to what I say;
When ye gang to the wall o' Stream
    O gang nae near the well-faur'd may.'[1]

III

'O haud your tongue, my gay ladie,
    Now speak nae mair of that to me;
For I nae saw a fair woman
    [That I cou'd] like so well as thee.'

IV

He's mounted on his berry-brown steed,
    And merry, merry rade he on,
Till that he came to the wall o' Stream,
    And there he saw the mermaiden.

V

'Ye wash, ye wash, ye bonny may,
    And ay's ye wash your sark[2] o' silk'—
'It's a' for ye, you gentle knight,
    My skin is whiter than the milk.'

VI

He's ta'en her by the milk-white hand,
    He's ta'en her by the sleeve sae green,
And he's forgotten his gay ladie,
    And he's awa' wi' the mermaiden.

VII

'Ohone, alas!' says Clerk Colven,
    'And aye so sair as akes my head!'
And merrily leugh the mermaiden,
    'O 'twill win on[3] till you be dead.

VIII

'But out ye tak' your little pen-knife,
    And frae my sark ye shear a gare,[4]
Row that about your lovely head,
    And the pain ye'll never feel nae mair.'

IX

Out he has ta'en his little pen-knife,
    And fraw her sark he's shorn a gare;
She's ty'd it round his whey-white face,
    But an ay his head it aked mair.

[1] Well-favoured (i.e. pretty) maiden.

[2] Shirt.

[3] Continue.

[4] Strip.

X

'Ohone, alas!' says Clerk Colven,
   'O sairer, sairer akes my head!'—
'And sairer, sairer ever will,
   And aye be war' till ye be dead.'

XI

Then out he drew his shining blade
   And thought wi' it to be her deid
But she's become a fish again,
   And merrily sprang into the fleed.

XII

He's mounted on his berry-brown steed,
   And dowie,[5] dowie rade he hame,
And heavily, heavily lighted down
   When he to his ladie's bower he came.

XIII

'O mither, mither, mak' my bed,
   And, gentle ladie, lay me down;
O brither, brither, unbend my bow,
   'Twill never be bent by me again!'

XIV

His mither she has made his bed,
   His gentle ladie laid him down,
His brither he has unbent his bow,
   — 'Twas never bent by him again.

(*The Oxford Book of Ballads*, ed. Arthur Quiller-Couch, page 126)

If you will look at the opening stanzas of Coleridge's 'The Rime of the Ancient Mariner' (pp. 21ff. in the set text), it will be obvious to you that, in a very broad sense, Coleridge is producing an imitation of this 'medieval' type of ballad. He was not the first to do so, for in 1765 Thomas Percy published a collection of ancient ballads and songs under the title *Reliques of Ancient English Poetry*, and this started a fashion for such imitations. We shall postpone further discussion of 'The Ancient Mariner' till later (page 37 below).

Will you now read Wordsworth's 'Lucy Gray' (page 48 in your set text) and listen to it on the cassette? Are there not some obvious resemblances to 'Clerk Colven'—for instance the style of this stanza?

> The wretched parents all that night
> Went shouting far and wide;
> But there was neither sound nor sight
> To serve them for a guide.

(Also, of course, some enormous differences, but these do not happen to be our concern here.)

Now please re-read the 'broadside' ballad 'Victory' discussed by Brian Stone in Unit 1, and then read Wordsworth's 'The Reverie of Poor Susan' (set text, page 1). Is there not, again, a distant resemblance, no doubt a conscious one, on Wordsworth's part—for instance in the jingling rhythm, and in the deliberately naive phrasing of 'And a single small cottage, a nest like a dove's,/The one only dwelling on earth that she loves'? There is a popular-song-like feeling to the whole thing. (And does not Blake's 'Holy Thursday' have a rather similar resemblance to a broadside ballad?)

---

[5] Dolefully.

14

Dove Cottage, Grasmere, from a drawing by Dora Wordsworth, the poet's daughter. (Reproduced by permission of the Trustees, Dove Cottage, Grasmere)

All we are trying to do is to make the point that, on the one hand, the title 'Lyrical Ballads' is meaningful (though obviously many of the poems in that collection—for instance, 'Michael' or 'Lines Composed a Few Miles above Tintern Abbey'—may not seem to have much connection with the ballad); and on the other hand, what Wordsworth and Coleridge are doing with the ballad form is something quite personal to themselves. Though there is one rather more specific point perhaps worth making: traditional ballads, whether of the medieval or broadside type, seem to imply or require music (singing to a tune or at least chanting to an instrument), whereas this is not the case with 'Lucy Gray' or 'The Reverie of Poor Susan' or even 'The Ancient Mariner'. And if so, then Wordsworth and Coleridge would seem to be basing their imitation upon what the ballad looks like on the printed page. The similarity seems to involve such features as repetition (of words and phrases) which can obviously be seen as well as heard.

Next, will you read the very informative account which Coleridge gave of the origin of *Lyrical Ballads*, in his *Biographia Literaria* (1817)? It is printed in the Prose Booklet, pp. 29ff.

At this point a warning is called for. It would be quite wrong to imagine that a taste for ballads, or an interest in 'the truth of nature' (or in simplicity, or the humanitarian) were unique to Wordsworth and Coleridge. They were, in fact, a familiar feature of the magazine poetry of the day. Thus it was not in this that they were innovators; and indeed what was truly innovatory and revolutionary in their work would have tended to escape the eye of contemporary readers. Robert Mayo makes this point well in an article 'The Contemporaneity of the *Lyrical Ballads*':

> . . . the reader of that day would tend to construe most of the contents of the *Lyrical Ballads* in terms of . . . modes of popular poetry, with which he was already familiar.

> He would, for example, if the poetry departments of the magazines are any index, regard as perfectly normal a miscellany of ballads on pastoral subjects (treated both sentimentally and jocularly), moral and philosophic poems inspired by physical nature, and lyrical pieces in a variety of kinds describing rural scenes, the pleasures of the seasons, flora and fauna, and a simple life out-of-doors . . .

> . . . the more one reads popular poetry of the last quarter of the eighteenth century, the more he is likely to feel that the really surprising feature of these poems in the *Lyrical Ballads* . . . is their intense fulfilment of an already stale convention. (pp. 71–72)

Will you now read the Preface to the 1802 edition of *Lyrical Ballads* (see Prose Booklet, pp. 10ff.) and the prefatory note in the Prose Booklet explaining how the Preface came to be written?

The Preface is a demanding piece of reading, and we shall have to spend a certain amount of time on it, but let us try immediately to apply certain of its points to the poems in your Wordsworth selection, to test some of the 'purposes' Wordsworth claimed for his poems.

> **. . . to choose incidents and situations from common life . . . and . . . to make these incidents and situations interesting by tracing in them, truly though not ostentatiously, the primary laws of our nature: chiefly, as far as regards the manner in which we associate ideas in a state of excitement.** (page 11)

The phrase 'the manner in which we associate ideas in a state of excitement' is at first sight rather obscure, and indeed there lies behind it a whole philosophical theory, known as 'Associationism', propounded by the philosopher David Hartley. According to Hartley, physical sensations of pleasure and pain become associated in our minds with things only indirectly related to pleasure and pain, and it is by this means that we acquire *intellectual* pleasures and pains and develop a moral sense. If this is true, then it is obviously very important to make the right impressions and associations early in life.

Wordsworth was much influenced by David Hartley, and, at the risk of over-simplifying a philosophical issue, let us draw your attention to the last stanzas of 'Strange fits of passion have I known'. (Please read the poem, set text, page 45, and listen to the cassette reading.) What Wordsworth is recreating here is actually a familiar phenomenon. The lover's mind, in the poem, is in a particularly receptive and sensitive state (as lovers' minds tend to be), and hence a quite insignificant event (the moon suddenly disappearing behind his beloved's cottage roof) sets off in him a powerful and disturbing train of 'association'. The sudden vanishing of the moon suggests, by association, *sudden death*, provoking in the lover an irrational pang of fear which rudely awakens him from his (perhaps dangerously cosy) daydream of love and security. — We seem to be not too far off in considering this an example of what Wordsworth is referring to in the phrase 'the manner in which we associate ideas in a state of excitement'. And at the same time, the familiarity of the phenomenon suggests that there is something 'primary' about the psychology which is revealed—something we all, perhaps, share.

What about some of the other *Lyrical Ballads*? Consider, for example, 'Anecdote for Fathers' and 'We are Seven' (set text, pp. 11 and 15). These poems illustrate, fairly plainly, Wordsworth's aim of making the incidents of common life interesting 'by tracing in them, truly though not ostentatiously, the primary laws of our nature'.

They suggest, moreover, the process by which the childish mind is formed. The poems have, though, often been criticized for their apparent triviality. Let us consider if this criticism is fair, or whether they are perhaps more than simple little 'case-histories', pressed into service to 'prove' a psychological theory. We will take 'We are Seven' first, if only because it became a wildly popular poem during the Victorian period (it was one of Dickens's favourites) but has since come in for a good deal of mockery and critical disdain. What is it about, and how successful do you think it is—in general, and in terms of Wordsworth's aims, as suggested above?

Discussion

The poem is about childhood, that much is obvious. The narrator tells of a chance meeting with an eight-year old 'cottage girl', that is to say, a girl from a rural labouring background. It is an encounter that could happen to anyone.

As it happens, Wordsworth based the poem on a meeting which took place on one of his walking tours in the west of England five years before its publication. The adult narrator stops to talk to her and asks, idly, as any adult might, how many brothers and sisters she has. She replies 'seven in all', but it emerges, while they converse, and the adult pursues his train of thought, that two of these seven are dead. The adult tries, naturally enough, to point out to the little girl that, if two are dead 'Then ye are only five.' But she refuses to take the point, and goes on stubbornly insisting they are seven, despite his attempts to dissuade her.

To many people, in Wordsworth's day and our own, this has seemed so much boring and childish nonsense. But one must take care about confusing the *account* of something childish, with childishness itself. Which means distinguishing between what the child and the narrator say, in the poem, and what the poem says. It is worth remembering that one of Wordsworth's major early works was a play (*The Borderers*): he was interested in *dramatizing* states of mind and character, and this is shown in a number of poems in *Lyrical Ballads*.

How might you defend the poem? A common Victorian defence was expressed in terms of a response to the little girl's 'natural' sense of the immortality of the soul; like Little Nell in *The Old Curiosity Shop*, she is imagined playing around the 'green' graves, an image with associations of growth, even resurrection, that contradict the physical facts. And one might even bring in, to support this view, the more well-known and later 'great' poem, 'Ode: Intimations of Immortality from Recollections of Early Childhood', in which Wordsworth addresses the child in that poem as 'Thou, over whom thy Immortality/Broods like the Day' (lines 119–20). Here we have (you might argue) a stage in Wordsworth's development of the view that there is a 'natural piety' in childhood, which we as adults lose, and need to pursue; an instinctive faith which we have lost, and can barely understand or grasp. Hence the puzzlement of the adult narrator in 'We are Seven'.

But, if we re-read the poem, do we find after all that that is what it says? Look especially at the last two verses. The thing to notice is that it is *the adult*, not the child, who uses the phrase 'in heaven', and who insists upon it. Moreover, it is the adult who is stubborn, almost exasperated, to find that he has been 'throwing words away' when he wishes to convince the child of his view, which is the familiar one that the dead survive in heaven. There is, to him, an astonishing matter-of-factness about the child's attitude, which 'simply' (only it does not seem quite so simple, now) accepts death, without fear or sorrow. Hence it does not trouble her to sit in the twilight and eat her supper in the graveyard near her home. Her memories are of the life she and her brother shared, not so much of his death:

> 'And when the ground was white with snow,
> And I could run and slide,
> My brother John was forced to go . . . '

The first verse of the poem in fact states its subject so clearly that it is easy to miss on a first reading:

> — A simple child,
> That lightly draws its breath,
> And feels its life in every limb,
> What should it know of death?

The child takes its feeling of life for granted, and is undisturbed by the idea of death. This is one of the 'primary laws of our nature', revealed by the child under the pressure of questioning. Wordsworth himself recalled (in a 'Note' to the 'Immortality Ode') that 'Nothing was more difficult for me in childhood than to admit the notion of death as a state applicable to my own being.'

In the Preface (page 11) Wordsworth warned his readers that they might 'frequently have to struggle with feelings of strangeness and aukwardness' as they read the poems in *Lyrical Ballads*; such poems, he anticipated, might not be considered poetry at all. Nevertheless, he was evidently quite confident of his judgement in writing and having published 'We are Seven': when a close friend tried to persuade him not to include it in *Lyrical Ballads*, on the ground that it could only harm his reputation and make him look ridiculous, he replied that it could take its chance.

'We are Seven' is, in a sense, a test case. But let us turn, now, to 'Anecdote for Fathers' to see if it confirms Wordsworth's purpose: to see if, once again, an apparently trivial, insignificant event yields some insight into the 'primary laws of our nature'. The poem is obviously comparable with 'We are Seven': it deals with a similar situation, in which an adult questions a child. This time the 'state of excitement' engendered by the pressure of the adult's questions leads the child to produce what is clearly a lie (the original sub-title was 'showing how the art of lying may be taught'): he would, he says finally, rather be at Kilve, because there's 'no weather-cock' there—an idea generated by the association suggested to him when he raises his head and catches sight of a 'broad and gilded vane' glittering upon the house-top. Clearly his father's persistence (subtly stressed earlier in the poem by the repeated gesture of catching his son's arm) has forced the child into an absurd and transparent lie, but *is* it only the boy who is absurd? What is the *tone* of the adult's words? Surely that of a rather pompous, obtuse man, who has been, in fact, sent up rather wonderfully by his son's blunt reply. The childish mind is not the only focus of Wordsworth's interest; but that of the adult, too. As William Hazlitt remarked in his essay on 'Mr Wordsworth' (*The Spirit of the Age*, 1825), 'the incidents are trifling . . . the reflections are profound'.

Hazlitt's response to the *Lyrical Ballads* was deeply appreciative: 'Fools have laughed at, wise men scarcely understand them,' he observed. Wordsworth's aim, in raising such trifling incidents of everyday life into the important subject-matter of his poetry, Hazlitt considered a 'levelling' impulse, connected with the 'revolutionary' movements of the age, and based upon a 'principle of equality'. This would, of course, not appeal to everybody; on the contrary. Wordsworth was taking a risk in writing about such subjects in such a way; but, as we have said, it was a risk he was evidently prepared to take—and to defend, as his Preface reveals. He knew what he was doing.

Each of his poems in the *Lyrical Ballads* 'has a purpose', he wrote. What was it?

. . . to follow the fluxes and refluxes of the mind when agitated by the great and simple affections of our nature. (page 12)

This observation he then explicitly related to 'The Idiot Boy', in which, as he put it, he traced 'the maternal passion through many of its more subtle windings'. But before we turn to that poem, let us look at another example, also mentioned by Wordsworth himself in the Preface—'Simon Lee' (set text, page 13). Does it suggest the movements of the mind 'when agitated by the great and simple affections'? What *are* the 'great and simple affections' expressed in this poem?

Discussion

The last lines of the poem take us to the emotional heart of it:

> — I've heard of hearts unkind, kind deeds
> With coldness still returning;
> Alas! the gratitude of men
> Hath oftener left me mourning.

'Gratitude' and 'mourning': certainly we are dealing with the 'great and simple' affections; but what is there in 'gratitude' to leave us 'mourning'? It's helpful, as with the preceding poems we've discussed, to consider the pose adopted by Wordsworth's chosen narrator, in order to understand the movements, the 'fluxes and refluxes' of the mind revealed in this poem, as they lead up to this strange and powerful conclusion. What we appear to have is a vigorous, healthy young man brought to contemplate his opposite, an elderly, weak and poor survivor of an earlier age, barely able to move, much less cut the tangled root of a rotten old stump—a job the young man is quick to execute for him. But before we get to that point, we have narrowly skirted, if not actually fallen into, some almost ludicrous feelings:

> An old Man dwells, a little man, —
> 'Tis said he once was tall.

Wordsworth is *deliberately* offering us the possibility of a laugh at the outset, so as to enable us to get over it, and accept the sobering 'reality' of the ordinary, the everyday, which, when deeply reflected upon (as Hazlitt suggested), reveals the more profound feelings of humanity. This does not mean that humour is banned; rather, that we should not rush to find it. The tone of the poem is what guides our responses; and this is by no means obvious or simple, as a careful reading soon suggests.

It is notable, for example, that the first and fourth verses reflect a serious irony about Simon Lee's position: the second reference to Ivor-hall is tellingly different from the opening:

> His Master's dead — and no one now
> Dwells in the Hall of Ivor;
> Men, dogs, and horses, all are dead;
> He is the sole survivor.

The rhyme-echo in 'survivor' and 'Ivor' is deliberate, and suggests that, although the high-flown associations of 'sweet shire' and 'pleasant Ivor-hall' are no longer, this man is still there, the lowly dependent, in his (the paradoxical phrasing neatly brings it out) 'liveried poverty'. The monosyllabic sombreness of 'men, dogs, and horses, all are dead' enforces the inextricability of the personal and the social. The old man's former vigour played its part in a world now gone. An *era* has been suggested by Wordsworth's serious, reflective tone. This connects with other poems in the sequence, other lonely figures, from 'The Old Cumberland Beggar' to 'Michael': what they seem to suggest is the underlying permanence of human emotions, in the midst of larger social changes. Simon Lee's memories, his reliance on his wife—these maintain a spark of life. By plumbing the depths of feeling, we plumb the depths of a situation too.

Notice, again, the play on 'kindness' in the poem. The ordinary, human 'kindness' offered apparently quite casually by the young man in the poem, is associated with that general human impulse to help another which makes us part of a common human*kind*. This provides some of the weight behind the concluding words: it's all too uncommon that 'kindness' should be offered, hence the sadness that even such a positive emotion as gratitude invokes. There is the further point, perhaps, that the stubborn old root is associated in our minds with the old man himself, waiting for the sharp axe of vigorous time to deliver him from his pathetic body—something the young narrator may not be aware of, but we are.

We come now to *language*. Wordsworth's choice of everyday and humble subject-matter inevitably involves an attitude to *language*. He was not oblivious of the life of the city, as that wonderful, later sonnet, 'Composed upon Westminster Bridge' (set text, page 115; recorded on the cassette), suggests. But it is in rural life that he finds what he most wants to write about to illustrate the generically human: 'low and rustic life was generally chosen' for the *Lyrical Ballads* because 'in that condition the essential passions of the heart find a better soil in which they can attain their maturity, are less under restraint, and speak a plainer and more emphatic language'. Such a language, Wordsworth felt, was a 'more permanent and a far more philosophical language' than that frequently used by other poets.

In the Preface, he proposed

> **to imitate, and, as far as is possible, to adopt the very language of men.** (page 13)

The language of poetry should be, he said,

> **a selection of the language really spoken by men.** (page 14)

What do these utterances mean? Let us see if a consideration of some aspects of 'The Idiot Boy' (with 'The Thorn', the poet's own favourite) helps explain. Please read 'The Idiot Boy' (set text, page 17) and consider, for example, the second verse: what is the narrator's tone, and which words, exactly, give us that tone? Are they appropriate to the subject of the poem?

Discussion

The tone is plain, straightforward: that of a simple person asking simple questions; and the words themselves are plain, simple, colloquial. 'Bustle' and 'fret', for example: good strong verbs which, reinforced by the repetition and rhyme we expect in a ballad, suggest the feel of ordinary, everyday speech, 'the very language of men', the 'language really spoken by men'. The subject of the poem could easily lend itself to a sensational, 'Gothic' treatment, a possibility the poet heads off, as it were, by means of a direct address to us, his readers, in lines 312–36 (page 25). Dropping the role of the narrator immersed in the tale he is telling, now that Betty's anxiety has reached a peak, he steps forward and puts to us the stale marvels of familiar 'literary' balladic discourse: Johnny and his horse roaming the high cliffs, or like a silent 'horseman-ghost' travelling along the valley, or even (most improbably, considering what we have heard of him so far, but the narrator tries it on us) turned into 'A fierce and dreadful hunter' or the galloping 'soul of evil'. The exaggerations imply the ironic paradoxical truth which, as Wordsworth goes on to reveal, is both more ordinary and yet more surprising. Betty finds Johnny safe. On their return home, Susan is better. And when the 'idiot boy' is asked what happened to him, his reply is:

> 'The cocks did crow to-whoo, to-whoo,
> And the sun did shine so cold!'
> — Thus answered Johnny in his glory,
> And that was all his travel's story.

The happy issue has its own strangeness, but it is a strangeness—the plain diction insists—inherent in the everyday. Under the stress of his situation, Johnny, like the children of 'Anecdote for Fathers' and 'We are Seven', has made odd associations, between cocks and owls, the sun and the moon, which reveal a perception of life quite different from our own: *that* is what is unexpected and surprising in his story, not any wild roaming in the trackless deserts of familiar fantasy.

Significantly, 'The Idiot Boy' aroused more hostility and incomprehension among critics and readers at the time than any other of the poems in *Lyrical Ballads*. Wordsworth was particularly distressed by the fact that Coleridge himself singled it out for damning attention. In *Biographia Literaria*, Chapter XVII (see Prose

Booklet, page 37) Coleridge described the mother as 'an impersonation of an instinct abandoned by judgement', that is, as an imitation of mother-love gone mad; furthermore, he remarked, the author had not 'taken sufficient care to preclude from the reader's fancy the disgusting images of *ordinary morbid idiocy*', so that overall what was presented was 'rather a laughable burlesque on the blindness of anile dotage, than an analytic display of maternal affection in its ordinary workings'. It is hard not to suspect that an important factor in Coleridge's surprisingly unsympathetic response to his friend's verse was the disgust engendered by the choice of such words as 'burr, burr, burr,' the boy's 'idiot' sounds, which Coleridge (and others who shared—and share—his view) would have preferred not to have thrust at him in a poem 'uncounteracted', as he said, by any 'description of the boy's beauty'. But Wordsworth prefers to give us exactly those words—or even sounds—which might offend what he himself referred to as 'false delicacy'. This is the language which 'truly' arises out of the characters and situation, and he does not flinch from offering it.

Of course, there are words in 'The Idiot Boy' which may seem improbable in the sense that we do not expect them to be in everyday use among people like Betty Foy: words such as 'quandary' (line 168) and 'prefaced' (line 182), for example. Similarly, the syntax does not pretend to follow *exactly* the patterns of everyday speech. But within the limits of the chosen ballad form, lines such as these at least echo fairly closely and convincingly the phrasing of ordinary speech. Wordsworth's claim is to use a *selection* of the language 'really used' by people. He reveals the emotions of ordinary people 'in a state of vivid sensation' to an audience presumed to be unfamiliar with their world, rather than merely imitating exactly or literally their diction.

As he put it in the Preface, the poet's task is to bind together 'by passion and knowledge the vast empire of human society, as it is spread over the whole earth, and over all time'. A vast ambition, you may feel, yet to make the inarticulate love of mother and son articulate, as he does in 'The Idiot Boy', for instance, at least hints at what is possible. For Wordsworth, the universal human feelings can and should be expressed; and they are given shape and form by drawing on that universal human reservoir of expression, language. For him, poetry originated in primitive utterances of passion which, through organic causes, were 'naturally' rhythmic and figurative. The earlier view had been, to put it crudely, that metre and figurative elements were primarily ornaments to heighten pleasure—'What oft was thought, but ne'er so well express'd', as Pope succinctly and memorably put it. But for Wordsworth and many of his contemporaries there is even a sense in which the distinction between prose and poetry was a false one. He suggests this in the Preface (see Prose Booklet, page 14), offering Gray's lines in the 'Sonnet on the Death of Richard West' as a case in point. The language of the lines of 'any value', such as 'my lonely anguish melts no heart but mine', does not differ from prose, whereas the other lines, which include such 'curious' elaborations as 'the smiling morning' and 'reddening Phœbus', are 'poetical' in a way he rejects.

That Wordsworth evidently uses *different* (rather than no) techniques should be evident. Repetition and 'plain' speech, even descriptive comparisons, are constantly deployed to great effect. You might like to read 'The Thorn', for example (set text, page 29), another of the longer narrative poems in *Lyrical Ballads*, and ask yourself how it achieves its effects. Is there any reason why the narrator keeps repeating his description of the thorn, and the place in which it stands? What is the significance of the comparison, in the first verse, 'Not higher than a two years' child/It stands erect, this aged Thorn'? (Remember how much Wordsworth conveys by means of a puzzled or puzzling narrator, in the poems we have already looked at.)

Wordsworth believed that once the poet had chosen his subject, the appropriate language, rhythm and metaphor would 'naturally' arise. From this it follows that it is essential to poetry that its language be the 'natural' or spontaneous expression ('overflow') of the poet's emotional state.

> **... Poetry is the spontaneous overflow of powerful feelings: it takes its origin from emotion recollected in tranquillity: the emotion is contemplated till by a species of reaction the tranquillity gradually disappears, and an emotion, kindred to that which was before the subject of contemplation, is gradually produced, and does itself actually exist in the mind.** (page 18)

The human, social sympathy with the common lot expressed in the poems we have on the whole referred to so far may seem to be contradicted by the more personal, individual emphasis of the process described by Wordsworth here. But 'Strange fits of passion' (already discussed from another point of view, see page 16 above) offers a rather neat example of the interrelationship of these sides of Wordsworth at this stage of his career. The first five stanzas are simple, narrative and pedestrian, as, according to Wordsworth's theory of poetry, they are quite entitled to be. But then, at stanza 6:

> My horse moved on; hoof after hoof
> He raised, and never stopped:
> When down behind the cottage roof,
> At once, the bright moon dropped.

One is aware of a quickening of feeling. That apparently meaningless or tautologous repetition, 'hoof after hoof', is oddly mysterious, even eerie; and the very careful placing of words in the last two lines creates tension and conveys a thrill of awe and fear. Now the fact that this is so exactly bears out Wordsworth's theory. In the course of writing the poem, the poet's 'tranquillity [has] gradually disappear[ed], and an emotion, kindred to that which was before the subject of contemplation, [has been] gradually produced'.

None of the poems in *Lyrical Ballads* is a mere, bald narrative; and none simply a lyrical outpouring of emotion. Most of them reveal a tendency towards either the 'ballad' or the 'lyrical', however; towards the 'objective', social world on the one hand, or the more 'subjective', inner world on the other. In general it was the second edition (1800) of the collection, revised and expanded by more than a third, in which may be found Wordsworth's more personal and inward poems, perhaps the most well-known of which are the so-called 'Lucy' poems, which include 'Strange fits of passion'. There is a new tenderness and intimacy about these poems which is very striking, and which bears out Wordsworth's notion that certain personal feelings, when recollected by the poet subsequently, come to re-exist in the mind.

There has been much speculation about the identity of the subject of the 'Lucy' poems, but there is no satisfactory evidence that she was a real English girl whom the poet loved, and who later died. It seems more probable that the subject is his sister Dorothy, although that would not explain her death. But perhaps this is being too literal-minded in any case; the 'death' may represent the death of feelings, rather than an actual death; and may refer to his affair with Annette Vallon ten years before, for example. What is known is that most of the poems were composed while Wordsworth was in Goslar with Dorothy in 1799. Goslar is in Germany at the foot of the Harz mountains, and brother and sister were forced to spend a severe winter there, isolated and alone in poor lodgings. They may well have spent much of their time reflecting on the past, and on their childhood together. Certainly it was there that Wordsworth began his great work about his childhood and its effect upon him, *The Prelude*. There is a sense in which the entire *Prelude* is about 'emotion recollected in tranquillity'.

But let us turn to another example, 'She dwelt among the untrodden ways' (set text, page 46). It seems simple, as simple as some of the other *Lyrical Ballads* we have mentioned. But is it? And where (if at all) does the poet's 'tranquillity' disappear, to be replaced by 'an emotion, kindred to that which was before the subject of contemplation'?

J. M. W. Turner, Buttermere with part of Cromackwater, Cumberland, a Shower. (*Tate Gallery, London*)

Discussion

To answer the second question first: there is a dramatic shift in tone in the penultimate line, isn't there: 'and, oh,/The difference to me!'? It is as if the gradual evocation of the 'maid' in all her strangeness and uniqueness is suddenly and shockingly overwhelmed by the reality of her death, which obliterates all else. The 'contemplation', the bringing into the present of past feelings, is not an easy or trouble-free experience: the pang of memory is sharp, because the original feelings themselves come back, and fill the consciousness. These lines are direct and unsentimental; not offering any false consolations, but 'facing' the plain facts.

Yet there is a curious, unresolved quality about the poem too. If the feeling of loss at its climax is clear and simple, the figure of the lost one is not, is it? Consider the first line: 'She dwelt among the untrodden ways'. It seems at first quite a simple, bald statement. But, why 'dwelt' instead of, for example, 'lived'? And what is the effect of 'among the untrodden ways'? That the subject of the poem should have 'dwelt' among 'ways' is unexpected, and suggests, by the use of semi-archaic, almost Biblical words, the image of a mysterious, secluded, innocent figure. 'Untrodden ways' is almost a contradiction, too: a 'way' is a path or road made by people walking or 'treading'; whereas 'untrodden' suggests something untouched and remote from people. There are other oddities, or ambiguities, about the poem. Consider the middle stanza: if the beauty of the violet is 'half hidden', it is also like the only star shining in the sky—something eminently visible and noticeable, surely? And what exactly does 'none to praise/And very few to love' mean?

There is a sense in which the subject of the poem is not so much a person, as a spirit—not necessarily supernatural, but an embodiment of certain feelings. The apparent simplicity of the poem has a Blakean tendency to suggest strong and deep feelings which it is hard, if not impossible, to pin down in any other words. Even the reference to a 'real' river in the second line is not what it seems: there are rivers of this name in Derbyshire, Yorkshire and Westmorland. Wordsworth clearly chose the name as much for its suggestiveness as for its English, Lakeland associations (and for its rhyme): 'the springs of Dove' suggest that the subject of the poem haunts the sources of peace, spiritual and emotional; moreover, that 'she' is not attached to only one place, but to a number—all those places, perhaps, which are remote, secluded, unknown and peaceful. She is a part of the landscape, of nature.

The first draft of this poem was sent in a letter to Coleridge from Goslar. Soon afterwards, in another letter, Wordsworth included the 'sublime epitaph' (Coleridge's words), 'A slumber did my spirit seal'. In this poem, the mysterious implications of 'She dwelt among the untrodden ways' were deepened, and the suggestion seems to be that 'She' has become completely identified with nature, with 'rocks and stones and trees'. But, again, it is difficult to tie the meaning of the poem down, and its power seems to lie precisely in its ambiguity and suggestiveness. Both poems, then, are far from 'simple'; they appear to deal with small, rather trivial and elusive feelings, but their indirectness and power relates them to the largest issues, to life and death and nature. There is much more that could be said about them, about how much of the meaning of the poems is carried by the simplest words, by straightforward syntactical devices, and so on; but the important point should once again be clear. Wordsworth's ambitions, as expressed in his Preface, are evident in the *Lyrical Ballads*. This would be a good moment to consolidate your work on *Lyrical Ballads* by reading the article on the subject by Paul D. Sheats in Abrams, pp. 133ff. Note that there will be further discussion of the 'Lucy' poems on pp. 95ff. below.

Lyrical Ballads may be described as only the beginning of Wordsworth's career, if a very substantial beginning. Let us now look at one of the largest and most impressive poems in it, 'Michael', which suggests directions in which Wordsworth was to develop. 'Michael' is sub-titled 'a pastoral poem', which places it in a long tradition of poetry, reaching back to classical times, about the moral worth of rural life and, in particular, of the shepherd's life. But it is an ironic title, since what we are given is an account of the breakdown of rural independence by misfortune brought about by the larger social and economic forces at work in late eighteenth-century England:

> The Cottage which was named the EVENING STAR
> Is gone—the ploughshare has been through the ground
> On which it stood; great changes have been wrought
> In all the neighbourhood . . .
> (lines 476–79)

If Wordsworth's poems seem to emphasize the dispossessed, the lonely, the vagrant, it is because he was registering a change in rural life as he witnessed it. This dimension is evident in a number of *Lyrical Ballads*, but especially in 'Michael'.

If we read, or re-read, 'Michael' (set text, pp. 62ff.), there is, isn't there, a new kind of narrative—can you identify what is new about it, compared to, say, 'The Idiot Boy'? Is it a matter of structure? Of how the poem is written? The verse-form?

Discussion

What may seem immediately striking is the *concentration* of effect here, for all that it is a poem of almost 500 lines. Partly, this is a result of the three-part structure of the poem: crudely, there is, to begin with, what one might call an address to the reader, in which the narrator points to the 'straggling heap of unhewn stones' that 'you might pass by,/Might see and notice not'; then there is the middle section, which tells the tale of Michael the shepherd, and the unfortunate circumstances which oblige him to send his beloved and only son away; and then a kind of coda, which returns us to the heap of stones, only now we know it to be the unfinished sheep-fold, the first stone of which had been laid by the shepherd's son. It has come to take on a human meaning.

'Michael' is in blank verse, unlike the other poems in the collection to which we have referred, but like 'Tintern Abbey'. As the example of Wordsworth's great predecessors, Shakespeare and Milton, had long before demonstrated, blank verse is a form of quite remarkable flexibility and range. Here it allows Wordsworth to 'tell a story'; but also to interweave the more personal reflections which, as we shall see, are to become more important for him than the social, or everyday. Can you identify an example, a passage from 'Michael' in which this happens? We would suggest lines 62–77: 'And grossly that man errs, who should suppose . . . The pleasure which there is in life itself.' It is the mind of man which comes to interest Wordsworth most, and in particular a sense of its largeness, its strength in adversity, its quality to survive—like a force of nature. This is what is strongest in the tale of 'Michael'; and it is what becomes a permanent interest in Wordsworth.

But—and it is a big 'but'—the minds of others, of the rural folk about whom he chose to write in *Lyrical Ballads*, were, he began to realize, of less interest to him than *his own mind*. If you look again at the opening section of 'Michael', you will notice, especially in lines 27–39, that Wordsworth reveals that it was by 'the gentle agency/Of natural objects' that he was led on 'to feel/For passions that were not my own . . . ' The 'heart of man, and human life', he was coming to realize, were to be discovered through his own past feelings; and indeed, it is *his* feelings, rather than the old shepherd's, which in the end are being offered to us as evidence

J. M. W. Turner, Lake Scene, Fallen Tree, *1800. (Tate Gallery, London)*

25

for the mind of man; *he* enters into the experience of others, as suggested to him by what he observes around him. Hence, the real events and emotions of his own life, referred to apparently only in passing here, become the massive study which is to issue in *The Prelude*. In and through the personal may be found the universal. And 'Tintern Abbey', a poem quite different in feeling from the narrative ballads, although at least anticipated by the 'Lucy' poems, shows him discovering this. We cannot read 'Tintern Abbey' in the same way as 'Michael', or 'We are Seven'; we cannot even read it in the same way as 'Strange fits of passion' or 'She dwelt among the untrodden ways'. It is a complicated, passionate and above all personal poem, quite remarkable, and unlike the rest of *Lyrical Ballads*.

'Tintern Abbey'

(By SE)

Please read 'Tintern Abbey' (set text, pp. 39ff.).

Wordsworth had first visited the Wye Valley during a solitary walking tour in August 1793. It was a period of great emotional stress for him. He had been obliged to abandon Annette Vallon in France, a lack of money forcing him back to England and away from the Revolution in which he had invested so much hope and so much enthusiasm. Since England's declaration of war on France in February 1793 he had sensed himself torn between his love of liberty and his patriotism, an anguish he was to explore in Books x and xi of the 1805 *Prelude*. He had not seen his sister Dorothy for over two years.

Wordsworth returned to the Wye with Dorothy in July 1798, after spending one of the most creative periods of his life at Racedown and Alfoxden in the company of Coleridge; the fruits of this period, in the form of *Lyrical Ballads*, were just about to be published.

Let us first consider lines 1–22. Like the traditional eighteenth-century topographical poem from which 'Tintern Abbey' springs, these early lines are packed with specific, concrete detail. Wordsworth's eye scans the landscape, cataloguing the sights from his vantage-point. This fact is very important, for we are never allowed to forget that these details are not the product of some disembodied eye but are the particular observations of the returning poet who occupies the 'foreground' of the picture.

> . . . and again *I hear*

> Once again/Do *I behold*

> . . . when *I* again repose/*Here*, under this dark sycamore, and *view* . . .

> Once again *I see*

One could almost use these early lines as a shooting script for a film, the camera starting in the foreground with Wordsworth and then tracking away from him into the middle distance or background, to be recalled once more to the foreground by another emphatic reminder of the observer's presence:

> The day is come when I again repose
> Here, under this dark sycamore, and view
> These plots of cottage-ground, these orchard-tufts,
> Which at this season, with their unripe fruits,
> Are clad in one green hue, and lose themselves
> 'Mid groves and copses. Once again I see . . .

Sometimes the detail is very precise; on one occasion we actually see Wordsworth in the process of correcting and sharpening his description. See if you can find it.

Discussion

The 'crispening-up' occurs in the lines:

> . . . Once again I see
> These hedge-rows, hardly hedge-rows, little lines
> Of sportive wood run wild . . .

It's not only in the precise cataloguing of topographical detail that Wordsworth resembles an eighteenth-century artist, for even his vocabulary here has an eighteenth-century ring to it—'sportive wood run wild' doesn't sound much like a line written by the author of the Preface to *Lyrical Ballads*.

Perhaps that last sentence was a little too emphatic. The imagery may well be comfortably eighteenth-century, the self-critical self-consciousness of that self-corrected line is not.

Although the poem begins with an auditory image, the predominant faculty is that of sight. Wordsworth 'hears' the 'inland murmur' but from then on the operative verbs are 'behold', 'view' and 'see'. It seems odd, doesn't it, that Wordsworth should give an auditory image pride of place at the beginning of the poem and yet not make any attempt to develop it through the next twenty lines? Take another look at the first twenty lines. Is it in fact the case that we get no further auditory information?

Tintern Abbey, engraved by J. Smith from a drawing by G. Holmes, 1807. (Mansell Collection)

Discussion

I think we do, though it's of a rather negative kind. We are told of the scene's silence. The one sound we are given is 'a soft inland murmur'. A murmur is itself a slight, wavering, indistinct sound; coupled with the adjective 'soft' it suggests something only just audible. The reader is thus alerted to the stillness and near-silence of the scene in which such faint, distant sounds can be heard. The other two auditory images are, as I have suggested, negative ones: 'the quiet of the sky' and 'wreaths of smoke'/Sent up in silence, from among the trees'. Note that the silence is particularly associated with the sky or things rising to the sky. The tracking camera of Wordsworth's attention moves not only outwards but upwards as well. It is noticeable that here, as in many of his other poems, Wordsworth's deepest spiritual experiences are often heralded by a sense of the stillness or silence of nature.

Did you notice, by the way, that seclusion, like quietness, runs like a thread through these early lines? Indeed, the two are often juxtaposed. There is, of course, the recurrent stress on the first person singular, which, when not counter-balanced by reference out to anybody else, can have a slightly oppressive, claustrophobic, isolating effect on the reader. As we have seen, the Wordsworthian 'I' occurs no fewer than four times in the first fourteen lines without the reader ever being offered an alternative or more disembodied view. The eye may drift out to the middle or background for a short while but, within a few lines, it will be brought up short with a specific time, place and person once more:

> . . . with the quiet of the sky.
> The day is come when I again repose
> Here, under this dark sycamore . . .

Apart from this, the seclusion theme occurs twice in this first section, both times coupled with images of silence:

> That on a wild secluded scene impress
> Thoughts of more deep seclusion; and connect
> The landscape with the quiet of the sky.

and

> . . . and wreaths of smoke
> Sent up, in silence, from among the trees!
> With some uncertain notice, as might seem
> Of vagrant dwellers in the houseless woods,
> Or of some Hermit's cave, where by his fire
> The Hermit sits alone.

'Well,' a critic might say, 'at least now we have a landscape inhabited by someone other than Wordsworth, we are losing some of that oppressive seclusion.' But are we? What is distinctive about the figures mentioned in these lines?

Discussion

The first thing one might say is that they are typical Wordsworthian figures in a landscape, examples of unaccommodated man: literally in the case of the vagrants who dwell in the 'houseless woods', and metaphorically in the case of the Hermit, who is, of course, himself isolated. The second thing to notice about these figures is that they are suppositious, for they are introduced by the phrase 'as might seem'. Unlike the Old Cumberland Beggar or the Leech-Gatherer, these figures hadn't been seen by Wordsworth; they are mere speculations. Amid all this welter of realistic detail the human characters who emerge at the end of this section are the products of his imagination alone. As his eye has tracked out to explore the landscape in front of him, so his imagination has followed, peopling it as it went.

In passing it is worth noting that, according to a number of contemporary sources, the landscape surrounding Tintern was far from under-populated. The smoke Wordsworth saw was almost certainly, as a contemporary guide book pointed out, from the fires of that most rural of industries, charcoal burning. Yet Wordsworth determinedly invents his own characters, which displace the real ones.

As has been said, the Romantic poets thought of the relationship of Man and Nature as a two-way process, and here we have an example of the poet's imagination colonizing the landscape. Can you now find an example, in this first section of 'Tintern Abbey', of the process working the other way round, of Nature influencing the poet's imagination?

Discussion

Take a look at lines 4–7. The syntax is a little confusing, but as a landscape can't have thoughts it must mean that the 'steep and lofty cliffs' give Wordsworth thoughts of a seclusion even more profound than the one he is observing.

These interpenetrations of the poet and the landscape prepare us for the change of mood and subject which occurs in the second section of 'Tintern Abbey'. It is to this we must now turn. What is the main difference between the section we have just been looking at and the material between lines 22 and 49?

Discussion

The most obvious difference, I think, is that all the specific detail of a real, physical landscape has disappeared and we are left with the effects that the memory of Wordsworth's first visit to the Wye has had upon him. In other words, in this passage the imagination has disconnected itself from nature and is now relating to the memory of a landscape rather than the landscape itself. This ability to recreate nature through memory and imagination is clearly very important to Wordsworth. Can you pick out what he has owed to the memory of this landscape?

Discussion

He lists three in an ascending order of significance:

1   Lines 27–30: it creates a feeling, strong enough to be physical ('felt in the blood'), which has a therapeutic effect on both body and mind, re-establishing tranquillity.

2   Lines 30–35: the suggestion that an unspecific general consciousness of nature teaches man a moral sense which operates automatically and unconsciously.

3   Lines 35–49: such memories can engender a trance-like state in which the burdens and confusions of our material world and bodily state are dissolved away and with a serenity of spirit we see through the surface of nature 'into the life of things'.

The most surprising thing here is the admission that it is only in this third grand and extreme state that the world seems intelligible.

> . . . that blessed mood . . .
> In which the heavy and the weary weight
> Of all this unintelligible world,
> Is lightened . . .

If this is the only state in which the world is rendered intelligible, then that fact must reflect back upon everything that has preceded it. The confident detailed description of the Wye Valley, the therapeutic calm and the subtle moral education offered by nature must be seen as surface phenomena of a world which for most of the time seems quite incomprehensible to the poet.

This might sound too gloomy an interpretation. After all, even if it is true, Wordsworth is claiming that ultimately, at least, in this third and highest state, things can be seen into and comprehensively understood. That surely is an heroically optimistic note on which to end this second section? It is, but now look at what follows immediately afterwards (lines 49–57). After the confidence of lines 41–49, how would you characterize this third, short section?

Discussion

It is one of doubt, and of a retreat from the high claims made in the previous section. Above all, it's a most unexpected piece of intellectual honesty. Until this moment 'Tintern Abbey' has looked like a conventional nature–philosophy poem which moves at a steady and stately pace from specific observations to grand, general statements of principle. But at this point progress is arrested, the confidence falters and the poem is revealed as something different and greater. We are not now, it seems, to have a neat, well-packaged presentation of Wordsworth's views, but rather a poem which explores the process rather than the end result of thought. The ideas in this poem are far from static; they are developed, questioned, doubted, re-formulated and doubted again. Nor are we witnessing just a clever intellectual game. Making sense of nature, spanning the gulf between man and nature, was a central concern for Wordsworth the man and Wordsworth the poet. This is what I meant by intellectual honesty. It is the power to 'see into the life of things' which Wordsworth most wants to believe in; it is, after all, the one gift from Nature which renders everything else 'intelligible'. But, by their very nature, such ecstatic visions are fleeting and are the proper subject for a rational mind's doubt and suspicion, particularly when recollecting in tranquillity. In 'Tintern Abbey', as in all the best Romantic poems, the poet's whole mind is engaged. Doubts, in part derived from eighteenth-century scepticism, and the sometimes desperate will-to-believe co-exist uneasily in this poem and force upon it that marvellous movement of, to use Wordsworth's own words, 'fluxes and refluxes'.

Wordsworth doesn't, of course, abandon all his claims for the power of Nature. Even if the final vision is 'a vain belief' he can nevertheless still find solace in his memories of the Wye Valley. The mention of this specific locale concludes the third part and seems to trigger the fourth part (lines 58–111), at least in so far as this next section returns the poet to the specific time and place at which the poem began. But he is not as he was. He is now assailed by the doubts and perplexities raised by the preceding lines, and these accompany the revival of the picture of the mind. 'The picture of the mind' itself, you will have noticed, accompanies, indeed, precedes the observer at the scene. In other words, what had been occasional and implicit in the earlier description of the Wye becomes constant and explicit now—the poet's mind and external nature are equal partners in the experience recorded.

> The picture of the mind revives again:
> While here I stand . . .

It's worth noting a couple of grammatical details here: first, the two partners in this romantic enterprise are separated by, and balanced around, a colon which keeps them distinct but close; secondly, the use of the word 'of' in 'picture of the mind'. The more usual phrasing would have been '*in* the mind'. But by using 'of' Wordsworth can have it both ways. The phrase as it stands means both a picture produced by the mind and someone's idea of what the mind is like. Wordsworth's theory of poetical diction, of the importance of ordinary, 'simple' language, did not, as some people have assumed, limit his vocabulary, for he was quite capable of using complicated words in a complex way when necessary. What it did do was encourage him to use some of the simplest words in our language—conjunctions and prepositions, for example—in unexpected, enriching ways; he makes apparently simple language work very hard indeed for its living.

The marvellous emotional mobility of 'Tintern Abbey' can be seen to full effect between lines 47 and 65, during which the poet moves from an ecstatic vision (47–49), through grave doubt (49–50), partial recovery (50–57) and uncertainty (58–61) to a growing sense of hard-won hope:

> While here I stand, not only with the sense
> Of present pleasure, but with pleasing thoughts
> That in this moment there is life and food
> For future years. And so I dare to hope . . .

Did you notice that it is at this precise moment, when the poet begins partially to recover his nerve, that for the first time the poem introduces the subject of the future? Before lines 64–65 it had been exclusively, almost oppressively, concerned with the present or the past. It is only a moment, for immediately afterwards the poem returns to retrospection, but it sows a seed which is to grow in importance as the poem moves to its end. But even at this moment of spreading hope Wordsworth's intellectual honesty will not allow either himself or the reader to rest in facile confidence. The poet doesn't just hope, he 'dares to hope', a much riskier and more self-conscious act.

Please read lines 65–111 again.

In this passage Wordsworth returns to the subject of the various types of relationship man can have with nature. He does this in a very personal and immediate way, by relating them to different stages of his own growth and development. In fact he describes three such stages. Take a little time and see if you can identify these, and jot down the characteristics Wordsworth associates with each.

Discussion

The poem does not list them in strict chronological order, for it sensibly starts from something already known by the reader, namely Wordsworth's first visit to the Wye. For the sake of the exercise we will list them in their 'proper' order:

1 When he was a boy his relationship with nature was like that of an animal's—physical and simple.

2 On his first visit to the Wye Valley he is more self-conscious than an animal, but the consciousness is emotional and sensuous, rather than intellectual, and it totally absorbs him.

3 On his second visit, his intellect comes into play: this, although it cuts him off from complete absorption in nature, allows him to see through nature to the forces and realities which underlie it.

Three things strike me in Wordsworth's description of his former state: its emotional ambiguity, its passion and its stoical honesty. Its passion is clear, I think:

> For nature then . . .
> To me was all in all . . .
>
> And all its aching joys . . .
> And all its dizzy raptures.

What about its ambiguity? Well, take a closer look at lines 72–85.

It may be pushing the argument too far to suggest that the exclusiveness of 'For nature then . . ./To me was all in all' is somewhat disturbing, although certainly its exclusion of humanity (unlike the third stage) might suggest a rather morbid, faintly escapist attitude. Certainly the use of that rather unexpected verb 'haunted' in line 77 darkens the otherwise ebullient mood. The near-oxymoron 'aching joys' perpetuates this undertow of ambiguity and is at the same time a very precise account of an experience, more common in those who are young, of a pleasure so intense and so high that it almost hurts. However, the feature that crystallizes this ambiguity occurs slightly earlier:

> . . . more like a man
> Flying from something that he dreads than one
> Who sought the thing he loved . . .

This could mean that the enthusiastic ferocity with which the younger Wordsworth threw himself into nature was so intense that it resembled something done out of extreme fear. Alternatively, it could mean that in 1793 Wordsworth's deep love of nature and his personal and political anguish were so intermixed that he was unable to tell whether he was running to Nature or away from Man. In fact it probably means both. It is certainly true, as you will find out when you read *The Prelude*, that Wordsworth's earliest, and in some cases most profound, experiences of Nature are as often coupled with fear as they are with joy, e.g.:

> In youth from rock to rock I went,
> From hill to hill in discontent
> Of pleasure high and turbulent,
>   Most pleased when most uneasy.
> ('To the Daisy': *Poetical Works*, ed. Hutchinson/de Selincourt, page 124)

What about stoical honesty? I think that it is expressed in Wordsworth's heroic acceptance that his intimate physical relationship with Nature, the one which, because it did not engage the mind ('no need of a remoter charm,/By thought supplied') and was untroubled by doubt, was gone forever. This admission of loss occurs early in the passage in a quiet, formal, controlled way:

> Though changed, no doubt, from what I was when first
> I came among these hills . . .

If this is all that honesty requires, it would be an easy virtue to accommodate within the poem. But it is not. Wordsworth must confront the confusing mixed motives that drove him to Nature, something he does in lines 71–72. Then comes the admission that he is so cut off from his earlier experience that even his art can't help him regain it:

> . . . I cannot paint
> What then I was . . .

Well, what was he? He was in that exemplary romantic relationship with Nature where the poet's feelings were so intertwined with the natural objects which caused them that it was impossible to say whether Nature was a part of Man or Man a part of Nature, where a mountain or a wood didn't just cause emotions but became the emotions themselves:

> . . . The sounding cataract
> Haunted me like a passion . . .
> Their colours and their forms, were then to me
> An appetite; a feeling and a love . . .

It is one of the great Romantic ironies that such states can be communicated only when they no longer exist. A self-conscious, self-critical intelligence is required for the writing of poetry, and it is clear that the intrusion of 'thought' is one of the things, perhaps the prime thing, which destroys such a state. Whatever the reason, Wordsworth had clearly lost that simple relationship with the landscape, and in the following lines he comes to a full and honest admission of that fact:

> . . . That time is past,
> And all its aching joys are now no more,
> And all its dizzy raptures.

Did you notice that the syntax is rather odd here? Why didn't Wordsworth say 'all its aching joys and dizzy raptures/Are now no more', or something to that effect?

Discussion

That hanging phrase, suspended out beyond the verb, is important. The two verbs are both punching home the reality of loss: 'time is past', 'are now no more'. The poignant 'aching joys' suggests the marvellousness of what has been lost but is controlled and 'rounded off' by the verb which follows it; an acceptance of loss is confirmed by the grammar. But then, just as everything seems neatly tied up, that second phrase bursts through as if Wordsworth couldn't quite hold it back. The grammatical oddity has also allowed Wordsworth to slip in that incantatory repetition, 'And all its . . . ' It is as if Wordsworth's determination to be honest to his feelings breaks through the well-mannered restraints of conventional grammar.

I wonder if, after this, one quite believes in Wordsworth's robust assurance of 'abundant recompense'? Certainly the elegiac tone of lines 83–85 belies the official claim that

> . . . Not for this
> Faint I, nor mourn nor murmur . . .

The following lines also help to qualify the tone of robust confidence:

> . . . other gifts
> Have followed; for such a loss, I would believe,
> Abundant recompense . . .

Look at the verb. It's not a straightforward assertion, 'I believe': the 'would' suggests an act of determination and will, implies a condition of belief which has had to be fought for.

This is not to suggest that Wordsworth was being dishonest when he asserted that his new relationship with nature offered 'recompense', but rather that the poem is being supremely honest in hinting that this recompense was achieved and sustained by an heroic effort of will in the face of acknowledged loss.

What does this new, mature relationship with Nature offer? How does it differ from the two states described earlier? Read lines 88–111 again and see if you can pick out some of the new features.

Discussion

The first thing that struck me was the intrusion of 'thought'. The fever has gone, and quietness and stillness and calm have come. In a sense this greater detachment was anticipated in the description of stage two. Did you notice the adjective which described the 'charm' brought by thought? It was 'remote'. Now the quietness of

33

the landscape, which was apparent at the very start of the poem, is converted into a moral quietism with a vocabulary to match: 'still', 'sad', 'chasten', 'subdue'.

As we should by now expect in Wordsworth's work, this stillness is a prelude to a moment of vision. Once more he is to describe that experience of seeing 'into the life of things', a combination of seeing deeper into Nature and seeing through Nature to something fundamental, something which 'interfuses', which runs through and binds together Man and Nature, everything that thinks and everything that is thought about. Did you notice, by the way, that Wordsworth, even at this moment of vision, keeps reminding us of the inevitably mixed nature of human experience? The 'joy' in line 94 doesn't 'move' or 'inspire', it 'disturbs' him.

Although Wordsworth is talking about a vision which seems to transcend Nature, he nevertheless uses images from Nature to express it. But it is a very different Nature from the one we were introduced to at the beginning of the poem. Look at lines 97–102. Look at the words on which the greatest stress falls. What features of his experience of the natural world is he now stressing?

Discussion

In three words: light, air, movement. They are all, of course, parts of the natural world, but they are so broad and so universal as to partake of the quality of abstracts, they are nowhere in particular and everywhere in general.

Did you puzzle about those unexpected adjectives in line 98? Why '*round* ocean' and '*living* air'? At this remarkable climax in the poem Wordsworth uses only one word that might be thought of as difficult—'interfuses'. All the others are simple; it is their unexpected combinations that allow them to carry so much meaning. An ocean is only 'round' when one views it on a global scale, which is the position Wordsworth wants us to view it from, as he is to go on to talk in almost universal terms:

> . . . And rolls through all things.

'Living air' might just mean air that gives the impression of being alive because it moves, but, given that we have been told that everything is interfused with a 'spirit', it is more likely that Wordsworth means us to take 'living' more literally. This, by the way, would not have seemed so peculiar to Wordsworth's contemporary readers as it does to us, for many of them would have had a smattering of classical learning, and Greek and Latin are full of references to the close connection between air and spirit, wind and the breath of God.

It is all part of Wordsworth's confidence in simple words' being able, given the right verbal context, to carry great meanings, that he works two other words in this passage very hard indeed. Which two words, and why?

Discussion

Between lines 97–102 'and' is used six and 'all' four times. The use of 'and' between each item in a list allows every item its full impact, particularly when the poem is read aloud; a comma, which is the alternative, allows elements in a list to be smudged over. The most important contribution that the repetition of both these words makes, however, is to offer a sort of grammatical model, or example, of what Wordsworth meant by 'interfuse'. The slow accumulation of those broad, magnificent aspects of reality in which the 'motion and the spirit' dwell gradually builds into a sense of a universe universally inhabited.

The occurrence of two other simple words in this passage deserves our attention. We are told of 'something' whose 'dwelling is the light of setting suns', etc. The last dwelling-place, we are told, is '*in* the mind of man'. This is what grammarians would call a false series, the preposition 'in' separating the 'mind of man' off from all the other, natural locations. In fact the 'in' marks the moment of another shift in the poem from outside nature to the mental interior of man, and prepares the reader for the dissolving of the divisions between mind and nature. When the poem dives into the 'mind of man', that mind is still grammatically distinct from the outside world; when the theme re-emerges two lines later, the mind and the object it thinks about are part of the same universal, unifying motion and spirit which 'rolls through all things'.

What about this extraordinary verb 'rolls'? As you read more of Wordsworth's poetry you will gradually become aware that, apart from imagery derived from the usual senses (sight, hearing, touch, taste, smell), Wordsworth employs a set of images based on what one might call a sense of certain physical forces, particularly of velocity and gravitation. This may sound obscure and silly but, when you have read 'Tintern Abbey', the first book of *The Prelude* and the 'Lucy' poems, try to list how many striking images you have come across based on the sensations of motion and balance, of turning, spinning and rolling, of dizziness and near-vertigo. I think you will be surprised at how many you find. Meanwhile, if you marry the global image of 'the round ocean' to a motion which 'impels' and 'rolls' you will get something very close to what I mean by a 'gravitational' image.

At this moment of visionary climax we might very naturally expect the poem to come to a triumphant conclusion. It does not. Instead, amazingly, it steps down and modestly returns us to the landscape we began with, though now fully acknowledging the 'interfusing', if I may borrow the word, of the senses and that which they perceive (although, interestingly, the 'mighty world' of the senses now takes precedence over the 'real' world which they perceive). With a return to the landscape comes a re-statement of the less ambitious claim that nature provides a sure foundation for morality. Here again, having returned us to a real landscape and a sound morality based on it, a self-respecting ode might properly end. But it does not; it sidesteps expectation and drives us off in a totally new direction. There are, it seems to me, two major differences between this last section and those which went before. Can you spot them?

Discussion

1 For the first time the poem broadens out to include another real human being, Wordsworth's sister Dorothy, who, we suddenly realize, had been there all the time but had remained unacknowledged until now.

2 The poem's emphasis shifts from a preoccupation with the relationship between present and past to a concern with the relationship between present and future.

The poem moves from its former to its final position by re-using some of its earlier material. For instance, after the first visionary moment of lines 35–49 we had Wordsworth stepping back and bringing everything into doubt once more with

> . . . If this
> Be but a vain belief . . .

Now, again after a moment of visionary confidence, we have Wordsworth falling back to a defensible position, rooting his security in the solidity of human affection. The doubt Wordsworth's poetic honesty forces him to admit to here is, however, of a calmer sort, less urgent, less threatening than the doubt in lines 49–50. The implication here is not, 'What if this is false?' but rather, 'It is not false, but it wouldn't matter if it were.' The vision is thus not so much denied as left to one side, suspended, while Wordsworth pursues a more immediate experience which is lodged in the relationship between himself, his sister and the landscape which surrounds them (lines 111–15).

What is this experience? It is fourfold, I think. First, in observing Dorothy's reactions Wordsworth can recapture something of his former relationship with nature. Secondly, as he has claimed before, they will share the benign moral influence of nature which feeds man 'with lofty thoughts'. Thirdly, when Dorothy has matured, the memory will provide 'healing thoughts' which will calm her spirit. Fourthly, if and when Wordsworth dies, he will live on in the memories engendered in Dorothy's mind, he will become an inhabitant of that landscape which is the fusion of memory and nature. Of course, these aspects are not as discrete as my crude paraphrase would suggest. They are all pulled together by being centred, not on Wordsworth, but on Dorothy and then on the two of them together in their common humanity.

I made a point, in discussing the previous section, of emphasizing the poet's determined honesty when describing his sense of the loss of a direct and immediate relationship with nature. Did you notice that, even in this final section where Wordsworth is opening out to his sister and to his future, he can't quite suppress the longing and the regret?

> . . . and in thy voice I catch
> The language of my former heart, and read
> My former pleasures in the shooting lights
> Of thy wild eyes. Oh! yet a little while
> May I behold in thee what I was once . . .

and

> . . . nor catch from thy wild eyes these gleams
> Of past existence . . .

Nor are we allowed to forget that most of life is not a rural idyll, and that Nature cannot be used as an escape. It can strengthen and console man, but it cannot change the human condition:

> . . . oh! then,
> If solitude, or fear, or pain, or grief,
> Should be thy portion . . .

(In passing notice how 'or' is doing the same job in this passage as 'and' was doing in lines 98–99.)

The final three lines of 'Tintern Abbey' are both complex and simple. If they combine Wordsworth, Dorothy, their memories of each other and of the landscape, they also do something very straightforward. They return the reader to the real Wye valley, to the

> . . . steep woods and lofty cliffs,
> And this green pastoral landscape . . .

from which the poem sprang. We return to

> . . . the very world which is the world
> Of all of us—the place where in the end
> We find our happiness or not at all.

But we return changed. Having understood the significance of the landscape to Wordsworth we see it through new eyes. In the words of T. S. Eliot:

We shall not cease from exploration
And the end of all our exploring
Will be to arrive where we started
And know the place for the first time.

As readers we too are now, like Wordsworth, 'revisiting' the Wye.

3   Coleridge as poet

Introduction

As has already been said (see page 11 above), Coleridge's main poetical output, and nearly all his most-admired poems, were the product of a very few years. The selection in your set text is arranged chronologically, and by the end of your work on this block you should have read your way through the whole *Selected Poems* at least once—if for no other reason, because the spectacle of Coleridge 'finding' himself as a poet is a fascinating one and reveals much about the situation of poetry in general in the 1790s. Also, for anyone with a feeling for the tragic, or tragi-comic, career of this extraordinary man, certain of the late poems and fragments—for instance 'Youth and Age' and 'Work Without Hope'—are moving personal documents.

We have already provided an account of 'This Lime-Tree Bower my Prison' (see page 11 above) and now proceed to a discussion of two poems of quite a different kind, 'The Rime of the Ancient Mariner' and 'Christabel', together with another of his 'conversation poems', 'Frost at Midnight'. Then, in the section on Imagination (pp. 98ff.) and again in the final sections of the block, we return to Coleridge and his ode 'Dejection'. (Note that our discussion of 'Dejection' requires you to read not only the version printed in your set text but also the much shorter version which Coleridge published: this latter version is to be found in the supplementary notes to the cassette readings from Coleridge.)

Do not forget to read the four essays on Coleridge's verse in the course anthology, Abrams (ed.), *English Romantic Poets*, or to consult the notes in your set text of the poems.

'The Ancient Mariner'

(By BS)

'The Rime of the Ancient Mariner' may well be the best-known narrative poem in English: its mystery and force have made it a 'natural' both for scholarly inquiry and for school treatment at various levels; and it has even been staged with success.

The version in which the poem is known, the one in your set book (pp. 21–44), is not the same as that originally published in 1798 as the first poem in *Lyrical Ballads* (the idea of which collection, by the way, was conceived after 'The Ancient Mariner' was written). The original version contained words of deliberately archaic vocabulary and spelling, as well as items of homely and gruesome detail, appropriate respectively to old ballad style and the late eighteenth-century taste for the 'gothick'. By 1800, influenced in part by hostile criticism, Coleridge had refined the poem a little. In *Sibylline Leaves* (1817), a later collection of Coleridge's poems, the epigraph from Thomas Burnet's *Archaeologiae Philosophicae* of 1692 appears for the first time, as in your set text, together with the prose marginal glosses and a few further textual changes. That the poem lived so continuously in its creator's mind gives it a personal significance which we must face, despite the risk of attaching undue autobiographical meaning to it.

The two key sentences in Burnet's Latin are the first: 'I can readily believe that in the sum of existing things there are more invisible beings than visible', and that beginning at 'Juvat'; 'Meanwhile, I do not deny that it pleases me sometimes to contemplate in my mind, as in a picture, the idea of a greater and better world: lest the mind, grown used to dealing with small matters of everyday life, should dwindle and be wholly submerged in petty thoughts.' And that takes us to the circumstances and ideas connected with the origin of the poem.

On 12 November 1797 Wordsworth, Dorothy and Coleridge set off on a walking tour along the Quantocks westward towards Watchet (the seaside village imagined as the home port of the Ancient Mariner) and onwards to Lynton, planning a poem on a supernatural theme, like the kind of German ballad which had lately become popular (in translation) in England. They wanted to earn a quick fiver to pay for their excursion by having it published in the *Monthly Magazine*, in which poems by Coleridge had already appeared. It was proposed as a joint work but, although the key idea, that of a sailor shooting an albatross and then suffering for his crime, was contributed by Wordsworth, the poem rapidly became Coleridge's sole responsibility, and he had written half the poem within eight days.

The first two editions of the poem, in 1798 and 1800, were prefaced by brief 'Arguments'. Perhaps you will consider what are the main differences between them? *1798*: 'How a Ship having passed the Line was driven by Storms to the cold Country towards the South Pole; and how from thence she made her course to the Tropical Latitude of the Great Pacific Ocean; and of the strange things that befell; and in what manner the Ancient Mariner came back to his own country.' *1800*: 'How a ship, having first sailed to the Equator, was driven by Storms to the cold Country towards the South Pole; how the Ancient Mariner cruelly and in contempt of the laws of hospitality killed a Sea-bird and how he was followed by many strange Judgements: and in what manner he came back to his own Country.'

Discussion

The main difference is the change from plain adventure summary, in which no 'strange' detail is given away, to a moralistic gloss which gives away the key episode. Like the Latin epigraph, like the prose gloss, the 1800 Argument heaps the poet's retrospective interpretation upon his own work: all these may distance you from the poem by pre-conditioning your reading of it. I personally find that they are true to the poem, but you must feel free to challenge them, or let them influence you slightly, if at all.

Prodigious reading by the untravelled Coleridge enabled him to envisage accurately and imaginatively the physical setting for his supernatural poem—such wonders as those now commonly known by children from television: Atlantic storms, the Sargasso Sea, the Roaring Forties, the frozen Antarctic, the vast emptiness of the Pacific, sailors' dread of being becalmed thousands of miles from land, the brilliance of tropical sun and moon and sky. In your first reading, which I suggest you reinforce by looking at James Reeves's fairly simple summary notes (pp. 136–39), go straight through the poem, allowing the verse, its forms, its setting, the narrative and its descriptive images, together with the progress of the Mariner's soul, to occupy your mind unencumbered, or at least not dominated, by 'interpretation'. That will rightly come later. As you go, lightly number the stanzas in each Part: that will make for easy reference later. *Now read the poem.*

Corposants (a kind of electrical discharge; cf. 'The Ancient Mariner', Part v, '. . . a hundred fire-flags sheen'), from Erasmus Francisci, The Wondrous Covering of Our Lower World, *Nuremberg, 1680. (Reproduced by permission of the British Library Board)*

I shall assume that, if this was your first acquaintance with 'The Ancient Mariner', you were struck, as many are, by three main things—the unerring rhythmical flow of the verse, the boldly graphic descriptions of scene and action, and the religious theme of sin and purgatorial progress towards atonement. Let us consider the first two to begin with, in relation to the poetic form to which Coleridge was avowedly responding in several compositions at the time—the ballad.

Quiller-Couch, the editor of *The Oxford Book of Ballads*, wrote: 'If any man, taking the ballad for his model, has ever sublimated its feeling and language in a poem . . . that man was Coleridge and that poem his *Ancient Mariner*.' 'Sublimated' is the word, because the poem is not as like a true ballad as Keats's 'La Belle Dame Sans Merci', which you read in Unit 1 (and to which we turn later in the course). In that poem, which we must yet recognize as a 'literary' ballad, to distinguish it from a true one, many of the features—progress entirely by dialogue, the subjects of magic and sexual passion, the characters of a knight and an enchantress, the brief and stark narration—are recognizably medieval.

In Coleridge's poem, instead of an unbending sense of fate dominating a tale of conventionalized characters, we have a complex and original spiritual sense of values dominating a character who suffers in an individual and sophisticated way. But the (considerably updated) 'language and feeling' are inspired by the model of the ballad.

It will help you now to re-read the ballad 'Clerk Colven' which was quoted on pp. 13–14 above. If you have access to the *Oxford Book of Ballads* you might also look at 'Sir Cawline' (page 14). (I mention the latter because Coleridge used its stanza variations, occasionally extending the four lines to five by doubling the third-line pattern, or adding a fifth and sixth, or even a seventh and an eighth, line on the pattern of the previous odd and even lines. Look at the third and fourth stanzas of Part II of 'The Ancient Mariner', and see how the subject-matter gains new emphasis, as well as completion, with the extra lines.) From those ballads you will get the idea that ballad is essentially story, and that ballad metre is the characteristic English form for popular verse story. Taking the work lightly, re-read Part I, and note what you think are ballad characteristics.

Discussion

✳ Here are a few such characteristics:

The narration of action is sufficient to itself—unexplained and unpsychologized (I think this is true of Part I only).

Dialogue is naturally set within the narration (stanzas 1–3).

Internal rhyming often features in the four-stressed lines (stanzas 2, 6, 7, 8, etc.).

Although there is detailed description, which one would associate with a more literary poem, it is presented as action narrative, its elements linked by the key continuator word 'and' of traditional oral story-telling (stanzas 11–14). Repetition is used as narrative link, and as intensifier (stanzas 1, 4, 5, and 10).

Such elements are found throughout the poem, and although no further exercises will be set on such strictly formal elements, it is important that you think about their effects as you study the poem. Before we leave Part I, here are stanzas 3 and 4 of the 1798 version, which were subsequently rejected. Can you suggest why?

> But still he holds the wedding guest—
>   There was a Ship, quoth he—
> 'Nay, if thou'st got a laughsome tale,
>   Marinere, come with me.'
>
> He holds him with his skinny hand—
>   Quoth he, there was a Ship—
> 'Now get thee hence, thou greybeard Loon!
>   Or my Staff shall make thee skip.'

The final version excludes all comic content, as well as the characterization of the Wedding-Guest, with the effect of concentrating attention on the Mariner and the spell-binding quality of the poem's opening.

Part I, the exposition, has given us a great double scene: one locally domestic, where the tale is told, and the other romantic and exotic, where the events of the tale unfold. We remain aware of both throughout the poem. The marvels of 'travellers' tales' will accommodate Burnet's ideas (remember the references to 'invisible beings' and 'a greater and better world'), and are measured against the common events of the English wedding scene. The Mariner having shot the Albatross in a sudden destructive fit, the natural and supernatural consequences follow in the rest of the poem, and we must selectively trace and discuss them.

A Strange Sight in the Element (*cf. 'The Ancient Mariner', Part II, '. . . The glorious Sun uprist'*), *from Gerrit de Veer,* The True and Perfect Description of Three Voyages, so Strange and Woonderfull, that the Like hath never been Heard of before, *Amsterdam, 1619. (Reproduced by permission of the British Library Board)*

To read a great poem is an experience from which we hope to gain a range of enriching meanings, rather than one overwhelmingly clear, single meaning. John Beer writes in *Coleridge's Poetic Intelligence* (page 147): ' . . . William Empson has remarked that if one is looking for the kind of practical moral action prescribed by the poem it is hard to get beyond the familiar Victorian "Don't pull Poor Pussy's tail, because God loves all his creatures." ' (Turn to the last stanza but two of the whole poem, which apparently supports that simplistic reading.) To penetrate to deeper meanings is hard, as Empson himself says, but it must be done; and it can be done, especially if one takes into account Coleridge's later opinion that such overt moralizing is a weakness in the poem.

To help you to do it, I assemble some biographical considerations which, if you wish to assess my selection or their validity, you may pursue with the aid of the appended bibliography.

'The quest for religious truth and the establishment of religious faith formed the master-current of his [i.e., Coleridge's] life.' (Basil Willey, *Samuel Taylor Coleridge*, page 11)

'Religious faith is an act of will, not of the understanding, thought Coleridge. The will is also involved in the awakening of Christian charity. The true philanthropist is one who has "encouraged the sympathetic passions till they have become irresistible habits".' (A. J. Harding, *Coleridge and the Idea of Love*, page 61, quoting from a lecture Coleridge gave in 1795)

'Night is my hell, Sleep my tormenting Angel. Three nights out of four I fall asleep struggling to lie awake—and my frequent Night-screams have almost made me a nuisance in my own House. Dreams with me are no Shadows, but the very Substances and foot-thick calamities of my life'. (Coleridge, *Unpublished Letters*; quoted by Whalley in *The Mariner and the Albatross*). Whatever else it may be, 'The Ancient Mariner', like 'La Belle Dame Sans Merci', is certainly a powerful nightmare.

In the repeated visions of horrific loneliness in the poem, we may find some reflection of the following: from 1794 until 1798 Coleridge was abused as a radical (especially so in *The Anti-Jacobin*) and accordingly was suspected of being a traitor by the local community, from which he was thus isolated, when he moved to Somerset just before starting work on 'The Ancient Mariner'. In addition, he was isolated from the radicals by his commitment to Christianity. Then, he had married Sara Fricker in 1795, and by the time he wrote 'The Ancient Mariner', he both knew that his marriage was a failure (largely, he believed, through his own faults) and yearned for the social harmony which he observed in the Wordsworth family.

A few more thoughts before you launch on your detailed reading of the rest of the poem. As we have implied, in the remark about 'Poor Pussy's tail', the shooting of the Albatross would hardly seem to deserve such prolonged and intense punishment as the Mariner receives. Why is it that a huge supernatural mechanism, which can even control the natural world, swings into action against the Mariner? If fantastic events in the poem may be taken as 'metaphorical or symbolical equivalents of psychological experience, or some form of visionary or imaginary re-orientation' (Harding, op. cit., page 60), what vision does Coleridge offer us? That is the main question.

Albatross, from the Cape of Good Hope, from Georges-Louis Leclerc, Comte de Buffon, Natural History of Birds, *vol.* x, *Paris, 1786. (Reproduced by permission of the British Library Board)*

As you ponder it during your reading, consider the following—not all of which I shall deal with specifically in my concluding discussion:

The various aspects of the physical world of the poem, and their relation to mental states and spiritual phenomena; the death, ghostly re-animation and 'final death' of the Mariner's fellow-sailors; the different supernatural persons, and their roles; the use and effect of the different narrative and moral perspectives as the tale unfolds (those of the poet, the Mariner, the Wedding-Guest, the sailors, the Hermit and his skiff-boat crew, the supernatural spirits, and the marginal glosses); the false end of the Mariner's penance (end of Part IV), and his continuing penance.

When you have completed your detailed second reading (and I suggest not till then), read the following discussion, which concentrates on Parts III–V and the ending of the poem.

Part II tells of the immediate consequence of the shooting of the Albatross. Nature, as if abhorring the act, suspends the beautiful animation of sea and sky, and turns the Pacific region into one of drought, 'slimy things' and nightly 'death-fires' (the characteristics of the Sargasso Sea usefully transferred from the Atlantic!). The ocean desert is Coleridge's most vivid symbolic scene of spiritual desolation and evil; another is the winter night-forest at the opening of 'Christabel'.

In Part III, with the arrival of the spectre-ship, the supernatural obtrudes visibly for the first time into Nature with a plan of apparently comprehensive punishment for the Mariner. His mates are all killed off, and the sound of their departing souls reminds him of the whizz of his cross-bow. But the eyes of the dead bodies stay open, to curse him in his loneliness, which makes him wish to die. That loneliness is there for the rest of the poem. It seems to me to mean, simply, spiritual rejection by both visible and invisible worlds.

Then, in Part IV, as so often in Coleridge's poetry, the Moon appears, to exercise *Christabel* beneficence (see the closing passages of 'The Nightingale' and 'Frost at Midnight'), and mighty relief comes with the Mariner's perception of beauty in the magical and moon-induced change in the appearance of the water-snakes.

It is worth looking at the detail of this important event (Part IV, stanzas 10–14). Consider its placing, the process within it, and the scenic and colour arrangements.

Discussion

It starts without warning, at a loathsome moment when the accursed Mariner wants only to die. The six lines from 'The moving Moon . . .' to ' . . . hoar-frost spread', the quietly thrilling movement in sky and sea with their implicit silver and gold, and the tranquil regularity of the verse, record a perception of extraordinary beauty. But the next three lines, to ' . . . a still and awful red', grimly recall the background of horror, In stanza 12, the Moon-colour is caught up in the movement of the water-snakes: 'elfish' reminds us that the experience includes the supernatural. Then the snakes with their lithe movements, which contrast with the previously 'rotting sea', transform the shadow of the ship, the base of horror, with their transmuted colours of 'Blue, glossy green, and velvet black', and finally and magically conquer the gloom with flashes 'of golden fire', which are of course powered by the Moon.

It is a crucial passage for the understanding of the poem. I think A. J. Harding's suggestion (page 42 above) is a good one. Freudian critics, for example, find sexual symbolism in the rearing of the water-snakes, and elsewhere. It also has its religious aspect. The Ancient Mariner can pray again, and with the real separation from the corpse of the Albatross, he would appear to be symbolically free, and hence purged of his guilt. Yet the redemptive significance of his apparently virtuous action in blessing the water-snakes is limited by the repeated 'unaware' (stanza 14) which governs it. Is it too easy an explanation of that illusion at the end of Part IV to say that nightmares don't end so simply? Perhaps nightmares simply don't end. That would help explain both the poem and Coleridge's lifelong preoccupation with it.

Let us return to that 'unaware'. It defines an action as sudden and unpremeditated as that of shooting the Albatross. But before the Mariner could pray, there was a spiritual movement in him—he perceived the exquisite order of creation as revealed and in part represented by the Moon. Note the lovely and significant gloss to stanza 10, which describes the Mariner's response to the 'greater and better world' of Burnet. 'Coleridge believed profoundly in a world which lay beyond human conception, and his way into it was through poetic or imaginative invention. What he could never *know* he could *imagine* out of the strength of his belief. So the spirit world that the Mariner accidentally reveals by shooting the Albatross is only an analogy for the poet's belief in that world' (Allan Grant, *A Preface to Coleridge*, page 124).

Thus to perceive a 'better world' only in the perspective of an abominable sin is peculiarly agonizing for the spirit; but it seems to be a common predicament of the religious. That experience is redoubled in Part V of 'The Ancient Mariner'. The bodies of the crew are re-aminated in ghostly style, but the wind which should healthfully move the ship is heard far off, not experienced by the Mariner and his companions. The latter are 'on the other side', and can be sweetly possessed by the beneficent spirits of the 'better world' (stanzas 14–17), while the sinning Mariner, excluded from that bliss though observing it, is relentlessly borne into a trance in which he hears his crime and future punishment spelled out by the Polar spirits (stanzas 23–26).

The ending of the poem At stanza 9 of Part VI, we are told in the gloss that 'The curse is finally expiated', but that is not my understanding; for in the very next stanza we have a terrifying image of the man aware of 'a frightful fiend' treading close behind him. And that fiend, it seems to me, is the force which impels the Mariner ever after to 'pass, like night, from land to land', compulsively telling his tale.

As the Mariner comes to the end of his narration, the sane and variegated natural world returns fully to the listener's consciousness (Part VII, stanza 18). The uproar of the other wedding-guests, the singing of the bride and her bridesmaids, and the vesper bell bidding to prayer, prompt a passionate yearning in the Mariner for the sociable joys acceptable to God from which he feels he will be for ever excluded (stanzas 20 and 21). The Wedding-Guest is so affected by the story that, at least for the time being, he too feels excluded:

> He went like one that hath been stunned,
> And is of sense forlorn:
> A sadder and a wiser man*
> He rose the morrow morn.

Thus, what purports by its title, structure and poetic processes to be a ballad about a sailor and the sea turns out to be the tragic testament of a sophisticated religious poet. Coleridge has been called 'the most notable practitioner of bad conscience in British letters' (Laurence S. Lockridge, *Coleridge the Moralist*, page 130). His poetry, memorable, shapely and controlled as the best of it is, expresses his sense of the waste of his mind and talents—for all that in other kinds of literary and verbal output (literary theory, criticism, letters, lectures, conversations with fellow-poets) that mind contributed more than any other to the Romantic movement in Britain. Right at the end, in his proposed epitaph, he referred to himself as one who 'Found death in Life', and asked for prayers that in his grave he might

---

* The old sense of 'sad' applies: serious, solemn.

Land of Ice, *from Friedrich Martens,* Voyage into Spitzbergen and Greenland, *Hamburg, 1675. (Reproduced by permission of the British Library Board)*

'find life in death'. You will remember that it was the Nightmare Life-in-death who successfully diced for the Mariner's soul (Part III, stanza 12). In the original version of 'Dejection' he wrote:

> Wherefore, O wherefore! should I wish to be
> A wither'd branch upon a blossoming Tree?

(i.e. upon the Wordsworths). That couplet was written in 1802. The note was constant. In 1825, the sad little poem 'Work without Hope' contains this:

> And I the while, the sole unbusy thing,
> Nor honey make, nor pair, nor build, nor sing.

Coleridge's own proposed remedy for his situation was love—the love that his Mariner failed to show the Albatross. He craved it himself, and believed that his faults—procrastination, drug addiction and so forth—hindered him in both the giving and receiving of love. 'The Pains of Sleep' (1803) ends thus:

> To be beloved is all I need,
> And whom I love, I love indeed.

Afterthought I mentioned Coleridge's prodigious reading. A book which illuminates the way Coleridge's 'shaping spirit of Imagination' (set text, page 101) transformed his reading and other experience into poetry is John Livingston Lowes's *The Road to Xanadu* (1927).

'Christabel'

(By PNF)

In the later eighteenth century there developed in Britain (and also in Germany) a taste for the medieval and the 'Gothick'. Certain distinct components in the taste soon became visible. There was, as has already been said, a keen interest in ancient ballads, stimulated by the publication in 1765 of Thomas Percy's *Reliques of Ancient Poetry*.[1] Then there was the related but separate fashion for the 'Gothick horror' novel, in which defenceless female victims are exposed to all

---

[1] Coleridge found the name 'Christabel' in the ballad 'Sir Cawline' in Percy's *Reliques*.

the terrors of 'medieval' oppression—are immured in castles and abbeys, complete with secret doors, dungeons and torture-chambers and haunted by headless nuns. You may perhaps have read Jane Austen's satire on this *genre* and its readers in *Northanger Abbey* (1818):

> 'But, my dearest Catherine, what have you been doing with yourself all this morning?—Have you gone on with Udolfo?'
>
> 'Yes, I have been reading it ever since I woke; and I am got to the black veil.'
>
> 'Are you, indeed? How delightful! Oh! I would not tell you what is behind the black veil for the world! Are you not wild to know?'
>
> 'Oh! yes, quite; what can it be?—But do not tell me—I would not be told upon any account. I know it must be a skeleton. I am sure it is Laurentina's skeleton. Oh! I am delighted with the book! ...'

Coleridge reviewed a number of such novels during the 1790s and he eventually became irritated with them, remarking wearily in a review of M. G. Lewis's *The Monk* in the *Critical Review* (February 1797): 'We trust ... that satiety will banish what good sense should have prevented; and that, wearied with fiends, incomprehensible characters, with shrieks, murders, and subterranean dungeons, the public will learn, by the multitude of the manufacturers, with how little expense of thought or imagination this species of composition is manufactured.'

Coleridge's 'Christabel' (set text, pp. 45–68; lines 1–68 are on the cassette) exhibits traits of both these fashions, or schools of writing, though I shall argue that in certain respects it is very different and perhaps could be considered the originator of a third school, of more lasting influence. It was certainly a most seminal poem. Walter Scott's 'medieval' verse was, on his own admission, inspired by 'Christabel'. Keats's 'The Eve of St Agnes', 'The Eve of St Mark' and 'La Belle Dame Sans Merci' show obvious signs of drawing upon Coleridge's poem. And more remotely it seems to be the ancestor of Tennyson's 'medieval' poems and of much Pre-Raphaelite painting and verse.

A point that is going to concern us is the fact that the poem is, anyway in a certain sense, incomplete and only a fragment. A curious history attaches to the poem. It is not quite certain when Coleridge began it. According to his own account in his Preface to the poem, he wrote the first part in 1797 and the second part in 1800, after his return from Germany; however, certain evidence suggests that he did not begin it till 1798 and after the writing of the 'Ancient Mariner'. More important, he once or twice spoke in letters of having written a lengthier poem than has survived. For instance he wrote to Thomas Poole (circa 11 October 1800) that it 'has swelled into a Poem of 1,400 lines'—which is more than twice the length of the published text. (However, he was not a notably truthful man.) The poem was not published till 1816, and he talked throughout his life of continuing it; and often in a tone which suggested that he knew, and had always known, how the story was to have gone on.

For an author to publish a poem that is incomplete, in this way—i.e. with the implication that he is unable to complete it—brings home to us an important truth, viz. that the writing of a poem, a complete one just as much as an incomplete one, is a process of discovery. The solution to an artistic problem does not come simply by deciding to solve it: it has to *found*, and sometimes it cannot be found—for reasons about which the artist may be as much in the dark as anyone else. (Though in the case of 'Christabel' we may say that a writer with less artistic conscience than Coleridge might have been tempted to fudge up a continuation and conclusion, knowing it not to be 'right'.)

But leaving aside the incompleteness, what about the poem as we have it, does it have *unity*? What is the relation of Part II of the poem, written a year or two later, to Part I? It is certainly somewhat different in 'feel'—for instance, the opening (lines 332–59) seems to be deliberately mocking the Gothick glooms and terrors of Part I. The sacristan tolling a knell for Christabel's dead mother becomes the occasion for a hearty and heartless joke on the part of the Devil, somewhat at the expense of our doleful tale; and the same sort of grim properties which were alarming in the night-scene reappear in lighthearted guise in Cumberland place-names—*Witch's* Lair, *Dungeon*-ghyll. Shall we regard this transition in tone as essential to the design of the poem? In a first draft of these units I said that it was, and a colleague attacked me, asking why was I so determined to find 'unity'. 'What the critic is supposed to do,' he remarked sarcastically, 'is to show the unity of . . . etc., and the reader used to literary criticism can see this coming several miles off; it's just a game.' I think he scored a point here, though what I am about to say may seem to show me reverting to the same error. It is that one can regard Part I of 'Christabel' as a complete poem, for all that it is so obviously an incomplete *story*. One can think of it as belonging, as you might say, to a certain *genre* of poems, the point of which is that they *pretend* to be incomplete. This is, at least how some of Coleridge's friends regarded Part I (Charles Lamb was quite angry with Coleridge for writing a Part II), and I find it possible to enter into their feelings. I love Part I, but when I ask myself what aspects of it are most unforgettable, the answer seems to be, not so much any episode in the story, as certain incidental—but evocative—lines. For instance the couplet 'She was most beautiful to see,/Like a lady of a far countrée.' In this, Coleridge is 'working' ballad-like naivety for all it is worth (and of course the fact that one feels this to be so stamps it as a sophisticated product of the 1790s and the Industrial-Revolution age), yet the lines seem beautiful and right, a subtle modern invention in an old mode. Or to take another example, the unobtrusive line 'And the Spring comes slowly up this way.' Here is a line which is purely modern in feel, not suggestive of a medieval ballad, but which seems to 'say' much more than its literal meaning. It is very evidently *not* just saying that Sir Leoline's castle lies in a far-northern latitude; it manages to evoke a place with very special (morbid and isolated) 'climatic' conditions, not just geographic ones but also human.

Let us look more closely at 'Christabel', and to begin with, at its curious—loose and irregular—metrical form. The form has great originality, and we feel that Coleridge speaks truly when he says in his Preface: ' . . . this occasional variation in number of syllables is not introduced wantonly, or for the mere ends of convenience, but in correspondence with some transition, in the nature of the imagery or passion.' Will you re-read this last paragraph of the Preface? The 'looseness and irregularity' which we mentioned extends, of course, to more than line-length, which is what Coleridge discusses here, and applies also to the pattern of strophes (see Glossary) and of rhymes.

To see how this loose and flexible form works, consider for instance the way' in lines 43–52, the movement of the poem begins to 'dance' in sympathy with the dancing leaf; how it grows hushed again; how, when the 'hour' of Geraldine's sinister dominance is ended, the verse-movement changes to one of boisterous gaiety, as the cheerful noise of the night-birds bursts out again. (That the voice of the owls should be jubilant and reassuring, instead of doleful, is a different point but worth pondering.) Notice again how the movement and chiming of rhymes becomes hypnotic and charm-like when Geraldine croons her spell:

> But vainly thou warrest
>   For this is alone in
> Thy power to declare,
>   That in the dim forest
> Thou heard'st a low moaning,
>   And found'st a bright lady, surpassingly fair;

and how the final two lines modulate into a kind of mummers'–play doggerel.

Coleridge, as he himself says, requires such a flexible verse-form for the better telling of his story and rendering of its 'passions'. However, it seems he needs it for another purpose too. He manages to involve us intensely in his story, with its terrors and mysteries, yet at the same time he remains outside it himself.

What is the story about? What is actually happening between Christabel and Geraldine, and are there unseen presences also at work (the dead mother? the distant lover)? Well, at one level Coleridge seems to be dropping clues that should lead us to construct a 'horrid' story of the supernatural of a kind that the girls in *Northanger Abbey* would greatly have relished. There is, first, the great question: who or what is Geraldine herself? And what is really going on in the 'hour' of her possession of Christabel?

We notice that Christabel, when overcome by a sinister vision of Geraldine (line 459), draws in her breath with a 'hissing sound' and then later (line 591) shudders aloud, 'with a hissing sound'. Is this perhaps a clue to something?

Discussion

Geraldine has been showing snake-like characteristics, so maybe, whatever Geraldine is, she is causing Christabel to turn into it also?

Why are we told that, in the morning, Geraldine's 'girded vests/Grew tight beneath her heaving breasts'? We know there is some mystery about her breasts, for Coleridge began to say so, only he stopped short: 'Behold! her bosom and half her side—/A sight to dream of, not to tell!' (lines 252–53). Later we shall be told obliquely what this sight was: 'Again she saw that bosom old,/Again she felt that bosom cold' (457–58); and the thought suggests itself that, if Geraldine's bosom was old and withered last night but is youthful and swelling by the morning, she was fed on something and may be . . . a vampire.

But why the serpent characteristics? Well, in ancient Greek and later mythologies there is a familiar figure known as a lamia—a serpent-like creature who seduces young men under the guise of a beautiful woman; and her purpose in so doing is to prey on their lifeblood. A lamia is in fact a form of vampire. (We shall meet with a famous one in a poem by Keats.)

Then, if bloodsucking vampirism is in question, may there not be some unsavoury connotation in the apparently innocent lines about the *blood returning* to Christabel's feet (323-25)? But if there are, they are certainly not spelled out; nor do we hear of any vampire toothmarks on Christabel, so we cannot be sure we are on the right track.

Consider, next, a point that must plainly have some importance: when we first encounter Christabel she is praying, for the welfare of her distant lover, at the foot of a mistletoe-hung oak-tree. No site could be more pagan (oak-trees and mistletoe were sacred to the Druids), and hence, though no doubt Christabel is praying to the Virgin Mary, it seems she is not above soliciting the help from other and less respectable sources also. Again, notice the sinister ambiguity given to the role of the dead mother. It appears that she is a guardian angel or 'daimon' to Christabel, still haunting the castle for her protection—in this, duplicating the motherly role of the Virgin Mary, to whom Christabel prays.

Coleridge, by the way, has a very striking remark in one of his Notebooks, dated 1810: 'My first cries mingled with my mother's death-groan, and she beheld the vision of glory ere I the earthly sun. When I first looked up to Heaven consciously, it was to look up after, or for, my mother.' It cannot refer literally to himself, for his mother did not die till he was 37, but it reminds us strongly of the last four lines of Part I of 'Christabel'.

But can we be quite sure that the dead mother is on the side of the angels? On her death-bed she prophesied that she would 'hear the castle-bell/Strike twelve' upon Christabel's wedding day (see lines 200–01). But, we reflect, twelve o'clock may be the wholesome daylight hour of noon but it could also be the 'witching' hour of midnight. Again, it seems that Geraldine has struck some kind of bargain with the mother (see 210–13), and when Christabel exclaims 'O mother dear! that thou were here!' Geraldine responds, rather oddly: 'I would . . . she were!' There are various possible ways of interpreting this. Will you see which occur to you?

Discussion

It could mean (1) that Geraldine would like the mother to be witness of her evil triumph; or (2) that Geraldine, though evidently in some sense an agent of evil, is an unwilling agent; or (3) that Geraldine first makes a conventional and hypocritical response to Christabel, then, feeling her dominance over Christabel, speaks out frankly, and warns the mother's rival spirit off.

All these possibilities we have been canvassing—vampires, lamias, diabolical mothers etc.—belong, in a broad sense, to 'Gothick horror'; and, though my earlier account of Gothick horror was an unfair caricature—for in fact some powerful writing was done in this vein—it does seem true that it is always to some extent a *game*. The thought nags at us, therefore, can this be all that Coleridge is up to? Do we not receive from the poem a sense of something truely *not* a game but impressive and serious? And if so, wherein does it lie?

My colleague Susie Meikle offers this suggestion: 'I wonder if there is not some use in discussing the ambiguity, and questions about the meaning, of "Christabel" and Christabel's experience in terms of the shifting relations brought out in the poem and the response of the older—supposedly "wiser"—generation to the situation. Could the erotic, sensual implications point towards a "rite of passage" of some kind for Christabel? The virgin learns something about/from/through Geraldine which is not actually expressed or articulated in the poem (just as the most intimate of such experiences are not) but which makes her especially vulnerable, now, in a way she had not hitherto been, to the rejection of her father's love.' As Susie Meikle rightly says, the poem is a deeply disturbing affair. Throughout Part I, and to the end of Bracy's account of his dream in Part II (563), Christabel has been endowed for us with a positive value of innocence, virtue and vulnerability. '*Then*,' Susie Meikle says, 'we discover that what we suppose to be the obvious meaning of the dream is totally reversed by Sir Leoline, who unquestionably takes *Geraldine* for the Dove! Aren't we, as readers, completely flummoxed by his interpretation, and isn't there a way in which we transfer that confusion on to Christabel herself and think that she must feel completely lost and confused in this world where the meanings of love, affection, security etc. are suddenly, inexplicably dislocated? It is as if Christabel were undergoing a nightmarish initiation into an adult world, which is baffling, but which she cannot help but enter—just as she unconsciously imitates Geraldine and loses her father's love, which, devastatingly, he transfers to the very object which caused his daughter to become hateful to him.'

You will observe that this approach places great emphasis on Part II, making Part I no more than a preparation, in an ostensibly 'supernatural' vein, for something more in the nature of a 'psychological novel'. (The implication would be that in Part I Coleridge is tempting us to place a supernatural explanation on events which, we discover later, belong to everyday reality.) And there is nothing implausible in that, perhaps, though it makes the poem more disastrously a fragment than do other readings and places great weight on some absent continuation. (If one is searching for a meaning at this 'psychological' level, further possibilities occur to one. Shall we regard these supernatural doings as, like the ghost in *Hamlet*, the expression of violent and incestuous conflicts going on in Sir Leoline's castle: could they, in some sense, represent jealous incestuous fantasies on the part of Christabel? Or again, might they be the refraction of the ancient and tragic quarrel between Sir Leoline and his friend Roland de Vaux and represent some mysterious attempt by Lord Roland to re-enter Sir Leoline's life?) The trouble with all such hypotheses is that they tempt us to downgrade the 'Gothick horror' sensationalism in the poem to the status of an inessential trimming, whereas, in whatever spirit, Coleridge seems indisputably to be playing the 'Gothick' game, for instance in the way he makes us hold our breath by artful halts at peculiarly alarming moments (see Part I, lines 250–54, 292–96). (In various manuscript versions, indeed, there is another line between the present 252 and 253, spelling out the crucial detail of Geraldine's black and withered bosom; but Coleridge evidently decided it would be more spine-chilling to omit it.)

My own feeling is that the poem, however it might have proceeded, would never have left us feeling that it *really* meant so-and-so—i.e. possessed a single deeper and 'serious' meaning towards which we had been led via more superficial thrills. (Though, on the other hand, this would be a reasonable, if very crude, way of describing 'The Ancient Mariner'.) It suggests itself to me that Coleridge wanted in 'Christabel' to create a thoroughly 'open' poem, inviting readings of many different sorts, according to the tastes of those reading it. Also that our instinct was correct, and the poem's 'incompleteness' is built-in. On this reading, Part II was an inspired addition, which drew out implications in Part I of which Coleridge had not originally been fully aware. It thus actually and retrospectively changed the nature of Part I and of the way we are meant to read it. Moreover, Coleridge might have added further developments and transitions at the same level of achievement of Part II and still have been no nearer 'completing' it. The 'seriousness', according to this view, would be of another kind, viz. an effort on Coleridge's part to project himself into the modes of thinking of the so-called 'Age of Faith' (the middle ages), and to link hands with it across the 'soulless' eighteenth century. What better means of doing so than by a story that can grip and involve its readers at the 'Gothick horror' level, and which exploits for that purpose a basic fact about the 'Age of Faith', i.e. that its Christianity managed to carry along with it all sorts of pagan elements?

We connect up here with the theme of Professor Sharrock's talk on 'The Overthrowing of the Mechanical Philosophy' (Radio Programme 5). The Victorian philosopher John Stuart Mill, who was brought up in the radical and Utilitarian school of thought of Jeremy Bentham, thus as an opponent of the conservative position to which Coleridge quite early moved, developed none the less a high opinion of Coleridge, saying that:

> He has been almost as truly as Bentham, 'the great questioner of things established'; for a questioner needs not necessarily be an enemy. By Bentham, beyond all others, men have been led to ask themselves, in regard to any ancient or received opinion, Is it true? and by Coleridge, What is the meaning of it? The one took his stand *outside* the received opinion, and surveyed it as an entire stranger to it: the other looked at it from within, and endeavoured to see it with the eyes of a believer in it; to discover by what apparent facts it was at first suggested, and by what appearances it has ever since been rendered continually credible . . . With Coleridge, . . . the very fact that any doctrine had been believed by thoughtful men, and received by whole nations or generations of mankind, was part of the problem to be solved, was one of the phenomena to be accounted for. ('Coleridge', pp. 99–100).

Mill's words are very apt to a poem like 'Christabel', which projects itself with such inquiring and imaginative sympathy into 'the Age of Faith'. Maybe there never actually was an 'Age of Faith'; but at least there has been something of deep importance, some powerful imaginative energy, inspiring the monuments and art of the middle ages, and Coleridge's poem helps us to make connection with it.

It is, for one thing, deliberately symbolical in a way that evokes the symbolism of medieval cathedral architecture and sculpture. Coleridge wants to reconstruct a vision of the world, not as an indifferent Newtonian machine, operated by general laws, but as something living, finite and responsive—as a place it is possible to feel at home in. In the poem Christabel is motherless and alone, sharing a castle with (so far as we are told) no more than a decrepit dog and an aged father. Nevertheless she is protected: the old mastiff bitch, and even the flames of the hearth, warn her of mischief, and the saints and the Virgin are *there*, just above her and within reach. Nature is active and her friend (as eventually it shows itself the friend of the Ancient Mariner), and 'the blue sky' (blue with the Virgin's colour) 'bends over all' protectively.

Needless to say, Coleridge, child of 'Enlightenment' ideas and product of the French Revolution, did not wish to revive ancient superstitions, indeed he was so far removed from them as to regard them with amused indulgence. Nevertheless, for good or evil, he was concerned—as a philosopher, but also as poet and critic— to revitalize the religious life and religious traditions of his country.

The fashion for Gothick horror, in the eighteenth century, went hand in hand with a taste for ruins. Owners of country houses would construct sham-medieval ruins in their grounds, and one could think of Coleridge's fragmentary poem as just such an artificial ruin. Much of the attraction of ruins, it may be said, is that they *are* ruined. Part of the pleasure lies in the knowledge that, to inheritors of the Reformation and the 1688 Revolution, these symbols of an oppressive *ancien régime* are ultimately no threat. In Coleridge we can perhaps see—as often with him—a superficial resemblance to eighteenth-century ideas but actually a reversal or transcendence of them, and what he takes pleasure in, in the Gothick, is not ruin but restoration.

'Frost at Midnight'

(By SE)

Please read 'Frost at Midnight' (set text, pp. 68–70) and listen to the cassette reading of it; and see if you can list two or three features of the poem which justify us calling it 'domestic' or 'conversational'.

Discussion

I would single out:

1   The poem's domestic setting: the cottage room, the fire, the baby.

2   The poem's tone and movement: the warm, affectionate response to the baby, the sense of immediacy in such lines as

> . . . The owlet's cry
> Came loud—and hark, again! loud as before.

3   The poem's being firmly centred on Coleridge's response to his surroundings as his mind ranges backwards and forwards in time.

How does the poem begin? Like 'Dejection' and Wordsworth's 'Resolution and Independence', with weather and nature, and nature acted on by weather. Unlike the aforementioned poems, it is the windless silence which is stressed here. Silence and solitude are, of course, the most characteristic pre-conditions for a romantic visionary experience but, uncharacteristically, they are here established at the very outset rather than worked towards. Indeed, so determined was Coleridge to underline this 'extreme silentness' that he committed a meteorological solecism. Frost is rarely if ever helped by wind, as wind in fact disturbs the conditions in which frost flourishes; 'unhelped by any wind' is therefore at best a rather redundant clause. But perhaps this flaw hardly matters, for the whole line is eclipsed by that extraordinary first image of the frost performing 'its secret ministry'. I think we might be able to work out, at least in part, why it should be 'secret'. After all, frost tends to form at night, in the dark and slowly, so it is 'secret' in the sense of being 'unobserved'. But why 'ministry', with its implications of the duty of conveying a sense of God to Man? The context of the image doesn't give us much help, for the poem seems to leave the image in isolation and goes off on another tack. The image, however, is used again unchanged right at the end of the poem, so that perhaps in some way the whole process of the poem is concerned with making sense of that image to which it returns. Anyway let's suspend analysis of this until it recurs, at which point, if our assumption is right, the question 'What does it mean?' will apply equally to the specific image and to the poem as a whole.

Take a look at the first 23 lines. These clearly set the scene, providing us with virtually all the 'physical' information we get in the poem: the operation of frost, the solitary poet with the sleeping infant in the cottage room, the preternatural silence, the 'low-burnt' fire. Also in these first 23 lines there is a transition, a shift from the poet's physical surroundings to something else. Now, I want you to read this first section again with the following question in mind: of the various elements of the material world described here, which two does Coleridge stress most and why? And—a connected question—where and how does the first transition occur?

Discussion

Simply in terms of the number of lines given over to their description, I would say that two aspects of the physical world which stand out in this poem are: the silence of the world *outside*, and the flickering life of the fire *inside*. It is an irony which will only be fully appreciated by those acquainted with the Wordsworthian idea of silence, stillness and solitude as essential components of the meditative and visionary experience, that the 'calm' is almost too great:

> 'Tis calm indeed! so calm, that it disturbs
> And vexes meditation, with its strange
> And extreme silentness.

The silence is not just intensive, it is extensive as well:

> Sea, hill, and wood,
> This populous village!

But Coleridge is not satisfied with the impact of this and, using all the informality and flexibility that the conversational poem permits, he reformulates it, allowing each aspect of the landscape full impact by wedging a comma and a conjunction between them:

> Sea, and hill, and wood,
> With all the numberless goings on of life,
> Inaudible as dreams!

This last simile introduces a theme which is to have significance later, but which is not allowed to develop yet, being held in check while the second 'physical' aspect is stressed.

The poem moves from the cold, silent, dark outside to the warm, silent, light inside. Gradually the reader's attention is being contracted from the expansiveness of 'Sea, and hill, and wood' to concentrate on one small aspect of the domestic scene, the fire. But even this is not the full contrast Coleridge is searching for; it's certainly small rather than large, it's warm rather than cold, but it, too, is calm and motionless—'and quivers not'. So the reader's attention is narrowed down again to 'the sole unquiet thing', the film of ash fluttering on the grate. Why does Coleridge home in on this minute, single example of unquietness? One might answer in a purely technical way, and say that Coleridge is about to use this specific detail as a sort of pivotal point from which he can redirect the poem or, in other words, effect a transition. But that would not explain why this detail was selected rather than any other. What explanation does Coleridge give?

Discussion

Its 'motion' in the otherwise universal 'hush of nature' makes it appear alive, it is 'the sole unquiet thing' (which separates it from the baby who 'slumbers peacefully') amid the calm, it appears to be the only thing in sympathy with the poet, who thus proceeds to identify with it:

> Methinks, its motion in this hush of nature
> Gives it dim sympathies with me who live,
> Making it a companionable form . . .

Did you notice the rather sombre ambiguity of 'unquiet'? While exclusively describing the 'film', it simply means 'not quiet'; but when, through indentification, it spreads to apply to the poet, it takes on the implication 'troubled' or 'disturbed' in mind or spirit. Coleridge pushes the identification into greater detail, and in doing so moves from the sombre to the absurd:

> Whose puny flaps and freaks the idling Spirit
> By its own moods interprets . . .
> And makes a toy of Thought.

'The Spirit', presumably Coleridge's, is 'idling', vulnerable to 'flaps and freaks', and, in an unquiet and idle moment, toys with an image which, ironically, turns out to be a just and accurate one, reflecting Coleridge's own desultory nature.

At this moment of accidental self-revelation the poem shifts towards the past, as Coleridge's memory, triggered by the 'film', takes command and recalls a time when such a phenomenon was not idle but, on the contrary, acted to fix and intensify both the memory and the imagination.

> But O! how oft,
> How oft, at school, with most believing mind,
> Presageful, have I gazed upon the bars,
> To watch that fluttering stranger!

Almost immediately, the poem shifts ground again, diving further back in time as he remembers day-dreaming at school of his earlier childhood. At this point the poem's backward movement ceases, the poet seemingly having found a point of rest in reassuring memories. Clearly the present, as represented in the first part of the poem, and the intermediate past of his schooldays ('the stern preceptor's face', 'pent 'mid cloisters dim') are in some way troubling to Coleridge, and only in the remote past can he find a secure happiness. Did you notice that this second transition was marked by a distinct reversal of imagery? What two sense-experiences whose absence was so stressed in the opening ten lines are here presented positively?

Discussion

The cold and the silence of the first ten lines are here converted to warmth and sound:

> . . . the old church-tower,
> Whose bells, the poor man's only music, rang
> From morn to evening, all the hot Fair-day,
> So sweetly, that they stirred and haunted me
> With a wild pleasure . . .

The phrase 'haunted me/With a wild pleasure' is, one suspects, an example of the influence that Wordsworth's vision of childhood was having on Coleridge at this time.

But a contentment rooted in the past cannot sustain itself indefinitely, and the poem shifts once more, forward this time, to his schooldays. The transition, which occurs in lines 34–35, is subtle. We are told that the memory of these things was 'soothing', but that itself suggests that we are no longer seeing them direct but have been forced to step back and see them in the context of schooldays where they have become just a temporary means of therapeutic escape. We are seeing them secondhand, as memories of memories. The bleak world of 'stern preceptors' and 'mock study' can corrupt the effects even of good things. The warm memories may originally have soothed Coleridge, but in the schoolroom next day their consequences are much darker—he is disorientated ('with mock study on my swimming book') and meditates darkly ('And so I brooded . . . '). Like Wordsworth in 'Tintern Abbey', Coleridge here is not celebrating memory as a wholly desirable thing, for its consequences can be ambivalent. Look at lines 34–36: can you find a simple poetic device which Coleridge is using to stress this ambivalence?

Discussion

The assonance of 's*oo*thing' and 'br*oo*ded' staples the two contrary effects of memory together.

But the darkest consequence of school life is implied, not here but two lines further on, where, of the three possible strangers presaged by the fluttering film, only one might properly be thought of as a real stranger—the unspecified 'townsman'. To put the other two, 'aunt, or sister more beloved', in the same category suggests some extreme form of emotional and physical separation. The 'beloved sister as stranger' theme is pursued in the following line, where the ultimate estrangement, brought about by death, is implied:

> My play-mate when we both were clothed alike!

Can you detect an ambiguity in this line?

Discussion

One of its meanings, in a culture which commonly dressed young boys to the age of three or four in 'skirts', is 'when we were young enough to be dressed alike'. Its second, metaphorical meaning is, however, more important. It was almost a theological commonplace to talk of Man as being 'clothed in flesh', of the human body in death being cast aside as the soul struggled out of its shabby clothing. So the line probably also means 'when we were both alive'. There would have been an added personal poignance to this linking of a dreary school and a lost sister for Coleridge: she died in the very year he finally left Christ's Hospital.

At this darkest point in the poem we have another transition. The theme of mortality, the spiritual deadness of Coleridge the schoolboy and the literal death of his sister, turns the poet to that most traditional symbol of human vulnerability, the sleeping child. We should not forget that any powerful image owes its strength ultimately to its being deeply rooted in reality. It was not just literary convention which encouraged Andrew Marvell to write 'The Picture of Little T.C. in a Prospect of Flowers' or Coleridge to turn to his sleeping son. If death was more frequent and more obvious in pre-industrial society than now, it was most frequent and most obvious in pre-industrial childhood, infant mortality commonly running at fifty per cent. Without suggesting that you run to a poet's biography in search of a poem's meaning (you won't find it there), I might underline this point by mentioning that Berkeley, Coleridge's second son born some three months after the writing of 'Frost at Midnight', died within nine months of his birth.[1]

Yet, paradoxically, although the transition is very traditional, the way in which the poem then develops is not. The child's 'gentle breathings' are mentioned, but rather than suggesting frailty, they are dynamic enough to

> Fill up the interspersed vacancies
> And momentary pauses of the thought!

and then, a few lines later, the breathing child is being identified with the breath of nature, the wind which doesn't just 'fill up' gaps but is, and goes, everywhere. Do you see what is happening? The 'deep calm' (which, as Coleridge has admitted, has disturbed him) has been broken up by the 'breeze' and 'the sounds intelligible/ Of that eternal language, which thy God/Utters . . . ', just as the urban image of being 'pent 'mid cloisters dim' has been broken open by the expansive images of the natural landscape:

> By lakes and sandy shores, beneath the crags
> Of ancient mountain, and beneath the clouds,
> Which image in their bulk both lakes and shores
> And mountain crags . . .

Traditionally the child's best hope was to replicate its father. In 'Frost at Midnight' the child is to improve on the father and, in some strange way, by doing so to redeem him. This may sound pretentious, so let's pin this idea down in the text. As Wordsworth in 'Tintern Abbey' was able to relive his earlier experience through Dorothy's reaction to nature, so Coleridge, as he imagines the experiences of his son, breaks through that sense of actual and emotional confinement and cold (generated by his memories of school) to a sense of movement and openness, an openness not just to the 'sky and stars' but to everything:

> Himself in all, and all things in himself.

The final transition is marked by a 'Therefore' which gives it the air of being a conclusion to an argument which, in a sense, it is. If 'God . . . doth teach/ Himself in all . . . ', then indeed everything is of significance and

> Therefore all seasons shall be sweet to thee . . .

It is an argument for close and unprejudiced attention to all things, an argument which, although ostensibly directed at his son, is clearly equally applicable to Coleridge. The poet illustrates and proves his argument by moving from generalities about the landscape to particular and exact details of weather and nature. We

---

[1] The note in your set edition wrongly identifies the slumbering child as Berkeley Coleridge. In fact the child must have been Hartley Coleridge, for Berkeley was not born until 14 May 1798. He died on 10 Febuary 1799.

have come full circle and are back to the real world inhabited by the poet and his son at the beginning of the poem, but it is a world seen through sharper eyes. No longer is it vague generalities such as 'Sea, hill, and wood' or 'lakes and shores/And mountain crags'; now we have sharply focused detail:

> . . . the redbreast sit[s] and sing[s]
> Betwixt the tufts of snow on the bare branch
> Of mossy apple-tree, while the nigh thatch
> Smokes in the sun-thaw . . .

Did you notice that the only generalized image in these last ten lines is the one referring to summer? The great symbol of emotional warmth and 'wild pleasure' that had dominated his desparately escapist memory ('the *hot* Fair-day') has been pushed into an undifferentiated background ('summer clothe the *general* earth . . .'), and what Coleridge now seems interested in are the pleasurable details to be found in darker seasons. Now, although what Coleridge is describing here is what he anticipates for his son, his descriptions are clearly of his own experience; after all, we have returned to what *he* had been observing at the beginning and to what his son, being too young and oblivious in sleep, could not see. In anticipating the education of his son by Nature, Coleridge has unconsciously re-educated his own senses and sees his own experience anew. The child has indeed, inadvertently, redeemed the father. The moral significance of this twist has a parallel in a radically different sort of poem by Coleridge, 'The Ancient Mariner'. Remembering your work on this latter poem, can you think of a turning-point similarly centred on a selfless act of contemplation?

Discussion

In Part IV the Ancient Mariner unselfconsciously blesses the water-snakes and, in doing so, releases himself from spiritual paralysis:

> A spring of love gushed from my heart
> And I blessed them unaware . . .
> The selfsame moment I could pray . . .

Another example of emotional restoration through imaginative sympathy can be found in 'This Lime-Tree Bower my Prison', which was discussed by Nick Furbank on page 11.

So Coleridge returns to the two subjects with which he began the poem—the frost and the quiet. Quietness is re-introduced in a new form, not as a long continuous calm and total absence of sound, but as a moment caught between two periods of movement during which one can hear the slight and delicate sounds of nature which are normally obscured:

> . . . whether the eave-drops fall
> Heard only in the trances of the blast . . .

(Note that 'eave-drops' is misspelt in your edition.) Given this example of quietness as a transitory and revealing state, a moment at which we can perceive the subtle details of nature, we are forced to view the poem's final image in a different light. 'The secret ministry of frost' is reintroduced, but this time (unlike the last) we are told what it is doing: it is hanging them (the eave-drops) 'up in silent icicles/ Quietly shining to the quiet Moon'.

This is a very specific sort of frost: not a generalized hoar frost, which dusts everything indiscriminately with white, but frost which organizes and imposes form on usually formless water. This ability to impart shape should remind us of one of the characteristics Coleridge attributes to his 'God revealed in nature' in lines 60–64. In lines 63–64 we have the following:

> Great universal Teacher! he shall mould
> Thy spirit . . .

To 'mould', to shape, is a quality of God revealed in all aspects of nature, even in the silent frost whose 'ministry' is, clearly, to teach of Nature's God in the smallest, quietest things. The quiet which ends the poem is unlike the silence which began it in just one respect: it is creative rather than disturbing. The generation of shape out of chaos can produce something as small as an icicle or as grand as the moon, but, in Coleridge's world, what they have in common is more important than what divides them. Thus in the final line the great and the little exchange their silence and their light:

> Quietly shining to the quiet Moon.

This marvellous tranquillity is not just the calm confidence of all-creating nature, it is also the spiritual peace achieved by and through human struggle. For somewhere on the universal scale of creation, somewhere between an icicle and the moon, we must place the poem we have just read: it too has imposed form on chaos and found meaning in apparent silence. 'Frost at Midnight' is not just a description of acute perception and creativity, it is also a very fine example of both these things in action.

You will find further work on poems by Coleridge later in these units: see pp. 98ff. and pp. 107ff. for his 'Dejection: An Ode', pp. 105ff. for 'Kubla Khan', and pp. 131ff. for 'The Eolian Harp' and other poems.

4   Wordsworth's 'Prelude'

(By LL)

Wordsworth's personal epic

The purpose of the following section of the units is to help you read *The Prelude* with the fullest possible understanding and appreciation. To do this, we shall begin at the beginning, with a discussion of the first book. Before proceeding further, you should read Book I very carefully: it is one of the finest things in English poetry, so you should enjoy the experience. To make sure that you have understood its arguments, I suggest you think of it in five parts, as follows: (i) lines 1–54; (ii) 55–115; (iii) 116–271; (iv) 271–640; (v) 640–end. (Passages from Book I are also recorded on the cassette.)

Exercise

Write down, very briefly, what you think each part is saying.

Suggested answer

Lines 1–54 are an expression of delight at escaping from the 'vast city', and at the fact that he is free to follow his own devices. Lines 55–115 continue the account of his wanderings, and his arrival in 'one sweet Vale', but they differ in not being written at the time. Wordsworth draws our attention to the fact that the opening passage was the spontaneous outpouring of a 'present joy', and that this is unusual for him. Lines 116–271 describe his longing to write a major work, and his long hesitation over choice of subject. As his uncertainty leads to listlessness and self-reproach, he asks 'Was it for this' that he grew up on the banks of his beloved Derwent, and that leads him to recollect the delights of his childhood, and so to recount some of his early memories. This forms the longest section of Book I, after which he explains, in the last 30-odd lines, that his purpose in this reminiscing has been to draw 'invigorating thoughts' from the recollections, and points out that he has at any rate got the poem started. For in the course of his long self-rebuke he has after all found the subject of his poem: it is to be the story of his own life.

This is a simple and effective rhetorical strategy. Uncertainty over choice of subject leads to a regretful, apologetic account of the blessing he seems to have failed to live up to, and that account turns out to be the subject. We might wonder, reading this, if that is the way it happened. Is Wordsworth re-enacting the way he discovered his subject, or had he (as my phrase 'rhetorical stategy' perhaps implies) planned the later development from the first? It so happens that we can answer this question. For a study of the manuscripts shows that the second half of the book was written first, and that the question 'Was it for this . . . ?' was written five years before Wordsworth had decided what to put in front of it. It was always intended as an autobiography.

Now the argument presented by that rhetorical question is of enormous importance for an understanding not only of *The Prelude* in itself, but also of its place in English poetry. To appreciate this, we need to know the model that lies behind it.

'The earth is all before me.' Is there anything familiar about this? To a reader who knows his Milton, it can hardly fail to recall the conclusion of *Paradise Lost*, when Adam and Eve are expelled from Eden: 'the world was all before them.' Milton's epic deals with the fall of man, and so with the beginnings of human history; and Wordsworth consciously chooses this concluding moment as his opening moment, to show that he is writing a different kind of epic, one which does not culminate in the human situation we know, but starts from it.

Once we have spotted the first Miltonic echo, we shall soon find many more. For instance, the remark that he was emboldened to trust 'that I might leave/ Some monument behind me which pure hearts/Should reverence' (VI: 67–69) recalls, almost certainly deliberately, Milton's hope 'that I might leave something so written to aftertimes, as they should not willingly let it die'. And, most important, the very hesitation about choice of subject is Miltonic. Milton is known to have dedicated himself early to the writing of a heroic poem, but to have spent twenty years settling on the subject. He writes at length about his hesitations, and the alternatives he has considered, in several of his prose works and Latin poems, and also in *Paradise Lost* itself: four of its twelve books begin with an exordium, or introduction, in which the poet speaks in his own person, discussing his fitness for the task. It may well be that Wordsworth was imitating the idea of the exordium in beginning his first book with a preamble of 54 lines on the delight of escaping from the city, and that the opening of Book VII, which recalls these lines and is also written on the spot, is meant as another exordium: though the contrast between exordium and poem cannot be so clear-cut when the body of the poem is also about the poet, and also in the first person. And it is quite certain that Milton lies behind Wordsworth's statement when pointing out that his theme is 'what passed within me':

> This is, in truth, heroic argument,
> And genuine prowess . . .
> (III: 182–83)

Just as Milton extended the subject-matter of epic (or heroic) poetry from pagan to Christian stories, so Wordsworth is extending it still further, from traditional stories to the growth of his own mind.

To do this was a radical innovation, and he knew it: indeed, the reason for calling our attention so fully to the Miltonic precedent is that we should see not only how traditional he is being, but also how new. 'It is a thing unprecedented in literary history,' Wordsworth wrote, 'that a man should talk so much about himself.' His reason for doing so was, he claimed, not self-conceit but humility. 'I began the work because I was unprepared to treat any more arduous subject.' The more arduous subject was the 'philosophical poem containing views of Man, Nature and Society' that he always regarded as his main poetic task, and to which *The Prelude* was to be a portico or ante-chapel. This philosophical poem was in turn to be divided into two, a narrative poem 'referring to passing events and to an existing state of things', and a reflective poem in his own person on 'whatever I find most interesting in Nature Man and Society and most adapted to poetic illustration'. The narrative poem was finished, and published in 1814 as *The Excursion*; of the reflective poem, known as *The Recluse* (though Wordsworth sometimes used 'The Recluse' to refer to the whole series, or to the last two), about a thousand lines were written: known as *Home at Grasmere*, they tell the story of how he first saw Grasmere as a child, and how he settled there in later life preparatory to starting on his major poem. They are in fact autobiographical, and like *The Prelude* can be thought of as a portico to the poem. Like *The Prelude*, they were never published.

All critics of Wordsworth agree that *The Prelude* contains some of his greatest poetry, and that much of *The Excursion*, after the first book, is worthy and tedious; for me, *Home at Grasmere* is at times very moving, with touches of the visionary

Wordsworth aged 48, chalk drawing by Benjamin Robert Haydon, c. 1818. (*National Portrait Gallery, London*)

intensity of *The Prelude*. It seems clear, therefore, that Wordsworth's attitude to his autobiographical poetry is the result of two contrasting feelings. On the one hand, he felt it was subsidiary to his great moral and philosophical work, and not worthy to stand on its own; he would only publish it after he had finished a work 'of sufficient importance to justify me in giving my own history to the world'. On the other hand, he could not manage the philosophical masterpiece, and could not make a success of the reflections on Man, on Nature and on human life, while his demon would not leave the autobiography alone. The 'unprecedented' drive to tell his own story in verse, though he was constantly driven to apologize for it, to himself and others, came direct from the springs of his poetic inspiration.

And was it unprecedented? Though no poet had previously written 8,000 lines about himself, autobiography was not in itself new. There are a few autobiographical diaries, or casual and intimate autobiographies, before the nineteenth century, but they are rare, and remained almost invariably unpublished (Pepys, Lady Anne Halklett, Boswell). Some (often posthumously published) were by men of affairs, but the overwhelming majority of autobiographies were religious, and usually Puritan; for the story of one's conversion, in a religion based on personal experience and believing in immediate contact with God, provided the equivalent

J. M. W. Turner, Morning amongst the Coniston Fells, Cumberland, *1798.* (*Tate Gallery, London*)

of a qualification for the ministry. Puritan spiritual autobiographies in the seventeenth century tend to conform to a fixed pattern: unregenerate youth, awakening (through a personal crisis or the hearing of a sermon), consciousness of sin and spiritual struggle, illumination and the acceptance of grace. We can see how important this common pattern is if we look at Wesley's views on the spiritual diseases which everyone brings into the world. The two worst are atheism and pride. Every man is by nature his own God. 'He worships himself. He is in his own conception absolute Lord of himself. He seeks himself in all things. He pleases himself . . . *His own will* is his only law.' Such is atheism. 'Another evil disease which every human soul brings into the world with him is *pride*: a continual proneness to think of himself more highly that he ought to think.' Clearly, these two 'diseases' belong closely together, for both involve an unregulated acceptance of the self.

Looking at the type of autobiography that this view produced, it is clear what the truly unprecedented venture would be: to tell the story of a life that neither had public importance nor was measured against any external theological pattern. The new autobiographer will be one who is not concerned with the public or religious significance of his story, but with his growth and development for its own sake; and he will not approach that development with any preconceived notion of the stages it will pass through. Had anyone ever done this?

One man thought he had, and thought he had inaugurated a new era in doing so:

> I have formed an undertaking for which there has never been a precedent, and after I have carried it out there will never be an imitator. I wish to show to my fellow-beings a man exactly as nature has made him; and that man is to be myself.

This is the famous opening of Rousseau's *Confessions*, published posthumously in 1782. It is preceded by a short Advertisement, in which he wrote:

> Here is the only portrait of a man, painted exactly according to nature and in all truthfulness, which exists, and which is ever likely to exist. Whoever you may be, whom my destiny or my confidence has made the custodian of this notebook, I beseech you by my miseries and by your bowels, and on behalf of the whole human race, not to destroy a useful and unique work which can serve as the basis for the study of man (something which has not yet begun), and not to take from the honour of my memory the one sure monument of my character which has not been defaced by my enemies . . .

The resemblances between Rousseau and Wordsworth have often been remarked on, both in their trust in Nature as an educational principle (Rousseau's *Emile* can be compared with Book v of *The Prelude* or Book i of *The Excursion*) and in this fact of telling their own life story so fully and openly. But there are also profound differences between them, and by stressing these we may perhaps be helped to a fuller understanding of Wordsworth.

Exercise

Rousseau's assertion is certainly very striking. Is it not *too* striking? Read it again, and ask if it contains any inconsistencies, or if any of its claims strike you, on reflection, as questionable.

Answer

There is, in the first place, a contradiction between the claim to uniqueness, and the claim to be inaugurating a new era: if no-one imitates his work, it can hardly turn out to be the basis for a new study. Then there is the subtler but more important contradiction, noticeable even in this short extract, that such a bold, even histrionic announcement of one's intention to be sincere is likely to render sincerity impossible. Genuine self-exploration is perhaps not compatible with the constant use (they almost seem to be Rousseau's favourite words) of *jamais*, *le premier*, *le seul* (never, the first, the only), which imply a constant (and pleased) attention to the newness of what he is doing. Such consciousness of what one is doing may be precisely what is *not* new, since it will either measure the self against external norms, or, as with Renaissance figures such as Montaigne and Thomas Browne, be aware of the eccentricity of not doing so.

Rousseau's heightened sense of his own importance reaches the point that Wesley would call atheism, and we call paranoia. This is clear from another of his books, the brilliant *Dialogues*, which is actually constructed on a principle that presupposes paranoia, a dialogue between that part of himself that imagines persecuting and uniqueness, and the part that remains in touch with sanity and society (these two parts are called 'Rousseau' and 'Jean-Jacques'). But there is also another form of self-exploration in Rousseau, for which we may take his fifth *Promenade* as our specimen. The *Rêveries du promeneur solitaire* (Reveries of the Solitary Walker) is a kind of sequel to the *Confessions*, and its title may seem to have a definite element of self-dramatization; but in the fifth and most famous of the *Walks*, we are given an experience of communion with Nature which turns out to be an experience of self-forgetfulness. Sitting on the shore of the Lac de Bienne, lulled into reverie by the ebb and flow of the water, Rousseau tells of two kinds of experience, the one merging into the other.

> From time to time was born some weak and brief reflexion on the instablility of the things of this world, of which the surface of the waters presented an emblem: but soon these light impressions were obliterated by the uniformity of the steady movement that rocked me, and which, without any active collaboration on the part of my soul, did not cease to hold me.

Here we see a transition from traditional reflexions on human life, in which the waves are an emblem of transitoriness, to reverie properly so called, in which he surrenders to the hypnotic movement, and moral reflexion is replaced by the state in which time appears to cease moving, and he is aware neither 'of privation nor of joy, of pleasure nor of pain, of desire nor of fear, but only the feeling of existence, a feeling which completely fills our consciousness'. This is something new in the history of sensibility, and makes the fifth *Promenade* an epoch-making document.

Turning to the English Romantics, we can now make a simple contrast. The self-dramatizing form of self-consciousness leads to Byron, the surrender to the 'sentiment de l'existence' leads to Wordsworth. The former is endemic in European Romanticism, the latter is a more elusive quality, and Wordsworth holds a unique place in its development. Here for instance are a few lines (not included in the final version of *The Prelude*) which describe an experience very close to that of the fifth *Promenade*.

> And feel a pleasant consciousness of life
> In the impression of that loveliness
> Until the sweet sensation called the mind
> Into itself, by image from without
> Unvisited, and all her reflex powers
> Wrapped in a still dream of forgetfulness.

There is nothing histrionic about *The Prelude*. Without flaunting the newness of its enterprise, it really is new. That his own development is important, and important in itself, is simply assumed, not asserted. It contains none of Rousseau's rhetoric of self-presentation.

The one element that can be seen as a deliberate rhetorical device is the Miltonic analogy, but in the respect with which Wordsworth treats his great predecessor, it is almost the opposite to the inconoclastic Rousseau. There is no doubt of Wordsworth's love for and debt to Milton's poetry; at the same time, he is showing us that the concern with his own development, which in Milton was a preliminary to the poem's subject, has now become the subject.

Spots of time

We have now looked at Book I, and discussed the nature and originality of Wordsworth's project. Before we look more closely at how he carried it out, you might like to get a general view of the poem, into which you can fit the discussions which follow. Clearly the best way to do this is to read it all through now, thus allowing your own impressions to interact with the interpretation you are offered in the rest of this part of the units. There is no substitute for the whole poem, but because your time is limited, and because some parts of *The Prelude* are more important than others, here is an abbreviated version which can serve as a basis: Books I and II, in full; Book IV, lines 247–345; Book V, 1–165, 389–442; Book VII, 589–end; Book VIII, 62–623; Book XI, 258–end. (All references are to the 1805 text.)

You should of course regard this as a minimum; and you may also want a general picture of what happens in the poem to give a sense of context to the parts we study carefully. The simplest way to get this is probably to begin with the titles of the books: it is clear from them that the first ten books take us chronologically through Wordsworth's life, from infancy through schooldays, student days at Cambridge, his final summer vacation (when he felt himself dedicated to poetry), his trip to the Alps, his experience of London, his time in France during the Revolution. The last three books no longer move chronologically but attempt to explain his mental crisis and recovery after his return from France, culminating in the reflections induced by his vision, when he climbed Snowdon at night, and his claim to have 'traced the stream' from birth into the light, lost sight of it, and 'given it greeting, as it rose once more' (XIII: 172). That is in a sense the conclusion of the poem; all that follows is an address to those he feels have meant most to him in his development—his sister Dorothy, his wife, and above all Coleridge, to whom the poem was originally dedicated.

Because the last three books attempt to explain the story, we shall start from them in asking how Wordsworth shows us the growth of his mind. For the most important concept in the poem is not introduced until Book XI.

Exercise

Before proceeding further, pause and re-read the second half of Book XI, 'Imagination, how impaired and restored', beginning at line 258.

Answer

The concept I am referring to is, as you have probably realized, that of 'spots of time'. Why is it so important to Wordsworth? After all, any autobiography is likely to concentrate on the important moments, and there will always be some that are more vividly remembered, that enjoy a 'distinct pre-eminence'. In setting forth his doctrine of 'spots of time', is Wordsworth offering us any kind of explanation of his development, or is he simply drawing attention to the fact that this is his life story? Is *The Prelude*, in other words, basically a narrative or a theoretical poem?

This is not an easy question to answer. As well as the difficulty of separating narrative from explanation in any autobiography, there is the important fact that

The Prelude grew, and changed in the writing. The growth of this very passage is interesting. Here it is as first written, in 1798:

> There are in our existence spots of time
> Which with distinct pre-eminence retain
> A fructifying virtue, when, depressed
> By trivial occupations and the round
> Of ordinary intercourse, our minds
> (Especially the imaginative power)
> Are nourished, and invisibly repaired.
> Such moments chiefly seem to have their date
> In our first childhood.

Comparing this with the 1805 version (you should of course have the text in front of you for the whole of this discussion), we see that a fuller description was added both of the trivial occupations and of the nourishing and repairing. The new detail which appears to convey most information is the statement of what he feels he has learned about the mind at such moments: that it is lord and master, and that 'outward sense/Is but the obedient servant of her will'.

Two spots of time are described after this introductory discussion. The first is the episode of the gibbet, culminating in the sight of a girl struggling against the wind, which must be one of the more moving passages in *The Prelude*, if not in all English poetry. The second describes how he waited impatiently for the horses that would fetch him home from school for Christmas, and how that episode merged with his grief and guilt at his father's death, and continued to haunt his memory.

What do these two marvellous passages tell us? Not, certainly, that the mind was lord and master. Even the terminology here used is of little help: it contrasts mind with outward sense, but the episodes are concerned with the interrelations of outward sense and *emotion*, and they come close to suggesting that outward sense is the obedient servant of the overwhelming emotion that colours what we see. The panic which Wordsworth felt when he stood on the site of the gibbet is

Caspar David Friedrich, Morning, *c. 1821. Note the imaginative coincidence of vision of the German Romantic painter and Wordsworth, though the two were unknown to each other. (Niedersächsisches Landesmuseum, Hanover)*

imposed on the later glimpse of the girl; the dreariness seems to exude from the landscape itself, just as the rhythm echoes the buffeting by the wind. The phrase that best sums up the effect occurs in the middle of the passage: 'visionary dreariness'. It is mysteriously appropriate, and as we ponder it we can perhaps see in it an appropriate ambiguity.

Exercise

Can you suggest what this is?

Answer

It was a vision of dreariness, created by the subjective state of the watcher (a vision is what normally can't be seen), and it was dreary to vision because of the wind and the bleakness (vision is the faculty of seeing). This is very powerfully suggestive: but what have *mind* and *will* to do with all this? The combination of those two terms implies an effort to master emotion or to control behaviour, and there is no question of that here.

The second visit to the naked pool, made years later 'in the blessed time of early love', was not in the original version. On this second visit the dreariness was, of course, gone. I do not think this is also intended as one of the spots of time. It was not itself of significance; what was significant is that the later pleasure, he believes, was 'more divine' for the earlier fear. Hence the conclusion (XI: 326–328) that

> . . . feeling comes in aid
> Of feeling, and diversity of strength
> Attends us, if but once we have been strong.

None of this was in the 1799 version. Once again an explanatory passage has been added; and once again, I suggest, it presents a superimposed moral. Whether the later, joyful emotion was strengthened by the earlier fearful one is something neither we nor Wordsworth could ever know; but surely we can be sure that the claim to have been strong is wholly inappropriate here. If we have to use such terminology, we must see that in fleeing from the gibbet site and looking round for his guide Wordsworth showed weakness, but though in a sense correct that would be almost as misleading: strength and willpower are simply irrelevant concepts in this description of overmastering emotion in a visionary scene.

My conclusion is that the power and interest of this passage does not lie in the attempt at psychological explanation. The claims that the mind is master or that he had been strong are merely superimposed, and do not, I suggest, direct our attention at what is really important—the mysterious hold which these spots of time have on his memory, and the tremendous emotional force that the verse recreates as it describes them.

Let us move now to the more theoretical passage (lines 329–45) that separates the two episodes. It too was added at some point between 1799 and 1805, and it too offers us a strange mixture of the commonplace and the powerful. There are expressions of bewilderment ('I am lost . . . ') along with clear conclusions, in particular the claim that man's greatness must come from himself, and the statement of his purpose in writing the poem (enshrining 'the spirit of the past/ For future restoration'). Now what exactly does that first claim mean—what, that is, would be the alternative to coming from oneself? Coming from Nature (or God)? Or coming from society? If it is the first, it belongs with Wordsworth's many discussions of the projective/realist contrast which is discussed later in these units (and it is a surprisingly unhesitant, even dogmatic example of this); if the second, it would be a contribution to Wordsworth's views on education, that in order to profit from books and teachers we must first look within—a very Wordsworthian view, but less appropriate than the first to what is here being discussed.

It is not for either of these conclusions that I have quoted the passage, but for what comes between them, the groping towards the elusive:

> . . . the hiding-places of my power
> Seem open; I approach, and then they close.
> (XI: 336–37)

These lines offer a particularly good opportunity to do something we have not yet attempted: compare the 1805 text of *The Prelude* with the final version, published on Wordsworth's death in 1850.

> . . . the hiding-places of man's power
> Open: I would approach them, but they close.
> (XII: 279–80)

Exercise

Make a careful note of the verbal differences between these versions, and comment on them.

Answer

First, I suggest, there is a doctrinal change: an increased confidence that his experience offers the basis for a general point clearly underlines the change from 'my power' to 'man's power'. The changes in the second line show Wordsworth tampering with the verbs, and particularly with their mood, and reveal his awareness that the act he is so desperately trying to recapture, being an *act*, must be expressed through a sequence of verbs. His first change ('seem open' to 'open') is surely an improvement, simply because by changing 'open' to a verb it postulates action in the object of his quest; the second ('I approach' to 'I would approach'), though one can see the rhythmic reasons for making it, is for the same reason unfortunate, since it makes the act less definite. As for the change from 'then' to 'but', it compels us to ask what the passage is a description *of*.

It certainly seems a characteristically Romantic passage; for a parallel, we can turn to Shelley's discussion of inspiration in his *Defence of Poetry:* 'the mind in creation is as a fading coal, which some invisible influence, like an unconstant wind, awakens to transitory brightness.' Shelley is describing the elusiveness of poetic creation ('A man cannot say, "I will compose poetry" '); Wordsworth too seems to be describing the act of expression, but what is he struggling to express? Is he trying to find out *what* the hiding-places are, is it insight on which the gates are closing, so that he is failing, or almost failing, to discover what the base is on which man's greatness stands? If so, 'but' is the more appropriate reading. Or is it a struggle to remember the early spots of time, to recall, before oblivion overtakes them, just what he saw at the naked pool? 'Then' would be at least as appropriate to this reading. Is the passage, in short, about understanding or remembering? Of course the answer is both; but it is worth pointing out that they need not be the same, and in another poet probably would not be: the sheer fact that Wordsworth does not distinguish them shows why remembering the spots of time is so important for him.

In exploring this passage, I have found it useful to compare the earliest with the later versions. It is now necessary to point out that this comparison can be extended to the whole poem, and if we do that we shall see that it is an even more central passage than we might have thought. For to begin with, *The Prelude* consisted of virtually nothing except spots of time.

The first version of *The Prelude* was written in the winter of 1798–99, when Wordsworth and his sister were living in isolation in Goslar, in Germany. It consisted of 978 lines, divided into two parts. Though he tinkered briefly with it

66

two years later, he then left it largely untouched until the thorough revision and expansion that turned it into the thirteen-book version of 1805. After that there were further revisions to turn it into the fourteen books that were published shortly after his death in 1850. Ever since the 1805 version was published in 1926, it has become common to compare the two, and (often) to prefer its freshness to the greater polish of the final version, and we have chosen it as the text for this course. The differences between the 1805 and the 1850 versions, however, are trivial in comparison with that between the 1799 version and the expanded version. It will be worth our while, therefore, to look briefly at the poem Wordsworth originally wrote.

This 1799 *Prelude* begins, as we have already seen, in mid-sentence: 'Was it for this . . . ? It then moves into the following series of recollections: childhood bathing, trapping birds, rock-climbing, the boat at night, skating, card-playing, the drowned man in Esthwaite; then comes the 'spots of time' passage we have just discussed; then the gibbet and the girl with the pitcher, waiting for the horses at Christmas, looking out to sea at evening, and finally an account of how the memories, whether or not they lead to self-understanding, are precious because of the feelings associated with them, ending with the line about making infancy 'a visible scene on which the sun is shining'. That ends the first part; the second part corresponds fairly closely to Book II as we now have it.

It is clear then that the original *Prelude* was confined to childhood, and consisted of what are now the first two books minus the opening 271 lines, plus the episode of the drowned man (now Book V, lines 450–81), the spots of time passage, and the two spots of time that now follow it in Book XI. There are linking passages in the first part, very similar to those we now have in the first book, though with some interesting differences: thus

> . . . ye Beings of the hills!
> And ye that walk the woods and open heaths
> By moon or star-light . . .

becomes by 1805 (I: 428–31):

> Wisdom and Spirit of the universe!
> Thou Soul that art the Eternity of Thought!
> That giv'st to forms and images a breath
> And everlasting motion! . . .

The almost pagan quality of the first version has here given place to what we can call pantheism (pantheism can be briefly defined as the doctrine that God and Nature are identical); and the change is accompanied by the tone's growing more solemn as well.

What Wordsworth did when he expanded the poem, therefore, was to add the introductory section; to continue the story to about the age of twenty-five; to remove some of the spots of time to later books, and to add others—some of them, such as the vision of the dawn that he came to see as his moment of dedication to poetry (IV: 327–45), among the finest and most famous passages of the whole poem; and to add a good deal more in the way of explanation and analysis. This last was added in stages: much of the pantheism ('Soul of Nature') is there by 1805, as is much of the insistence on the moral benefits of Nature, but the explicitly Christian passages do not appear until later.

There was always some explanatory commentary interspersed with the memories, but the way it has grown can be seen by a simple arithmetical comparison. The original first part of 1799 has 464 lines, and contains at least nine spots of time—if we include the childhood bathing (now I: 291–304) and the fishing and kite-flying (now I: 505–524), which are repeated rather than single memories, it contains eleven. The thirteenth and last book of the 1805 version has 445 lines, and consists of one spot of time (the ascent of Snowdon—admittedly one of the longest and most famous), followed by an analysis of its significance that is very much longer than the episode itself, that soon leaves behind all the details of experience, and that leans very heavily on established moral terminology. Look for instance at XIII: 140–42:

> To fear and love,
> To love as first and chief, for there fear ends,
> Be this ascribed . . .

Virtually all the spots of time are solitary, communings with nature that involve no contact with other human beings. Is it not odd, then, that he claims that he was learning to love? This claim too seems to me a piece of moralizing imposed on the earlier text, rather than growing out of it.

Few critics of Wordsworth would deny that *The Prelude* is an uneven poem, and that the truly marvellous passages are, for the most part, the spots of time, which were already there in the 1799 version. In expanding this to nine times its length, Wordsworth felt he was making it a more ambitious poem, telling the story of his life more fully and with fuller understanding; and most readers have accepted this claim. I would like to conclude this section by suggesting a less orthodox view. This is that the original two-part poem has a strong claim to being considered as the authentic *Prelude*. In it the spots of time have not yet been dispersed among ever longer stretches of discussion which, when they lose touch with the actual memories, are in constant danger of becoming vapid and moralizing; and the central subject, the growth of a poet's mind, is presented with just enough (often implicit) commentary to constitute a powerful, exploratory and ultimately mysterious account of his development. To enable you to decide for yourself if this claim is justified, we have printed as an appendix (pp. 140ff.) the First Part of the 1799 *Prelude* (there is no need to reprint the second, since it corresponds closely to the second book you have read). After reading this through, you will be able to judge if I am being merely eccentric in wishing Wordsworth had left it as it was.

Robbing the traps

After this wide-ranging discussion of *The Prelude* as a whole, it is now time to look closely at a particular episode. This is of course an exercise you can perform for yourself, and perhaps already have: choose one of those that seem to you particularly powerful, familiarize yourself with the text, and then ask yourself how the emotional effect emerges from the language. We shall choose as our example the episode of the trap-robbing (I: 305–32). It is not as complex as, say, the marvellous episodes of the boat-stealing (372–427) or the ascent of Snowdon (XIII: 1–90), but it is very moving, and small enough to be exhaustively discussed. Now you should pause and read the passage, preferably several times, and at more than one sitting, until you feel you know it well.

Exercise

When you are ready to formulate your response, pay particular attention to the diction (kind of vocabulary used) and the moral (if any) that is being drawn; and ask yourself just what we are being told about the episode.

Answer

What is most striking about this passage is, perhaps, its sense of movement. The poet is constantly and restlessly on the move, and the mention of the 'open

Caspar David Friedrich, Landscape in the Riesengebirge, with Rising Mist, *c. 1822. (Neue Pinakothek, Munich. Photo: Bildarchiv Foto Marburg)*

heights' and the 'smooth green turf', by their sense of spaciousness, reinforce the wide-ranging movement already conveyed by the verbs (even more strongly in the 1799 version, which contains

> . . . hurrying on,
> Still hurrying, hurrying onward.)

Wordsworth's autobiographical poetry tends to show him, in youth, in a state of restless motion, most famously in 'Tintern Abbey' (67–72):

> . . . when like a roe
> I bounded o'er the mountains, . . . more like a man
> Flying from something that he dreads than one
> Who sought the thing he loved.

This restlessness is often conveyed with a note of apology or self-rebuke, but Wordsworth cannot disguise the fact that it represents his most intense experiences, more intense (and often issuing in more powerful poetry) than the maturity to which it later yielded. The self-reproach is seen here in the concluding lines, in which his sense of vague guilt is projected on the landscape in the form of the mysterious sounds that surround him. These concluding lines, with their images of the 'low breathings', are an excellent example of how poetry can be both vague and precise. The suggestiveness and mystery central to so much Romantic poetry appear to lead to the view that imprecise statements will be more poetic, because more haunting, than firm and clear-cut ones; but at the same time, we are accustomed to value poetry for the precision with which it is able to convey an effect in exactly the right words. The paradox in this is exemplified—and explained— by lines such as these. What exactly the poet heard is left uncertain; the experience never quite crossed the threshold of perception, and the passage would lose its mystery if the sounds were either clearly perceived or clearly explained. How wrong it would have been to fall back on ready-made concepts, and use words like 'guilt' or 'uneasy conscience'. Yet the language conveys perfectly that half-perceived and half-understood experience: 'undistinguishable' is an exact rendering of what happened, and the shift from 'sounds' to 'undistinguishable motion' suggests the straining to pin down which of the senses will best capture the experience. The last line extends the haunting by the way it steals back from the sounds to the land itself. The experience is vague, but the language is precise.

Several of the effects of the passage depend on diction, and to explain this we can remind ourselves of a well-known fact about English vocabulary. Almost all English words come from one of two sources, either Anglo-Saxon, or Latin (either direct or via French). The Anglo-Saxon words are usually common, concrete, familiar ('fair', 'grow', 'frost', 'breath', 'snap'), and even when not frequently used have an earthy ordinariness about them (think of 'clink' or 'plump'). The Latinate words tend to be more abstract, longer and (even when very common) sound more formal. Since English vocabulary is so rich, and since there are often Saxon and Latinate terms for the same thing, we have a choice of which store of vocabulary to draw on. One result of this for poetry is the possibility of shifting from Saxon to Latinate diction, or vice versa, and this passage makes brilliant use of such shifts. Take the sentence beginning 'On the heights': the first line and a half are pure Saxon, then we get 'I plied/My anxious visitation', in which all three of the words that carry meaning are Latinate. This is wholly appropriate for the shift from physical movement to the moral significance of his actions. The plain descriptive but resonant sentence 'Moon and stars/ Were shining o'er my head' is wholly Saxon, as is the beginning of the next, until we come to the Latinate 'trouble'. Perhaps we can say that Wordsworth troubled the still night in the way Latinate diction troubles the simplicity of our Saxon language.

I have already suggested that the moral conclusions drawn by Wordsworth when he reflects on the influence of Nature tend to be superimposed and misleading; and this passage provides a good example. Why did he feel the indeterminate guilt, the uneasiness, that led to the disturbing experience of the last lines? The passage tells us that this followed on stealing the bird from someone else's trap, but it is hard to believe that Wordsworth's Nature would care much about who the bird belonged to once caught. The offence against Nature, if there is one, must consist in the trapping itself. The same point can be made about the boat-stealing episode, for the parallels between the two are very close. Just as in the trap-robbing he 'seem'd to be a trouble to the peace', so in the boat-stealing he tells us

> It was an act of stealth
> And troubled pleasure.

And both episodes end with the poet haunted by mysterious feelings of guilt. It would be very superficial to attribute the nightmares and disturbing forms of lines 417–27 to the fact that he had taken a boat which did not belong to him. In some mysterious way (too mysterious for any rational self-reproach to be possible) the child's very presence on the lake was an offence. At their profoundest level these experiences, like all the crucial experiences of the poem, are below understanding.

Beauty and fear

What have the spots of time got in common? By trying to answer this question, we will surely learn a good deal about Wordsworth's view of his own development. At the least, we shall learn what kind of experience mattered most to him. And this is a question you can, once you have got to know the poem, begin to answer for yourself. Even if you have only read the abridged version which I suggested as a minimum, you will have come across most of the spots of time.

Exercise

As you reflect on them, can you suggest qualities they all share, or that will divide them into contrasting groups?

Answer

One very obvious point is perhaps worth making to begin with. None of the episodes has any external importance: a biographer would never know they were significant, if Wordsworth had not told him. We can see this very clearly by looking at the two spots of time which are connected with important external events, one public and one private: the death of Robespierre (x: 466–566), and the death of his father, which we have already referred to (xi: 346–89). In both cases, it is not the obvious importance of the event as an event that makes it one of the spots of time; what matters is how one event links with another in Wordsworth's memory. In the case of the death of Robespierre this is very striking, and tells us something significant about the poem.

No fewer than three books of *The Prelude* are devoted to the French Revolution; they tell the story of how his earlier hopes led to disillusion, culminating in a period of agonized inner conflict, during which he 'yielded up moral questions in despair', and from which he was gradually rescued by concentrating, under his sister's guidance, on his vocation as a poet. This might suggest that the French Revolution was of crucial importance in Wordsworth's development, and yet I did not include it in the parts I suggested you concentrate on. Did that give a false impression of the poem?

There are some powerful passages in the French Revolution books (you might like to look at x: 38–82, for instance), and of course you should if you possibly can read the whole *Prelude*. All the same, I think the decision not to concentrate on them can be defended, for a reason that will become clear if we look more carefully at the death of Robespierre episode.

Exercise

Make a short summary of what happened, and of what precedes and follows it in the poem, before you read on.

Answer

Perhaps you did not bother to mention one obvious point: that Wordsworth describes not the death of Robespierre, but how he learned about it. This was from a group of travellers he happened to meet when visiting the grave of his childhood teacher in Furness; we are prepared for the receiving of the news by a detailed account of his childhood memories and his reflections at the graveside, and although the news itself is followed by an account of the hopes he now felt for the future of France, we are told nothing of whether these hopes were realized; as we move towards the climax, politics are left behind, and we are reminded that it all took place on the very spot where he had ridden as a child. The last line is a deliberate echo from Book II: 'We beat with thundering hoofs the level sand'— and in the 1850 version, Wordsworth even ends the book at this point. A public event has been turned into a private event.

In all the remaining spots of time, no external event of any importance is even mentioned. Romantic biography, of which *The Prelude* is so central an example, has very little connexion with conventional biography, for it deals with material that is otherwise inaccessible to the biographer: not with the events which look important from the outside, but with those which felt important when experienced. For this reason, there seems no particular need to inform ourselves about the events of Wordsworth's life when reading *The Prelude*.

Our next point about the spots of time is one that divides them into two groups. Wordsworth himself makes such a division when he describes the means used by Nature in his growth (I: 362–71), on the one hand 'seeking him/With gentlest visitation', on the other employing 'severer interventions, ministry/More palpable'. As you get to know the final two books, you will find that this contrast is returned to over and over: it is not a subsequent and superficial comment, but something that Wordsworth was always conscious of. Some of the experiences were of calm and joy, others were of fear, and often deeply disturbing. The first group includes the skating (I: 452–89), rowing on the lake to music (II: 170–93), morning walks (II: 341–71) and hooting at the owls (V: 389–413—discussed later, pp. 85ff.). The second includes many of the most famous passages: as well as the trap-robbing (already discussed) and the boat-stealing in Book I, the dream of the Bedouin (V: 49–139), the brooding on the September Massacres (X: 38–82) and both the episodes of Book XI. Both kinds of experience are characteristically Wordsworthian, but they reveal very different aspects of his sensibility.

The calm experiences are closer to Wordsworth the poet of Nature as he is usually thought of, for they suggest harmony with the world around him. Perhaps the crucial phrase for this feeling is 'the sentiment of Being', most strikingly used in II: 420:

> . . . I was only then
> Contented when with bliss ineffable
> I felt the sentiment of Being spread
> O'er all that moves, and all that seemeth still . . .

Similar passages can be found not only in *The Prelude* but in 'Tintern Abbey' (the famous account of the 'presence that disturbs me with the joy/Of elevated thoughts') and even in *Michael*, who felt 'the pleasure that there is in life itself.' This calm, almost contentless, awareness of one's own existence once again recalls the Rousseau of the fifth *Promenade*, and seems to be the equivalent in experience of Wordsworth's pantheism, the worship not of a transcendent God but of a presence immanent in the universe. Here are a few passages you might like to compare with these lines: II: 321–26, II: 359–71, the continuation of the lines just quoted as far as II: 434, IV: 150–55, and the following fragment, which was not included in the final version of the poem:

> By such communion I was early taught
> That what we see of forms and images
> Which float along our minds and what we feel
> Of active, or recognizable thought
> Prospectiveness, intelligence or will
> Not only is not worthy to be deemed
> Our being, to be prized as what we are
> But is the very littleness of life
> Such consciousnesses seemed but accidents
> Relapses from the one interior life
> Which is in all things, from that unity
> In which all beings live with God, are lost
> In god and nature, in one mighty whole
> As undistinguishable as the cloudless east
> At noon is from the cloudless west when all
> The hemisphere is one cerulean blue.

Exercise

Read through these passages again, looking carefully at the use made of images that present themselves to the senses, and at the comments about the poet's awareness of the external world. This will mean you are considering what Wordsworth has to say about images as they occur in perception; then ask yourself about Wordsworth's use of images *as a poet* and see if you can relate the two trains of thought.

Answer

I wonder if you are struck by the same thing as I am. The fragment above suggests that the 'forms and images' we see, like our active thoughts, are mere superficial accidents compared with our experience of 'the one interior life/Which is in all things'. This explains why the 'elevated mood' of II: 325 was 'unprofaned' by form or image, and the holy calm of II: 367 left the bodily eyes forgotten. We seemed to be concerned with an experience that has no sense-content.

But what is poetry if not a matter of form and image? How can experience be conveyed if the essential point about it is that there was no perceptible content? Wordsworth writes of 'bliss ineffable', and the original meaning of 'ineffable' is 'what cannot be spoken of'. Are we then concerned with an experience it is not possible to write about?

Since Wordsworth's most profound experiences are almost, at times, without sense-content, he seems cut off from most of the natural ways of talking about what happens to us. It is astonishing in that case how well he succeeds (II: 367–71):

> Oft in those moments such a holy calm
> Did overspread my soul, that I forgot
> That I had bodily eyes, and what I saw
> Appear'd like something in myself, a dream,
> A prospect in my mind.

It is not easy to describe how such writing works; perhaps the closest we can come is to say that it concentrates on the processes of consciousness. It is an attempt, at the same time, to remember and to understand, to recall what the experience was, and to understand what it was like—a close parallel to the discussion earlier of the lines

> . . . the hiding-places of man's power
> Open: I would approach them, but they close.

in which I suggested that the lines are struggling both to recall and to understand, and the two struggles are seen as one.

Another parallel with our earlier discussion is here possible. I have already suggested that vague and elusive experience can be expressed with precision, and something of the same paradox is seen in these 'mystical' passages. Look back at the fragment beginning 'By such communion', and in particular at its last three lines. Do they use forms and images? Asking that question, we see that the distinction Wordsworth is drawing can exist *within* sense-perception. There are no images or recognizable thoughts in the lines if we are looking for particular sense-perceptions, there is none of the 'infinite variety of natural appearances' that Wordsworth, in a famous but misleading remark, declared it was his aim to introduce into poetry. But the lines do describe a sense-perception, a very powerful one, of the kind that corresponds to an awareness of the one interior life. Once again, can we not say that the experience is indeterminate, the language precise?

Let us turn now to the other set of experiences, those that brought fear. They suggest to me a very different Wordsworth: a man suffering from deep anxieties, haunted by a frightened distress which he tries desperately to control. This is the Wordsworth who was fascinated by geometry—an unlikely passion, surely, for a man feeling himself in harmony with Nature, but all too likely for a man who can write (VI: 178–80):

> Mighty is the charm
> Of those abstractions to a mind beset
> With images, and haunted by itself . . .

The tribute to his sister Dorothy which Wordsworth inserted at the end of the final book confesses that he too exclusively 'sought that beauty . . . which/Hath terror in it', and praised her for softening the 'countenance severe' of his soul. All this suggests that the mind whose growth we watch in *The Prelude* was more deeply disturbed than is always realized, and that the powerful lines about the way the huge peak haunted him after the boat-stealing episode are central to the poem. The most convincing account of this side of Wordsworth's sensibility is that of David Perkins, who finds in him 'a suffocating, almost panicky fear that man is doomed to isolation from the healthful influences of his natural surroundings'. It seems an eccentric, even perverse account of our great poet of Nature, but the evidence for it is there, and in some of the finest poetry.

There would be no point in asking which is the 'correct' view of Wordsworth's relation to Nature. We could hold a war of quotations, setting against each other those passages which confirm the orthodox view of a Wordsworth who believes in benevolent Nature and the benign influence of mountain solitude, with Perkins's Wordsworth, for whom man (this is the most extreme statement of all) seems to be 'a kind of fungus momentarily clinging to the bleak immutable rock'. That would simply serve to show that both are real, and that Wordsworth, as he tells us, grew up 'fostered alike by beauty and by fear'.

The poetry of memory

One final point about the spots of time. Many of them include not only the experience that is being remembered, but also the process of remembering. We have already seen this in the case of the two episodes of Book XI, in both of which the original memory is overlaid by a subsequent memory, the two being contrasted in the case of the gibbet scene, merged in the case of the waiting for the horses. To look more carefully at this point, let us consider the opening of Book II, and especially the lines 27–33.

Exercise

Read them carefully and ask yourself what they tell us about the poet's relationship to his past. Do they seem to you to contain a paradox?

Answer

On the one hand these lines tell us of the gulf between the self who is writing and the childhood self he is recalling, the two separated by a gap that cannot be crossed. Yet the gap quite patently *is* being crossed, not only by the vividness with which the childhood games have just been described (' . . . to bed we went,/With weary joints, and with a beating mind'), but by the statement that the early days 'have such self-presence in my mind'. The two distinct Beings are both present in the same consciousness, and the experience of division is also an experience of unity—as is clear from the lines

A tranquillizing spirit presses now
On my corporeal frame . . .

(Notice the verb 'presses', by the way: the experience of remembering is felt as something bodily.)

Exercise

Look now at IV: 247–68. After reading this passage carefully, note down what seems to you the function of the simile: what is being compared with what, and how does the passage fit into the poem as a whole?

Answer

Long similes like this are a characteristic of epic poetry, and *Paradise Lost* is rich in them; and once again, Wordsworth is pouring new wine into the Miltonic bottle, following precedent, but in a way that illustrates his personal, untraditional subject-matter, as we see by addressing ourselves to the questions I have asked. It is a simile for memory, clearly: the person in the boat, making out the beauteous sights under the water, is like someone searching his memory. His inability to part 'the shadow from the substance' must correspond to the difficulty of remembering, and if we press the parallel we can say that the confusion between shadow and substance is like the confusion between what really is in the memory, and what only seems to be there (perhaps because it is part of the present, perhaps because we simply made it up). The line which most perfectly fuses tenor and vehicle in the comparison is surely 'Incumbent o'er the surface of past time', in which the person in the boat and the person remembering seem completely identified.

Now what is the passage doing in the poem? If you read on, you will see that it introduces the episodes that follow, telling us that they are as fair and as clear as any which preceded. But if that were all it were doing, it would seem a very elaborate passage for such a simple transition; it also surely connects with the poem as a whole, drawing our attention to what is really its main activity.

For *The Prelude* is a poem of memory, not only in the obvious sense that writing about one's early experiences requires the poet to remember them, but also in the sense that the process of remembering is itself part of the subject, so that the experiences emerge tinged with the fact that they are being recalled. This is the element in Wordsworth that anticipates Proust, and entitles us to say that the true parallel to *The Prelude* is Proust's great novel *A la recherche du temps perdu* (translatable as 'In Search of Lost Time' or as 'In Search of the Past'). Both authors regard the act of remembering as not only a parallel to but also as the basis of artistic creation.

You will recall the claim made in the Preface to *Lyrical Ballads*, that poetry takes its origin in emotion recollected in tranquillity.

> The emotion is contemplated till by a species of reaction the tranquillity gradually disappears, and an emotion, kindred to that which was before the subject of contemplation, is gradually produced, and does itself actually exist in the mind.

This could almost be a description of the recalling of some of the spots of time:

> —Unfading recollections! at this hour
> The heart is almost mine with which I felt
> From some hill-top, on sunny afternoons
> The Kite high up among the fleecy clouds
> Pull at its rein, like an impatient Courser . . .
> (I: 517–21)

Proust, for whom the difference between unconscious memory and the comparatively superficial voluntary memory was so important, would never have written 'unfading recollections'; but though Wordsworth makes this claim, the most vivid physical detail in the lines—'pull at its rein'—seems rather to suggest the sharp tug with which a forgotten memory shoots up into consciousness.

Even when Wordsworth is apologetic for the persistence with which he returns to his 'recollected hours', it is often in the firm tone of one who knows he is doing the right thing. An example of this is I: 657–63 (the passage, you will recall, which concluded the first part of the 1799 *Prelude*). Its culminating image,

> And almost make our Infancy itself
> A visible scene, on which the sun is shining . . .

contains, once again, no explicit admission that the memory had disappeared and been recaptured, but once again the vivid physical detail (in this case, the last line) suggests a discovery rather than a constant presence—especially if we connect this passage with the lines from Book XI we have so often reverted to:

> The days gone by
> Come back upon me from the dawn almost
> Of life . . .

Proust and Wordsworth are probably our two greatest poets of childhood, yet in neither of them is childhood given any special status. Many of Wordsworth's spots of time are from childhood, yet as Wordsworth extended the story into his mid-twenties he continued to find them, and he removed the statement that such moments 'chiefly seem to have their date in our first childhood'. A Freudian dealing with this material would probably claim that the emotional quality of the memories is due to something in the quality of the child's psyche, that is later buried or sublimated. Wordsworth claims something like this in the 'Immortality Ode' (see pp. 110ff. below), though in very different terms, philosophical rather than psychological, advancing a Platonic doctrine of pre-existence to explain the quality of childhood vision. *The Prelude*, however, certainly in its finest parts, refrains from psychological explanation: it knows nothing of how the memories operate, only that they do. This may disappoint some of the expectations of the modern reader, especially the modern Freudian reader; but that disappointment is so intimately bound up with the rewards of memory, that it is hard to wish the poem had been written differently.

Wordsworth and pastoral

In this section we shall look at Book VIII, in order both to study a further element in the poem itself, and to relate it to a different tradition.

Exercise

Before proceeding, turn to Book VIII, and read the whole if you have time, and at least lines 62–471, paying particular attention to what Wordsworth has to say about the shepherds, how he responds to them, and how the shepherds he knew contrast with those of poetic tradition.

Answer

You will perhaps have been struck by the fact that this book is less introspective than the others: it is concerned with the environment in which Wordsworth grew up, and there is a good deal about the countryside itself before we move to its effect on the poet. You will remember that the Preface to *Lyrical Ballads* announced

76

that humble and rustic life provided the best setting for observing the essential passions of the heart, and this book can be seen as an extended illustration of that claim.

As well as describing the rustic society of the north-west of England, Wordsworth contrasts it with other, more familiar, versions of the shepherd's life. Some of these are listed in lines 183–220: first, the legendary life of the shepherds ruled by Saturn in the Golden Age, then those of Shakespeare's plays *As you Like It* and *The Winter's Tale*, then the May Day revels of folk-lore that he had heard about but never seen. Then, beginning at line 312, he describes the carefree life of shepherds in 'old time', by the side of various Italian rivers (all of them mentioned in Latin poetry: Galesus by Virgil and Horace, Clitumnus by Virgil, and so on) and the glimpses he himself caught of an idyllic rustic existence when he was in Goslar.

Wordsworth's aim in compiling this list is to detach his poem from the pastoral tradition. The idyllic life of shepherds in a warm climate whose life is never strenuous, whose hardest task is carving a beechen bowl, is illustrated indifferently from fact, fiction or legend: such uncertainty belongs to pastoral, with its idealized view of a country life that is located in a more-or-less legendary past (the Golden Age) or in a more-or-less fanciful version of a real place (Arcadia). Wordsworth is following the spirit of this convention when he adds a Germany that he once briefly visited and never felt to be as real as his native England.

In contrast to this idyllic existence, the shepherds of the Lake District led a life that was strenuous, free and difficult, terrifying yet also inspiring. They were examples of 'Man free, man working for himself, with choice/Of time, and place, and object'. To designate the difference between this picture and that of the pastoral tradition, we can borrow the useful contrast made by A. O. Lovejoy and George Boas, in *Primitivism and Relative Ideas in Antiquity* (1935), and speak of soft and hard primitivism. The primitive life can be preferred to the sophisticated because it is simple, leisurely and idyllic: shepherds lead an unproblematic existence in which they play the flute, woo shepherdesses, and relax in carefree ease. That is the result of Theocritus's *Idylls*, Virgil's *Eclogues*, and much Renaissance poetry: it is frail, but delightful while it lasts. But the primitive life can also be praised because it is simple, austere and tough: shepherds lead an unproblematic existence in which they struggle for a living, drink water and eat simple fare, learn to be hardy, healthy and of stern character. That is the country life amid which Wordsworth grew up, among the 'snows and streams/Ungovernable', and the 'terrifying winds' of his native region.

Wordsworth is replacing a conventional version of shepherd life by one drawn from his own experience; yet it would be wrong to say that he is replacing an idealized by a real version. For in its way, his version contains as much idealization as the Forest of Arden. This is clear if we ask how much he appears to have known about the life of Lakeland shepherds. He does not seem to have spoken to them, or been familiar with their daily problems. What impressed him was the glimpses he caught of them through mist, or outlined against the setting sun. Though he did not give them Latin names, or see them through the eyes of Virgil, he admits that he had little contact with them; they were 'ennobled' by the way they loomed suddenly in front of him like not altogether human creatures, and he is thankful that they presented themselves to him 'thus purified' and (in a very revealing line) 'remov'd, and at a distance that was fit'. It is not surprising, in the light of this line, to learn that Wordsworth always had the reputation, in the Lake District, of keeping apart from his country neighbours. A volume of *Reminiscences* of Wordsworth and the peasantry of Westmorland, by one Canon Rawnsley, speaks of his seclusion, the distance he kept from their cottage homes and the rarity of his mingling with them, and even suggests that this enabled him to forget their faults when writing of them.

So in suggesting that Book VIII is less introspective than the earlier books, we must add that Wordsworth may not have been capable of truly emerging from himself to see rustic life as it was. He tells us frequently, both in *The Prelude* and 'Tintern Abbey', that love of Nature led him, in his maturity, to love of man. But 'love of man' does not often mean love of men. There is very little in *The Prelude* about contact with other people. This point is so striking that it has led one of Wordsworth's best critics, David Ferry, to say of Wordsworth, 'his genius was his enmity to man, which he mistook for love'. This may seem to you an extreme statement, but it calls attention, very strikingly, to Wordsworth's isolation. Coleridge described him as *spectator ab extra*, the spectator from outside. The Wordsworth of *The Prelude* thinks about people more than he talks to them, and he thinks about mankind more than he thinks about people.

You might in conclusion like to compare your reading of *The Prelude* with your reading of *Lyrical Ballads*. Our discussion has referred more than once to 'Tintern Abbey', which is obviously the poem that anticipates, and even overlaps with, his account of the growth of his own mind. But 'Tintern Abbey' is not typical of *Lyrical Ballads*, most of which tell stories of rural life to illustrate the primary laws of our nature, and in which the poet himself does not appear. They show us a different side of Wordsworth's complex genius, one in which, you may feel, he interests himself not only in man but in men. Or does he? We will leave you with the question.

5 Imagination

(By LL)

Coleridge's theory of imagination

The following section deals with the literary theory of Coleridge and Wordsworth, and in particular with their idea of imagination. The subject is interesting and important in itself, as helping us understand the Romantic view of literature, and as part of the development of theories of the mind; but poems are of course more important than theories of poetry, and our eventual aim will be to use the theory as a way in to their poetry. But our starting point is theory, and we shall therefore begin with Coleridge's famous definition of imagination in Chapters XIII and XIV of the *Biographia Literaria*. It needs careful reading.

> The IMAGINATION then, I consider either as primary, or secondary. The primary IMAGINATION I hold to be the living Power and prime Agent of all human Perception, and as a repetition in the finite mind of the eternal act of creation in the infinite I AM. The secondary Imagination I consider as an echo of the former, co-existing with the conscious will, yet still as identical with the primary in the *kind* of its agency, and differing only in *degree*, and in the *mode* of its operation. It dissolves, diffuses, dissipates, in order to re-create; or where this process is rendered impossible, yet still at all events it struggles to idealize and to unify. It is essentially *vital*, even as all objects (*as* objects) are essentially fixed and dead.
>
> FANCY, on the contrary, has no other counters to play with, but fixities and definites. The Fancy is indeed no other than a mode of Memory emancipated from the order of time and space; while it is blended with, and modified by

that empirical phenomenon ot the will, which we express by the word CHOICE. But equally with the ordinary memory the Fancy must receive all its materials ready made from the law of association.

*   *   *

This power, first put in action by the will and understanding, and retained under their irremissive, though gentle and unnoticed, controul . . . reveals itself in the balance or reconciliation of opposite or discordant qualities: of sameness, with difference; of the general, with the concrete; the idea, with the image; the individual, with the representative; the sense of novelty and freshness, with old and familiar objects; a more than usual state of emotion, with more than usual order; judgement ever awake and steady self-possession, with enthusiasm and feeling profound or vehement; and while it blends and harmonizes the natural and the artificial, still subordinates art to nature; the manner to the matter; and our admiration of the poet to our sympathy with the poetry. (Vol. I, page 202; vol. II, page 12)

There are two main everyday uses of the term 'imagination'. The first is that which says 'You just imagined that', or 'It didn't happen; it was just my imagination.' This usage contrasts imagination with reality, and it gives us the adjective 'imaginary' (i.e. not real). The second usage is that which refers to a poet or an artist as having a rich or fertile imagination. This refers to the power necessary for creating works of art, and it gives us the adjective 'imaginative'.

Exercise

Are these meanings of the word found in the passage?

Answer

The first, surely, is not there at all; and the second is what Coleridge calls the secondary imagination. It is clear, is it not, that the power described in the second extract ('to which,' Coleridge says, 'we have exclusively appropriated the name of imagination'), the power which balances 'sameness, with difference', is the same as the secondary imagination which 'dissolves, diffuses, dissipates, in order to re-create'; and that this is the faculty that creates poetry, the quality that we normally call 'imagination' in literary discussions.

Exercise

What then is the primary imagination?

Answer

The crucial sentence is that which asserts 'the primary IMAGINATION I hold to be the living Power and prime Agent of all human Perception'. This may sound surprising, but it is plain enough: imagination is the power that enables us to perceive the world. So far from regarding imagination as the faculty which misleads us into mistaking fictions for truth, Coleridge sees it as the faculty that puts us in touch with reality. Does this seem odd to you?

It may be at variance with everyday usage, but it is not an eccentricity on Coleridge's part: he derives it from his reading in philosophy, for in Hume, and still more in Kant, imagination is the faculty that bridges the gap between sensation and thought, enabling us to organize the data provided by our senses. By themselves, the senses would give us a world that was merely chaotic; by itself, the intellect would not be able to put any real content into the world. This involves a view of perception as active and creative, not as a mere passive acceptance of the external world: a view that derives from Kant, for whom all perception involved the imposition of certain 'constitutive categories' on an external world which would be unintelligible without them. For Kant, the world is not passively perceived; perception involves the mind's activity, and the faculty which does the ordering is called the synthetic imagination. Towards the end of his life, Coleridge wrote: 'the pith of my system is to make the senses out of the mind—not the mind out of the senses, as Locke did'. This is to declare himself a Kantian.

But though there is philosophical warrant for Coleridge's view, it was an innovation in literary criticism. For the mainstream of eighteenth-century thought, imagination was often regarded with suspicion. The following passage from John Locke's *Essay concerning Human Understanding* represents something like eighteenth-century orthodoxy:

> By *real ideas*, I mean such as have a foundation in nature; such as have a conformity with the real being and existence of things, or with their archetypes. *Fantastical* or *chimerical*, I call such as have no foundation in nature, nor have any conformity with that reality of being to which they are tacitly referred.

To this sturdy and commonsensical tradition, imagination (or fancy: the eighteenth century did not distinguish the terms) is misleading and dangerous, and ought always to be controlled by the judgement.

We shall return later to Coleridge's distinction between imagination and fancy. You will have noticed that he treats the latter with the same condescension that eighteenth-century critics displayed to both. Fancy is not related to the 'prime agent of all human perceptions', and is not an active constitutive faculty.

Exercise

Please read another passage from the *Biographia Literaria* (Chapter VII).

> Let us consider what we do when we leap. We first resist the gravitating power by an act purely voluntary, and then by another act, voluntary in part, we yield to it in order to light on the spot, which we had previously proposed to ourselves. Now let a man watch his mind while he is composing; or, to take a still more common case, while he is trying to recollect a name; and he will find the process completely analogous. Most of my readers will have observed a small water-insect on the surface of rivulets, which throws a cinque-spotted shadow fringed with prismatic colours on the sunny bottom of the brook; and will have noticed, how the little animal *wins* its way up against the stream, by alternate pulses of active and passive motion, now resisting the current, and now yielding to it in order to gather strength and a momentary *fulcrum* for a further propulsion. This is no unapt emblem of the mind's self-experience in the act of thinking. There are evidently two powers at work, which relatively to each other are active and passive; and this is not possible without an intermediate faculty, which is at once both active and passive. (In philosophical language, we must denominate this intermediate faculty in all its degrees and determinations, the IMAGINATION. But, in common language, and especially on the subject of poetry, we appropriate the name to a superior degree of the faculty, joined to a superior voluntary controul over it.) (Vol. I, pp. 85–86)

Does this refer to the primary or the secondary imagination?

Answer

The faculty that enables us to think by joining together our passive reception of sense-impressions, and our active synthesizing of them by imposing the necessary conditions for empirical knowledge, sounds very like Kant's synthesizing imagination, and the reference to 'philosophical language' may well be an admission of its Kantian origin. (We shall not bother about Coleridge's more immediate debt to other German thinkers—Schelling and Schlegel—since the concepts are primarily Kantian.) Now clearly, in Coleridge's terminology, this must be the primary imagination. It is concerned with our apprehension of the external world, that is, with perception; and it is contrasted with the 'superior degree of the faculty' that the term is appropriated to 'in common language, and especially on the subject of poetry', which is clearly the secondary imagination.

Organic and mechanical

We move now to a closely connected point about literary creation; and we can begin from a conventional eighteenth-century critic:

> It would be no less absurd, for a poet to violate the *essential* rules of his art, and justify himself by an appeal from the tribunal of Aristotle, than for a mechanic to construct an engine on principles inconsistent with the laws of motion, and excuse himself by disclaiming the authority of Sir Isaac Newton. (James Beattie, *Essays on Poetry and Music*, 1776)

Since the Romantics, writing a poem has not often been compared to constructing an engine. In drawing the parallel, Beattie refers to 'rules': what are the rules of poetry? The most famous 'rules' in the seventeenth and eighteenth centuries were the dramatic unities of time, place and action, that were (quite wrongly) attributed to Aristotle. Beattie may not be defending these particular rules, though he may well have considered the unity of action to be one of the 'essential' rules of the art; but he is certainly claiming scientific status for some sort of rules, as did Pope in his *Essay on Criticism*, that defence of clarity, good sense and decorum:

> Those rules of old, discovered not devised,
> Are Nature still, but Nature methodized.

Newton's laws could also, surely, be described as 'Nature methodized'.

Here, on the other hand, is Coleridge:

> Yes, not to acquire cold notions—lifeless technical rules—but living and life-producing ideas, which shall contain their own evidence, the certainty that they are essentially one with the germinal causes of nature,—his consciousness being the focus and mirror of both,—for this does the artist for a time abandon the external real in order to return to it with a complete sympathy with its internal and actual. ('On Poesy or Art', 1818; reprinted with *Biographia Literaria*, ed. Shawcross, vol. II, pp. 258–59)

Lifeless, technical rules are here contrasted with the true exercise of the imagination. Though Coleridge does not here use the term, the idea of abandoning the external real in order to return to it is an exact parallel to 'dissolves, diffuses, dissipates, in order to recreate'. Poets, for Coleridge, do not need rules, because the imagination operates not mechanically but organically. What does this contrast mean?

> The difference between an inorganic and an organic body lies in this:—In the first—a sheaf of corn—the whole is nothing more than a collection of the individual parts of phenomena. In the second—a man—the whole is the effect of, or results from, the parts; it—the whole—is everything, and the parts are nothing. (Coleridge, *Table Talk*, 18 December 1831)

The word 'organic' comes from a Greek word meaning 'tool', but that origin seems to have disappeared in the Coleridgean use. So important to him is the emphasis on 'living and life-producing ideas' and on the 'germinal causes of Nature', that a good deal of his criticism, indeed of much Romantic criticism, describes literature in terms that are metaphorical when used of writing but would be literal if used of a plant.

On this point, Romantic thought scored what has often seemed a definitive victory. Literary theory said 'good riddance' to the mechanical doctrine of association of ideas (see page 16 above), just as Coleridge (who had been attracted to it in his youth) came to reject it totally as a psychological theory. Here is a letter to Southey in which we can see this rejection at work:

> While I wrote that last sentence, I had a vivid recollection, indeed an ocular spectrum, of our room in College Street, a curious instance of association. You remember how incessantly in that room I used to be compounding these half-verbal, half-visual metaphors. It argues, I am persuaded, a particular state of general feeling, and I hold that association depends in a much greater degree on the recurrence of resembling states of feeling than on trains of ideas, that the recollection of early childhood in latest old age depends on and is explicable by this, and if this be true, Hartley's system totters . . . I almost think that ideas *never* recall ideas, as far as they are ideas, any more than leaves in a forest create each other's motion. The breeze it is that runs through them—it is the soul, the state of feeling. (Coleridge to Southey, 7 August 1803)

Perhaps a brief subversive comment is in order at this point. No victories are definitive in the history of ideas, and we live now in the age of cybernetics. The enormous revolution that computer programming has brought about in our understanding of mental life could be described as a resurgence of the mechanical analogy: for a programme consists, essentially, of the splitting up of complex mental operations into their constituent parts. If we add the point that modern biology now explains so many organic processes in mechanistic terms, we can ask ourselves if the organic analogies we owe to the Romantics have had their day. Neo-Romantics may take comfort in the fact that computers have not yet been programmed to write poetry.

But however great the eighteenth-century stress on rules and precedents, on competence and professionalism, in literature, they also had a very old doctrine which tells us that poetry cannot be written simply by taking thought.

Exercise

Can you suggest what this is?

Answer

I am thinking of the idea of inspiration. Literally, to be inspired is to be 'breathed on' by Apollo or one of the Muses or (if the context is Christian) by the Holy Spirit. This belief goes back at least to Plato, and there has never been a time when some version of it was not held: it serves to remind us that the powers required to write true poetry are never within the poet's complete control and that no analysis can succeed in telling us that they are. And Coleridge himself has left us one of the most marvellous accounts of the inspired poet ever written, in his description, at the end of 'Kubla Khan', of what it would be like to possess true poetic powers:

> I would build that dome in air,
> That sunny dome! those caves of ice!
> And all who heard should see them there,
> And all should cry, Beware! Beware!

His flashing eyes, his floating hair!
Weave a circle round him thrice,
And close your eyes with holy dread,
For he on honey-dew hath fed,
And drunk the milk of Paradise.

It is difficult to imagine anything further removed from the poet of Beattie, who needs to learn the rules of his art as a mechanic learns to construct an engine.

It is time, surely, that we looked at some actual lines of poetry, and we can begin with those which Coleridge himself quotes. In an earlier discussion of fancy and imagination (*Biographia*, Chapter IV; see the Prose Booklet, page 32) he quotes as an example of fancy Otway's

Lutes, lobsters, seas of milk, and ships of amber

and as an example of imagination Shakespeare's

What! have his daughters brought him to this pass?

along with 'the preceding apostrophe to the elements'. Both are attempts to express madness. The first is almost a piece of nonsense-verse: the list of items is joined together by associations that lie on the surface—first alliteration, then a string of marine associations, then a deliberate distortion of colours. It is fun, but obviously not an example of unifying power. Coleridge has chosen it as an extreme contrast to the line from *King Lear*, which has no verbal ingenuity, and expresses an overmastering emotion, the obsession with his daughters' ingratitude. If you turn up the apostrophe to the elements (*King Lear*, III. ii):

Rumble thy bellyful! Spit, fire! spout, rain!
Nor rain, wind, thunder, fire, are my daughters.

you will see that the imaginative unity comes from the old king's dominant emotion. Now turn back to the letter to Southey, with its marvellously illuminating metaphor: there Coleridge claims that to explain how ideas are joined together by looking only at the ideas themselves, as the theory of association does, is like explaining the movement of leaves without mentioning the wind. And we are told what the wind corresponds to: it is feeling.

Clearly there is a connexion between the theory of imagination, and a theory which attributes central importance to the feeling or emotion that holds a vision of the world together. Such a theory gives us the view that poetry is the expression of emotion, a view that, as the Romantic movement progressed, came to be more or less orthodox. For John Stuart Mill, writing in 1833, poetry is 'the expression or uttering forth of feeling', for John Keble (1838) it is 'the indirect expression in words . . . of some overpowering emotion'. The seeds of this doctrine are undoubtedly present in Wordsworth and Coleridge: in Wordsworth's famous description of poetry as the 'spontaneous overflow of powerful feelings', and in Coleridge's claim (*Biographia*, Chapter XV) that 'images . . . become proofs of original genius only as far as they are modified by a predominant passion', a claim perfectly illustrated by Lear's speeches during the storm.

We are beginning to see that central to the Romantic view of literature is a cluster of ideas that could no doubt exist independently but tend to go together: the ideas of imagination, of inspiration and of the expression of emotion. What they have in common is that they play down the conscious and the rational elements in poetry. Neo-classic critics, or those who set a high value on reason as an element in poetic creation, are likely to be suspicious of these ideas, and it is certainly the case that they provide the origin of some of the intense irrationality and anti-intellectualism that we associate with the modern movement. But though Nietzsche and D. H. Lawrence may be the descendants of Romanticism, they would have astonished their ancestors, for the ideas of imagination, of the centrality of emotion and of the inspired poet are seldom if ever used by Wordsworth and Coleridge to attack reason. For them, powerful feelings overflowed into an expression that did nothing to subvert rational understanding; indeed, both of them have a strong strain of good sense that reminds us that there is continuity with neo-classic thought as well as reaction against it. This is clearly seen in Wordsworth's interest in tracing 'the primary laws of our nature', a very similar idea to the neo-classic belief in general laws of human nature; and in Coleridge's constant insistence that Shakespeare's judgement was equal to his genius. The first Romantics were by no means the most extreme.

Wordsworth's view of imagination

Imagination is not such a central concept in Wordsworth's criticism as are nature and feeling, but it is fully discussed in the 1815 Preface, the relevant part of which is reprinted in the Prose Booklet (pp. 24ff.).

Exercise

Ask yourself, as you read this, how the ideas there set forth compare with Coleridge's.

Answer

Wordsworth, like Coleridge, begins from the operation of the mind, insisting that imagination is not simply the faculty of reproducing absent objects, but involves 'processes of creation or of composition, governed by certain fixed laws'. The most important of these processes is that of

> consolidating numbers into unity, and dissolving and separating unity into number,—alternations proceeding from, and governed by, a sublime consciousness of the soul in her own mighty and almost divine powers.

If you compare this with Coleridge's definition (which you should be very familiar with by now), you will surely be struck by how close they are. Imagination is here contrasted with fancy in much the same way as by Coleridge: when for instance Wordsworth writes that 'fancy does not require that the materials which she makes use of should be susceptible of change in their constitution, from her touch', does this not sound very like Coleridge's claim that 'fancy has no other counters to play with, but fixities and definites'? And when it comes to finding examples of imagination, Wordsworth chooses the same aspect of Lear's madness that Coleridge was to use.

And how is imagination manifested in the actual text of a poem? The orthodox eighteenth-century answer would have been, through the use of marvels, fictions, impossibilities and what Addison called 'the fairy way of writing'. Coleridge's greatest poems, of course, give us just this, and the eighteenth century would have had no difficulty in identifying 'The Ancient Mariner', 'Kubla Khan' and 'Christabel' as poems of imagination. But it is clear from all we have just discussed that Coleridge's view is nothing like this, and if you have read the plan of *Lyrical Ballads* in Chapter XIV of the *Biographia* (see Prose Booklet, pp. 33ff.) you will know that he was concerned to emphasize the similarity between his own poems of the supernatural and Wordsworth's poems of the everyday. And Wordsworth's view is nothing like this either, as we can see from his declaration that *Peter Bell* was written

> under a belief that the Imagination not only does not require for its exercise the intervention of supernatural agency, but that, though such agency be excluded, the faculty may be called forth as imperiously, and for kindred results of pleasure, by incidents within the compass of poetic probability, in the humblest departments of daily life. (Epistle Dedicatory to *Peter Bell*, 1819; *Poetical Works*, ed. Hutchinson/de Selincourt, page 188)

And the examples of imagination in action given in the 1815 Preface are drawn indifferently from poetry of the marvellous and poetry of the ordinary, with no attention being paid to the distinction.

Exercise

Now read over what he says about the lines from Virgil, Shakespeare and Milton, and his own lines about bird-song, in order to discover how Wordsworth believes imagination is manifested.

Answer

The examples of *hang, brood* and *buried* are all metaphors. It looks as if Wordsworth believes that imagination is expressed through metaphor: a point to bear in mind when we come to discuss his poetry, since it is not obviously rich in metaphors.

Poems of the Imagination

We turn now to Wordsworth's poetry. When he collected his poems in 1815 he classified them in groups, mainly according to the faculty that they were based on: Poems founded on the Affections, Poems of the Fancy, Poems of the Imagination, etc. And among these last, he singled out two for particular discussion in the Preface, 'There was a Boy' and 'Resolution and Independence'. We can therefore be guided by him in our choice of poems.

'There was a Boy' was separately published in the 1800 *Lyrical Ballads*, and also forms part of *The Prelude*. You will find it in Book v, lines 389–422. Please read it carefully (and listen to it on cassette) before proceeding.

To write a poem about a child, his sports and his untimely death, is (and was) not unusual; but the reader who expects a picturesque sketch of childhood and its games will be surprised and perhaps disappointed by this poem, in which so little happens. Such a reader was Francis Jeffrey, the influential editor of the *Edinburgh Review* (see the Prose Booklet, extract 3), whose austere eighteenth-century taste was irritated by Wordsworth's 'unpoetic' and matter-of-fact simplicities. Here are Jeffrey's remarks about the poem:

> The sports of childhood and the untimely death of promising youth, is also a common topic of poetry. Mr Wordsworth has made some blank verse about it; but, instead of the delightful and picturesque sketches with which so many authors of moderate talents have presented us on this inviting subject, all that he is pleased to communicate of the rustic child, is, that he used to amuse himself with shouting to the owls, and hearing them answer. To make amends for this brevity, the process of his mimicry is most accurately described [Jeffrey then quotes lines 395–99]. This is all we hear of him; and for the sake of this one accomplishment, we are told, that the author has frequently stood mute, and gazed on his grave for half an hour together! (From *Edinburgh Review*, April 1808; reprinted in *William Wordsworth: A Critical Anthology*, ed. Graham McMaster, pp. 99–100)

It is clear that Jeffrey considers the poem trivial; yet there seems to be a reluctant admiration wrung from him by the description of the mimicry. Here in contrast is Coleridge's response to the lines:

> The blank lines gave me as much direct pleasure as was possible in the general bustle of pleasure with which I received and read your letter . . . That

> > Uncertain heaven received
> into the bosom of the steady lake,

> I should have recognized anywhere, and had I met these lines running wild in the deserts of Arabia, I should have instantly screamed out 'Wordsworth!' (Coleridge to Wordsworth, 10 December 1798)

The enthusiasm of this contrasts strongly with Jeffrey's coolness, but there may not be much difference in their perception of what the poem is doing. It is not really a poem about childhood, let alone about that particular child, it is a poem about the relation between subjective experience and the external world. For that reason the concluding lines about the boy's death, though they turn it into a pleasingly sentimental childhood poem, are not really very important. Its beauty belongs neither there nor in accurate description (though it has that) but primarily in the careful, loving account of how the external world is perceived. Read the opening lines again: do they not begin to gather strength, and to sound like poetry, as they concentrate on our reception of the scene?

> > . . . when the stars had just begun
> To move along the edges of the hills . . .

Already we are participating in the boy's awareness of the world around him, already that curious act of intense concentration has begun. Indeed, *concentration* is perhaps the central element in the experience: the boy concentrates intently on what he is doing, and we concentrate with him. And it is the sudden suspension of this concentration, when the pause of silence comes, that enables him to become aware of the 'visible scene' with an intensity not otherwise possible. It was the description of this awareness that produced the Wordsworthian quality Coleridge so triumphantly recognized.

By what verbal means does the poem produce this powerful effect? As so often when Wordsworth is writing at his best, the question seems almost unanswerable: the most haunting lines are so close to ordinary speech. It is not difficult to find some very striking writing—lines 399–404, for example, where the repetitions and the pauses produce a marvellous imitation of the echoing noises of boy and owls. But the climax of the poem is much harder to characterize, though perhaps it is more haunting still. Look again at the following (406–09):

> Then sometimes, in that silence, while he hung
> Listening, a gentle shock of mild surprize
> Has carried far into his heart the voice
> Of mountain torrents . . .

These lines drew from Thomas de Quincey a comment so illuminating that it almost seems a creative act equivalent to the poet's own. De Quincey singled out one word for special attention: before reading on, ponder the lines carefully to see if you can suggest which word contributes most strikingly to their power.

Here is de Quincey's comment:

> The very expression 'far' by which space and its infinities are attributed to the human heart, and its capacities of re-echoing the sublimities of nature, has always struck me as with a flash of sublime revelation.

How right he is. The word 'far' gives to the inner world of our experience the same quality of extension that the outer world possesses. It suggests that the watcher's awareness of the visible scene has some resemblance to the reflection in the lake; and it gives a physical reality to the act of perceiving.

Wordsworth's own comment on the poem, in the 1815 Preface, is as follows:

> In the series of Poems placed under the head of Imagination, I have begun with one of the earliest processes of Nature in the development of this faculty. Guided by one of my own primary consciousnesses, I have presented a commutation and transfer of internal feelings, co-operating with external accidents, to plant, for immortality, images of sound and sight, in the celestial soil of the Imagination. The Boy, there introduced, is listening, with something of a feverish and restless anxiety, for the recurrence of those riotous sounds which he had previously excited; and, at the moment when the intenseness of his mind is beginning to remit, he is surprised into a perception of the solemn and tranquillizing images which the Poem describes.

It is clear that we were right in concentrating on the process of perception when looking for the centre of interest of the poem; and how trivial, in comparison to his rendering of sense-experience, seem the 'delightful and picturesque sketches' that Jeffrey wanted.

'Guided by one of my own primary consciousnesses': the wording of this holds a clue that we can follow up. The poem is about perception itself, and claims that the interaction between internal feelings and external accidents is what feeds the imagination. If we now turn back to Coleridge's distinctions, the conclusion seems inescapable: we have here a poem of the primary imagination.

I suggested that Coleridge might have derived the concept of the primary imagination from his interest in Kant's philosophy; now we see that another origin is possible (there is no need to choose between them): the way Wordsworth's poetry conveys the apprehension of the external world. Since the poet whose work he so deeply admired and wished to explain was so concerned with how we perceive, he may have had very good cause to place perception at the centre of his theory of imagination.

'Poems of the Imagination' contains one other poem that formed part of the *Prelude*. Under the title 'The Simplon Pass', twenty lines of what later became Book VI are here published. These lines are much less self-contained than 'There was a Boy', and since we have the complete *Prelude* it seems foolish to discuss them in isolation. You should therefore now read the whole account of crossing the Alps (*Prelude*, Book VI, lines 488–572).

Exercise

You will easily see that the account falls into three parts: try to characterize each briefly.

Answer

Lines 488–524 are straightforward narrative, matter-of-fact, even pedestrian. Lines 525–48 are an invocation to imagination, celebrating its glory and trying to fathom its workings. Lines 549–72 (the part that was separately published) return us to the Alps, but in a very different style: after eight lines of narrative we are given an exhilarated account of the sublimity of the mountain landscape.

J. A. Koch, The Schmadribach Waterfall, *1821–22. (Neue Pinakothek, Munich. Photo: Direktion der Bayerischen Staatsgemäldesammlungen)*

The second part—the invocation—has become one of the most famous passages of the *Prelude*, but some details in it are puzzling. In particular, what is meant by 'here' (line 527) and 'now' (line 531)? Did Imagination come athwart him when questioning the peasant and learning that they had crossed the Alps, or when writing the poem nearly ten years later? The mention of 'Before the eye and progress of my Song' suggests the latter reading, but the use of the preterite tense ('came', 'was') strongly suggests the former, and I suspect that 'lifting up itself . . . ' is a rather clumsy prolepsis, taking us to the moment of composition while still talking about the past. At line 531, however, the present tense makes it clear that this is the moment of composition. The most likely interpretation, then, seems to me the following: Imagination came athwart me in the Alps, and I felt lost as in a cloud on hearing the news; now, as I write the poem, I relive

Ludwig Richter, The Watzmann, *c. 1825.* (*Neue Pinakothek, Munich. Photo:
Direktion der Bayerischen Staatsgemäldesammlungen*)

that moment, but feel a glory as I see through the cloud. Then come the powerful
lines (532–36) on the light of sense going out in flashes: another fading-coal
image (you will remember that we found the same point made in *Prelude*, XII,
lines 279–80 (1850), when he saw childhood only in glimpses: this is clearly an
important image for Wordsworth). Imagination here is the faculty that almost
succeeds—even, for a moment, succeeds—in grasping a visionary experience.

And so to the lines that became a poem of the Imagination. No conventional
reader of eighteenth-century poetry would feel quite at home with them, for
description is almost completely subordinated to expressing the emotional impact
of the scene. The lines describe movement that appears not to move (as in the
marvellous line, 'the stationary blasts of water-falls') or the unmoving that seems

restless ('the rocks that mutter'd close upon our ears'). As it proceeds, the passage seems to grow more and more agitated, culminating in the statement that what he saw was like 'workings of one mind'.

Exercise

This is the really original image of the passage: have you come across anything similar elsewhere in the *Prelude*?

Answer

One of the most famous of the spots of time is the ascent of Snowdon that opens the concluding book. If you have not yet read, or have not lingered on, that passage, then take this opportunity to do so. There is no space for a full discussion of it here, but let me call your attention to its climax. After the moon has risen, and shown him the astounding scene of mist below him, he concludes (XIII: 66–70):

> A meditation rose in me that night
> Upon the lonely Mountain when the scene
> Had pass'd away, and it appear'd to me
> The perfect image of a mighty Mind,
> Of one that feeds upon infinity . . .

Caspar David Friedrich, Wanderer above the Sea of Mist, c. 1821. (Hamburger Kunsthalle. Photo: Ralph Kleinhempel)

We seem here, do we not, to have the same image as in VI: 566–69?

> The unfetter'd clouds, and region of the heavens,
> Tumult and peace, the darkness and the light
> Were all like workings of one mind, the features
> Of the same face . . .

What is this mind? In both passages, I suggest, we can read the lines in two ways. Is he being offered a glimpse of the mind of Nature herself, or is it an individual human mind? In both cases the writing would be remarkable, but not in the same way. In the first case, we are being given an insight into the nature of the universe that we can perhaps call pantheist, for the universe itself is seen as containing a kind of intellect infused through the whole. The fact that Wordsworth was strongly attracted by pantheism (the doctrine that God and Nature are identical) when writing *The Prelude* seems to make this the more probable reading, but I must confess myself drawn to the other. If we are seeing an image of an ordinary human mind, then the metaphoric power of the writing, rather than the doctrine itself, is central: the physical landscape takes on a mental life as a consequence of the imaginative power of the poet. He is not passing on a pantheistic insight, he is dissolving and dissipating in order to recreate.

'Resolution and Independence'

The other poem of Wordsworth's mentioned in the 1815 Preface is 'Resolution and Independence', from which he quotes to illustrate 'the conferring, the abstracting and the modifying power of the imagination'. Since it is certainly one of his major poems, we will follow his lead, and make it a central text for looking at the use of imagination in his poetry.

Exercise

Clearly you must begin by getting familiar with the text (set text, pp. 110ff.; recorded on cassette) and when you have done this I suggest you draw up a brief account (less than 100 words) of its argument.

Answer

This should have been very easy. 'Resolution and Independence' is a complex poem, as we shall see, but the main point it appears to be making is quite simple. The poet is subject to fits of despondency, and after setting out for a walk in happy mood, he is suddenly overtaken by a dejection he cannot explain, and that seems to him part of the fate of being a poet. At this point he meets an old man who earns his living by gathering leeches, an increasingly difficult task. He is so impressed by the resolution and independence he finds in the leech-gatherer that he laughs himself to scorn for his own dejection.

We know quite a lot about the origin of this poem. An entry in Dorothy Wordsworth's *Journal* on 3 October 1800 relates the incident which suggested it:

> We met an old man almost double. He had on a coat, thrown over his shoulders, above his waistcoat and coat. Under this he carried a bundle, and had an apron on and a night-cap. His face was interesting. He had dark eyes and a long nose. John, who afterwards met him at Wytheburn, took him for a Jew. He was of Scotch parents, but had been born in the army. He had had a wife, and 'a good woman, and it pleased God to bless us with ten children'. All these were dead but one, of whom he had not heard for many years, a sailor. His trade was to gather leeches, but now leeches are scarce, and he had not strength for it. He lived by begging, and was making his way to Carlisle,

where he should buy a few godly books to sell. He said leeches were very scarce, partly owing to this dry season, but many years they had been scarce—he supposed it owing to their being much sought after, that they did not breed fast, and were of slow growth. (*Journals of Dorothy Wordsworth*, ed. Mary Moorman)

The poem is dated 1802, so although this is clearly its germ, two years passed before it was actually written—an example of Wordsworth's method of building his poems on 'emotion recollected in tranquillity'. One change in particular which he made is very striking. The real leech-gatherer had taken to begging, but in the poem he continues, despite their increasing scarcity, to earn his living by hunting for leeches. This is clearly an appropriate change, fitting the old man's resolution and independence.

When the poem was finished Wordsworth sent it to Mary Hutchinson (his future wife) and her sister Sara. Their comments are lost, but we have his reply, in a letter to Sara of 14 June 1802: it is very full and interesting, and tells us a good deal about Wordsworth's view of his own poem:

My Dear Sara,

I am exceedingly sorry that the latter part of the Leechgatherer has displeased you, the more so because I cannot take to myself (that being the case) much pleasure or satisfaction in having pleased you in the former part. I will explain to you in prose my feeling in writing that poem and then you will be better able to judge whether the fault be mine or yours or partly both. I describe myself as having been exalted to this highest pitch of delight by the joyousness and beauty of Nature; and then as depressed, even in the midst of those beautiful objects, to the lowest dejection and despair. A young Poet in the midst of the happiness of Nature is described as overwhelmed by the thought of the miserable reverses which have befallen the happiest of men, viz. Poets. I think of this until I am so deeply impressed with it, that I consider the manner in which I was rescued from my dejection and despair almost as an interposition of Providence. Now whether it was by peculiar grace, a leading from above—A person reading this Poem with feelings like mine will have been awed and controlled, expecting almost something spiritual or supernatural. What is brought forward? 'A lonely place, a Pond', 'by which an old man *was*, far from all house or home': not *stood*, not *sat*, but *was*—the figure presented in the most naked simplicity possible. This feeling of spirituality or supernaturalness is again referred to as being strong in my mind in this passage. How came he here? thought I, or what can he be doing! I then describe him, whether ill or well is not for me to judge with perfect confidence: but this I can confidently affirm, that though I believe God has given me a strong imagination, I cannot conceive a figure more impressive than that of an old Man like this, the survivor of a Wife and ten children, travelling alone among the mountains and all lonely places, carrying with him his own fortitude, and the necessities which an unjust state of society has entailed upon him. You say and Mary (that is you can say no more than that) the poem is very well after the introduction of the old man, this is not true, if it is not more than very well it is very bad—there is no intermediate state. You speak of his speech as tedious: everything is tedious when one does not read with the feelings of the Author. *The Thorn* is tedious to hundreds; and so is *The Idiot Boy* to hundreds. It is the character of the old man to tell his story, which an impatient reader must necessarily feel as tedious. But, Good God, Such a figure, in such a place; a pious, self-respecting, miserably infirm Old Man tell such a tale!

My dear Sara, it is not a matter of indifference whether you are pleased with this figure and his employment; it may be comparatively so, whether you are pleased or not with this Poem; but it is of the utmost importance that you should have had pleasure from contemplating the dignity of this old man's character. Your feelings about the Mother, and the Boys with the Butterfly, were not indifferent: it was an affair of whole continents of moral sympathy. I will talk more with you on this when we meet—at present, farewell and Heaven for ever bless you. (*The Letters of William and Dorothy Wordsworth*, vol. I, pp. 366–67)

The first half of this letter gives us Wordsworth's account of the argument of his poem, and you should find it profitable to compare this with your own reading. Perhaps what is most striking about the letter as a whole, however, is its defensive tone. Although Wordsworth is not arrogant (he concedes that she may be displeased with the poem, while insisting that she must take the old man himself seriously) he writes as if Sara must be to blame if she has not responded fully, and his eagerness in spelling out what he meant (it sounds almost schoolmasterly at times) makes the letter an invaluable document.

You may be surprised—or perhaps on reflection you will not be—to learn that Wordsworth did revise the poem, and on lines suggested by Sara's criticism. The original manuscript is lost, but textual scholars have been able to reconstruct a good deal of the first version. There appears to have been much more about the old man, his work and his family, including the following lines:

> He wore a Cloak, the same as women wear
> As one whose blood did needful comfort lack:
> His face looked pale as if it had grown fair
> And, furthermore, he had upon his back
> Beneath his cloak, a round and bulky Pack . . .

This sounds as if it must be the stuff that Sara found 'tedious'. And not only did Wordsworth cut it out (along, probably, with a couple of other stanzas), he also inserted the marvellous ninth stanza ('As a huge stone . . . '), which now seems so central to the poem. It looks as if Wordsworth was willing to weaken the lesson that he claimed was the point of the poem, the 'fortitude, independence, persevering spirit, and the general moral dignity of this old man's character'. This point, I shall suggest, is very important.

Exercise

It is time now to look more closely at the text of the poem, and ask whether the poem we have corresponds to what we would expect after learning of its origin and Wordsworth's own comments. Have you already begun to form an opinion about this?

Answer

The old man does not appear until stanza VIII, so no fewer than seven stanzas are devoted to the opening description of 'having been exalted to the highest pitch of delight . . . ; and then as depressed . . . to the lowest dejection and despair'. Now for the purpose of the poem's lesson, there is no need to mention the exaltation and delight at all: the poet 'laughs himself to scorn' when he compares his dejection with the old man's resolution. The poem itself, however, is unimaginable without this up-and-down movement: the first three stanzas are filled with excitement and bustle, and the poet's exaltation is presented as corresponding to the exhilarating weather after the storm. What we are shown in the first 50 lines is a movement that can be called manic-depressive, an alternation between heights and depths that is as apparently arbitrary as the weather, and then, because it doesn't always fit the weather, even more so. This alternation is presented as the poetic temperament: the poets mentioned in stanza VII are Chatterton and Burns, but it is difficult not to believe that he was thinking even more of the unstable Coleridge.

What is the effect of these seven stanzas? They suggest surely that the up-and-down movement is too powerful to resist. It is as inevitable as, then more mysterious than, the alternations of the weather; it springs from the deepest level of the poet's being. Surely the injunction to pull himself together, to take a lesson in resolution and independence, seems superficial in comparison. If the poet does succeed in laughing himself to scorn at the end, one suspects it may be because the seesaw has moved again, and his 'old remembrances' have gone from him wholly.

I am beginning to suggest that the poem Wordsworth wrote does not altogether correspond to the moralizing poem he claimed to have written. I now want to take this point further, and as the next step I suggest we look at the actual quality of the poetry.

Exercise

Read the poem again, and note down the stanzas, from stanza VIII to the end, that seem to you most powerfully written and most mysteriously impressive.

Answer

This is a subjective matter, of course, and not everyone will have chosen the same; but I shall be surprised if your list does not include some at least of the following: stanzas IX ('As a huge stone . . . '), XI (especially 'Motionless as a cloud . . . move at all'), XVI and XIX. If you did not include these, read them again now, and see if you can make out why to so many generations of readers they have seemed the most memorable part of the poem. They are the lines in which the old man is mysteriously transformed into another kind of creature, into a dream figure, into a dimly understood presence. In these passages, in which we are given the overmastering impact of the leech-gatherer, the poet seems unable to see or hear him properly: it is hardly surprising to read in stanza XVI:

> But now his voice to me was like a stream
> Scarce heard; nor word from word could I divide.

Solitary wanderers are common figures in Wordsworth's poetry: the old soldier at the end of Book IV of *The Prelude*, the Wanderer, who is the chief personage in *The Excursion*, the Old Cumberland Beggar—they are usually old men. The leech-gatherer takes his place quite naturally among these, and, having already read Coleridge's 'Ancient Mariner', you may feel a resemblance between that wanderer ('I pass like night from land to land') and this old man, pacing 'About the weary moors continually'. Indeed, there is hardly a Romantic poet, in England, France or Germany, who does not offer us portraits of solitaries and wanderers. And what they have in common is alienation and mystery, not resolution or independence.

It is now time to turn to another, and more important, comment by Wordsworth on his own poem, that in the 1815 Preface. He there quotes stanza IX, along with the end of stanza XI ('Motionless as a cloud . . . ') as examples of 'the Imagination employed upon images in a conjunction by which they modify each other'. Here is what he says:

> In these images, the conferring, the abstracting, and the modifying powers of the Imagination, immediately and mediately acting, are all brought into conjunction. The stone is endowed with something of the power of life to approximate it to the sea-beast; and the sea-beast stripped of some of its vital qualities to assimilate it to the stone; which intermediate image is thus

treated for the purpose of bringing the original image, that of the stone, to a nearer resemblance to the figure and condition of the aged Man; who is divested of so much of the indications of life and motion as to bring him to the point where the two objects unite and coalesce in just comparison.

The operation of imagination, according to this passage, consists in the transformation of one object into another. It clearly also performs the function which Coleridge attributed to Wordsworth's poetry in the *Biographia*, Chapter XIV:

to give the charm of novelty to things of every day, and to excite a feeling analogous to the supernatural, by awakening the mind's attention from the lethargy of custom, and directing it to the loveliness and the wonders of the world before us.

Though the terminology is different, this is the same function as recent structuralist criticism calls 'defamiliarization'. There can hardly be a poem of Wordsworth's that awakens the mind's attention, and excites a feeling analogous to the supernatural, more successfully than this one.

So far, everything we have pointed to in the poem illustrates the theory of imagination very well: the parts I have picked out as the most imaginative do dissolve, diffuse, dissipate in order to recreate, and they give the charm of novelty to things of every day. But what has all this to do with the moral that Wordsworth so earnestly commended to Sara Hutchinson? Fortitude, independence, persevering spirit and moral dignity are familiar concepts, which do not require the mind to awake from the lethargy of custom; and the difference between good and bad behaviour may have little to do with the poetic imagination.

I therefore suggest to you, as the conclusion of this discussion, the following comment on 'Resolution and Independence'. (You may not agree with it, but if you don't I hope you will find it a useful stimulus to working out your own view; and if you want a rather more orthodox comment, you have of course got Wordsworth's own letter to Sara). The apparent argument of the poem is conventional: it preaches a moral lesson, and ends with self-rebuke. The most brilliant parts (the opening stanzas, and the passages in which the old man takes on a visionary, prophetic, even non-human quality) are those which have least to do with this moral. Wordsworth the moral teacher was capable of writing very conventionally, and with no imagination.

The Lucy poems

The group of five poems that are usually known as the 'Lucy poems' are among Wordsworth's most loved and best known. In the 1815 classification, three are placed among Poems Founded on the Affections ('Strange fits of passion have I known', 'She dwelt among the untrodden ways' and 'I travelled among unknown men') and two among Poems of the Imagination ('Three years she grew in sun and shower' and 'A slumber did my spirit seal'—probably the two finest). We will treat them all as a group, adding two others: 'Louisa', which stands immediately before them among Poems Founded on the Affections (we know that Wordsworth took great trouble over the order of his poems), and 'To a Young Lady' ('Dear Child of Nature'), which was originally intended to form part of the same poem. The five Lucy poems are on pp. 45–48 of your set text (and four of them are recorded on the cassette); the other two, which are not in the set text, are reproduced here.

Louisa

After accompanying her on a mountain excursion

I met Louisa in the shade,
And, having seen that lovely Maid,
Why should I fear to say
That, nymph-like, she is fleet and strong,
And down the rocks can leap along
Like rivulets in May?

And she hath smiles to earth unknown;
Smiles, that with motion of their own
Do spread, and sink, and rise;
That come and go with endless play,
And ever, as they pass away,
Are hidden in her eyes.

She loves her fire, her cottage-home;
Yet o'er the moorland will she roam
In weather rough and bleak;
And, when against the wind she strains,
Oh! might I kiss the mountain rains
That sparkle on her cheek.

Take all that's mine 'beneath the moon,'
If I with her but half a noon
May sit beneath the walls
Of some old cave, or mossy nook,
When up she winds along the brook
To hunt the waterfalls.

(*Poetical Works*, ed. Hutchinson/de Selincourt, pp. 85–86)

To a Young Lady

Who had been reproached for taking long walks in the country

Dear Child of Nature, let them rail!
—There is a nest in a green dale,
A harbour and a hold;
Where thou, a Wife and Friend, shalt see
Thy own heart-stirring days, and be
A light to young and old.

There, healthy as a shepherd boy,
And treading among flowers of joy
Which at no season fade,
Thou, while thy babes around thee cling,
Shalt show us how divine a thing
A Woman may be made.

Thy thoughts and feelings shall not die,
Nor leave thee, when grey hairs are nigh,
A melancholy slave;
But an old age serene and bright,
And lovely as a Lapland night,
Shall lead thee to thy grave.

(Ibid., page 173)

Exercise

Read all seven poems, and note what seem to you the most striking similarities.

Answer

I think you will have found that the poems not only belong together, they illuminate one another far better than any commentary can do. The most striking common points, surely, concern solitude, closeness to Nature and death. Almost all these women live in or seek out isolation from the rest of humanity; and all of them are described as peculiarly—and movingly—intimate with Nature: they take long walks, they leap among the rocks, they could all surely be the subject of this beautiful stanza from 'Three years she grew':

> 'She shall be sportive as the fawn
> That wild with glee across the lawn,
> Or up the mountain springs;
> And her's shall be the breathing balm,
> And her's the silence and the calm
> Of mute insensate things.'

In four of the Lucy poems the girl dies, in the remaining one ('Strange fits of passion') the poet suddenly and unaccountably cries to himself, 'If Lucy should be dead'; 'To a Young Lady' concludes with the touching image of

> But an old age serene and bright
> And lovely as a Lapland night,
> Shall lead thee to thy grave.

Now this cannot be accidental: there must be some profound connection between solitude, closeness to nature, and death. It suggests, does it not, that love of Nature is a kind of refusal of life? This point has been made by David Ferry, in his brilliant study of Wordsworth, *The Limits of Mortality*. This is what he says of the women of these poems:

> Death is the natural culmination of what they have been developing toward. They are distinguished from ordinary human beings, from the speaker who declares his love for them, by the extraordinary completeness of their relation to eternal nature, and they die only to go home where they belong.

To illustrate this point, let us look more closely at 'Three years she grew'.

Exercise

I would now like you to reread this poem, and to sort out the facts in it. When did Lucy die? Is she alive or dead during most of the poem? What are the 'three years' of the first line?

Answer

If I am not mistaken, you will have found this exercise surprisingly difficult. One would expect that grasping such basic facts would be easier than understanding the poem's philosophy and the relationship to nature that it explores. But the reverse turns out to be the case; the mysterious intimacy with the floating clouds, with the rivulets, with the stars of midnight, surely makes an immediate impact, and reminds us of the Wordsworth of the first two books of *The Prelude*. All that is clear enough; but what exactly happened to Lucy?

In the first place, is she three years old? The opening lines seem to say that: or is it a reference (not otherwise elucidated) to her living in the countryside but not having yet attained intimacy with nature? More serious, when Nature announces 'She shall be mine, and I will make/A lady of my own', is she referring to life or death? The last stanza fails to make this clear, for the lines

> Thus nature spake—The work was done—
> How soon my Lucy's race was run!

are ambiguous. The most natural reading is surely to take 'the work was done' as referring to the same thing as the subsequent line, so that Nature is announcing Lucy's death. But it is possible that they are saying: 'Thus Nature spake, and the work of turning her into a child of Nature, intimate with the landscape, was done—*but* how soon (after that) her race was run.' It is forcing things a bit to imagine a 'but' there, but it is just possible. If now we turn to the body of the poem, it is striking how many details could refer either to a living girl's closeness to nature, or to a dead girl's becoming part of nature. Almost every stanza has such a touch: think for instance about

> 'And her's shall be the breathing balm,
> And her's the silence and the calm
> Of mute insensate things.'

Did Wordsworth intend this? Well, I will admit that, on one level at least, Wordsworth seems to have intended the poem to be about Lucy alive: 'lean her ear' (line 26) suggests this, as does the swelling of her bosom (line 33—this also indicates, does it not, that she is not intended as a child) and, most compellingly for me, the fact that she shall be sportive *as* the fawn seems to exclude any pantheistic suggestion that the dead Lucy is actually part of the fawn. But we must beware of setting up some external standard of what the poet 'meant' as if that had more authority than what he actually wrote. The ambiguities with which the poem is fraught are there, and are largely responsible for its power. And they do very strikingly confirm Ferry's point. Intimacy with nature is described in a way that constantly suggests death, and even the possibility that she is a child may not be wholly accidental. The reason why there is no 'but' in the second line of the last stanza may be that what Nature has said seems to lead inevitably to Lucy's race being run. As Ferry puts it, 'they died of their mysticism; or their mysticism itself was a kind of death anyway, of which their physical deaths were only the most concrete expression.'

'Dejection'

The Poems of the Imagination include some of Wordsworth's finest: 'Nutting', 'Ruth', 'Tintern Abbey' and 'Peter Bell', among others. Try and read (or re-read) some of these for yourself. You may find it interesting, for instance, to re-read 'Tintern Abbey' in the light of this discussion of imagination; or, when you come to revise Coleridge's 'Ancient Mariner', to read it along with 'Peter Bell', which was intended as a kind of counterpart to it. What we need to do now, however, is to turn to Coleridge's own poetry to see what use we can make of the idea of imagination when discussing it. It will be best to look not at one of the obviously imaginative poems of the supernatural, but at one of his more personal poems. I have therefore chosen 'Dejection: an Ode'.

On 4 April 1802 Coleridge wrote (we can even say 'poured out') a verse letter of 340 lines to Sara Hutchinson, Wordsworth's future sister-in-law, with whom he was in love; in October he published a much shorter version (139 lines) in the *Morning Post*. This version leaves out most of the autobiographical material, including a long passage on his childhood, and an account of his domestic woes, and conceals the identity of the woman he is writing to. There is of course no reason why he should not have done this, and indeed it seems to show a true understanding of the difference between a personal letter (even one in verse) and a poem intended for the public; but unfortunately the actual abridgement was done clumsily, so that the argument of the published version is not as consistent as the original. That is one reason why we have given you the fuller version, sprawling as it is. (This is the version in your set text, Reeves.) You will be asked to read this original version later in these units. For the present, however, please refer to the abridged version, reprinted in your supplementary notes accompanying the cassette readings.

Exercise

Now read the poem (and listen to the cassette reading). You might like to do this forthwith, even before looking at my suggested questions. Then, on subsequent readings, ask yourself the following:

1   The poem is clearly concerned with the relation between emotion and the external world. Can you pick out some lines that show a correspondence between the two, and lines which show the lack of such correspondence? Which is more prominent?

2   What is the function of the wind in the poem?

3   What is meant by 'in our life alone does Nature live'?

4   Is there any nature poetry in 'Dejection'?

5   Finally, what is being asserted about the imagination? Is it the same idea of imagination as in *Biographia Literaria*?

Answers

These questions are not easy, but they should take you to the heart of the poem.

1   The first stanza describes a tranquil evening. A quiet wind produces a 'dull sobbing' from an Aeolian lute (this favourite eighteenth-century toy was a kind of harp placed out of doors, that emitted a musical sound as the wind passed through it). But it looks as if a storm is brewing, and the poet longs for it to come, in the hope that it will 'startle this dull pain, and make it move and live'. It might seem at first that emotion and external scene correspond, and that the lute is expressing his own grief as it 'sobs', but as we read on we see that there is a contrast, or lack of correspondence, between the inner and outer world. Indeed, this is the main theme of the middle part of the poem, and is explicit in stanza II, which tells us how unresponsive he is to what, we now realize, is a beautiful sunset. The stanza concludes with an explicit statement of this lack of correspondence: 'I see, not feel, how beautiful they are!' Clearly that is to be the main subject of the poem.

2   The wind makes two appearances in the poem. In stanza I it is a 'dull sobbing draft', whose sole function seems to be to agitate the Aeolian lute and produce a sound that corresponds with the poet's emotion. One gets the impression that if it was not for the lute he would not even be aware of the wind, so that it is the lute, the artificial object, which really expresses his feelings for him, rather than the natural object, the wind. Stanza VII, however, tells us that the storm has broken, indeed 'long has raved unnoticed', and at the same time transfers attention from the poet to the wind itself, the 'mad Lutanist', and the feelings it conjures up. This time there is no attempt to match the scene to the poet's emotion; the actions and feelings which are described are conjured up by the wind, and are an attempt to depict its associations. If we call this a correspondence between emotion and external scene, it is no longer in the same sense: the poet has now removed himself from the poem. For this reason, stanza VII is less personal; it seems more conventional, and less important in what has up to then been a deeply personal poem.

3   The line 'And in our life alone does Nature live' is central to the poem. We can take a term from psychology to designate what it is saying, and call it a projection theory. The poet is aware of his lack of response to the beauty of the evening, and insists that the failure is due to him. Outward forms do not arouse emotion in us, it is we who bestow our feelings on them.

This is certainly not the doctrine found in Coleridge's earlier poems. In 'This Lime-Tree Bower my Prison' he asserts that Nature (by which he must surely mean something outside himself) 'keep[s] the heart awake to Love and Beauty'—exactly what it is failing to do in 'Dejection'. And in 'The Nightingale' he attacks the kind of poetry that imposes its own feelings on nature, urging the poet to surrender 'his whole spirit' to external influences. There seems no question in these poems that Nature lives independently of our life, and influences it.

On the other hand, the doctrine stated in 'Dejection' is a kind of psychological equivalent to the philosophical position which, as we have seen, Coleridge held. His constant insistence on the active role of the mind in acquiring empirical knowledge, his Kantian view of perception, his belief that 'man comes from within, and all that is truly human must proceed from within', attest a consistency throughout his career. And there is one poem which expresses the same position, the lines 'To William Wordsworth', written in 1807 after hearing him recite *The Prelude*, where he says:

> . . . Power streamed from thee, and thy soul received
> The light reflected, as a light bestowed . . .

Clearly we shall not find complete consistency in Coleridge on this point. What of Wordsworth? The question whether our awareness of the presence of Nature derives from something really there, independent of us, or whether we project our own hopes, fears and feelings and imagine we are receiving an outside influence, is frequently raised in *The Prelude*, especially in Book II. Wordsworth is usually rather careful to say that he does not know which is the true explanation, and that it perhaps does not matter because there is no doubt of the reality of his experiences.

There is no logical reason why belief in the constitutive activity of the mind in perception should go with a projection theory about religious or spiritual forces, or why the view that we receive sense-impressions passively should go with a 'realist' theory (i.e. the view that such forces are really there); but it would not be surprising if they did go together, if a thinker's view on perception and his view on spiritual influences corresponded, active with active, passive with passive. In the case of Coleridge, there seems to be a persistently held philosophical position, but much inconsistency about the projective/realist issue. Can this be explained?

Two explanations are possible. One is advanced by Thomas MacFarland in his study of 'The Symbiosis of Coleridge and Wordsworth'. He believes that Coleridge really held the active (and the projective) view, that Wordsworth really held the passive (and the realist) view, but that their reciprocal influence was so great that each declared, on occasion, for the other's position. There is no doubt about the influence, which MacFarland documents very impressively (they even wrote bits of one another's poems), but a view like this can never be finally proved. The other possibility is that though Coleridge's philosophical position was consistent, he really did not hold a firm position on the projective/realist issue, and his insistence on the projective view in 'Dejection' may itself be a sign of the psychic malady from which he is suffering. Try re-reading the third stanza in the light of this view: can it now be seen as ambiguous?

Yes, there is a possible ambiguity which, once we have noticed it, suddenly seems very obvious (almost like the duck/rabbit perception trick). 'And what can these avail?' ('these' of course means the beauties of the external scene), 'It were a vain endeavour', 'I may not hope'—why are these hopeless statements made with such certainty? The endeavour is vain because of his dejection: nothing seems to help. The endeavour is vain because he is looking the wrong way round: external factors do not govern our inner state. These two readings are both very close to each other and very far apart: they are different ways of making the same point, yet the one lays all the emphasis on a philosophical theory, the other on his hopeless state of mind. If you say the lines over to yourself several times, you may even begin to feel that the strong emotional power of 'what can these avail?' has something to do with this ambiguity: we can see it one way, then another, each equally hopeless. Even though the opening of stanza IV goes on to offer an explanation in terms of theory, we can hardly get the emotional explanation out of our mind. It is after all a poem not about philosophy but about dejection.

4   This question is clearly an invitation (and I hope you took it so) to consider what we mean by 'nature poetry'. There are two senses of the term which do not seem to apply to 'Dejection'. One is description of the natural world. There is not a great deal of direct description in the poem, and what there is serves to make a point or indicate a contrast. Thus the description of the moon (lines 9–14) is inserted as a prediction, a suggestion that a very different scene is preparing; and the careful description of the sunset exposes his unresponsiveness, so that the suggestion of intense scrutiny ('the western sky,/And its peculiar tint of yellow green') sounds as if it comes from a watcher with lack-lustre eye.

Another sense of the phrase 'nature poetry' is the kind of celebration of the spiritual influence of nature that is so important in *The Prelude*, and this, as we have seen, is quite explicitly not present: its absence is the main subject of the poem. Stanzas II–V seem to bring in much of the usual material of nature poetry, but not to use it (not to be able to use it) in expected ways. Perhaps therefore one way of indicating the poem's subject is to say that it is about the inability to write nature poetry.

5   Finally, imagination. The term is used to stanza VI, which we will now look at more closely. It is a lament for the drying up of feeling, the fact that afflictions have not only robbed him of mirth but, more seriously, suspended 'my shaping spirit of Imagination' as a result of his habit of 'abstruse research'. (Did you notice, by the way, that on this occasion Coleridge seems to use 'fancy' as a synonym for 'imagination'?) Now since the poem is concerned with this lack of emotional response, he may well feel he is unable to exercise the co-adunating power that should hold the visible scene together: his inability to 'feel how beautiful they are', which he attributes to his lack of joy, could equally be seen as a lack of imagination.

Our discussion could stop here; but I cannot resist adding one last point. If the poet's imagination has really been suspended, how did he write the poem? This is a common paradox in poems that lament the poet's failing powers but that nonetheless succeed in doing what they claim they cannot do (Yeats's 'Circus Animals' Desertion' is a famous modern example). After all, if the primary imagination is really 'the prime agent of all human perception', then it was at work in showing Coleridge the 'green light that lingers in the west', and the secondary imagination turned it into the very moving lines about his own inadequacy. I do not say this to score a point over Coleridge, but to indicate a necessary paradox in the poetry of dejection.

Imagination and fancy

I have claimed that Wordsworth and Coleridge agree essentially in their view of imagination. Do they also agree about fancy? Coleridge seldom speaks of fancy except in derogatory terms, treating it usually as a foil to imagination. It is not easy to conceive of him including a section of Poems of the Fancy in his own works, as Wordsworth did. The following passage, from a letter to his friend Sotheby in 1802, makes his position clear:

It must occur to every reader that the Greeks in their religious poems address always the Numina loci, the Geni, The Dryads, the Naiads, etc, etc. All natural objects were *dead*, mere hollow statues, but there was a Godkin or Goddessling *included* in each. In the Hebrew poetry you find none of this poor stuff, as poor in genuine imagination as it is mean in intellect. At best, it is but fancy, or the aggregating faculty of the mind, not imagination or the modifying and coadunating faculty. This the Hebrew poets appear to me to have possessed beyond all others, and next to them the English. In the Hebrew poets, each thing has a life of its own, and yet they are all one life.

Pagan mythology is seen as inferior because it adds the name of a deity or local spirit to the natural scene, almost like a label. It works by means of mechanical aggregation, and as we would expect, the point is made in order to set off, by contrast, the power of imagination. Now Wordsworth has also given us his views on Greek mythology.

Exercise

Here is a passage from *The Excursion*; read it carefully, and try and note down what Wordsworth is saying about the origin of myths, as well as whether his view is the same as Coleridge's.

> Once more to distant ages of the world
> Let us revert, and place before our thoughts
> The face which rural solitude might wear
> To the unenlightened swains of pagan Greece.
> —In that fair clime, the lonely herdsman, stretched
> On the soft grass through half a summer's day,
> With music lulled his indolent repose:
> And, in some fit of weariness, if he,
> When his own breath was silent, chanced to hear
> A distant strain, far sweeter than the sounds
> Which his poor skill could make, his fancy fetched,
> Even from the blazing chariot of the sun,
> A beardless Youth, who touched a golden lute,
> And filled the illumined groves with ravishment.
> The nightly hunter, lifting a bright eye
> Up towards the crescent moon, with grateful heart
> Called on the lovely wanderer who bestowed
> That timely light, to share his joyous sport:
> And hence, a beaming Goddess with her Nymphs,
> Across the lawn and through the darksome grove,
> Not unaccompanied with tuneful notes
> By echo multiplied from rock or cave,
> Swept in the storm of chase; as moon and stars
> Glance rapidly along the clouded heaven,
> When winds are blowing strong.
> (*Poetical Works*, ed. Hutchinson/de Selincourt, page 635)

Answer

This view is not logically incompatible with Coleridge's. You no doubt noticed that Wordsworth used the term 'fancy'. He too believes that pagan gods and goddesses are fictions, added to the scene by the watcher. But how different the tone! Wordsworth writes with deep sympathy about the process of myth-making: the herdsman invents the figure of Apollo because he is so deeply moved by the distant music he hears, the hunter invents Diana out of his delight in the moon. Wordsworth refers to the pagan Greeks as 'unenlightened' (meaning, I presume, since this is the later, orthodox Wordsworth, that they were not Christian), but though the process of myth-making is not one he wishes to indulge in himself or use the results of, it is presented as deriving from a genuine emotional response to nature. Indeed, the experience of the hunter who fancies that he sees the beaming Goddess with her nymphs is strikingly like Wordsworth's own:

> . . . as moon and stars
> Glance rapidly along the clouded heaven,
> When winds are blowing strong.

These lines would not be out of place, would they, in the first book of *The Prelude* —say in the trap-robbing episode we discussed earlier (page 68)?

Wordsworth is such a strong believer in immediacy, in the direct expression of his feelings and experiences, that we would not expect him to be attracted to literary conventions and artifices, or to the use of classical mythology. But when he can see myths or quaint stories as the product of a genuine feeling for nature, he treats them with sympathy. It is therefore a characteristic strategy of his poetry (and one that is common in other Romantics too) to convey a delighted awareness of the origins of legends, a rediscovery of the power of traditional devices. The point is made quite explicitly in these lines:

> —The Poets, in their elegies and songs
> Lamenting the departed, call the groves,
> They call upon the hills and streams to mourn,
> And senseless rocks; nor idly; for they speak,
> In these their invocations, with a voice
> Obedient to the strong creative power
> Of human passion.
>
> (*The Excursion*, I, 475–481; *Poetical Works*, op. cit., page 596)

This situation is particularly frequent in the Poems of the Fancy. In these we see Wordsworth toying with ingenious conceits, with legends that have a strained or quaint moral, or (as in these lines) with the pathetic fallacy, the figure by which non-human creatures and even objects are seen as sharing the poet's emotion. There is more to such devices, he tells us, than one might at first think. But it is clear that they are not his own way of writing, and most of the poems in this section seem to be offered without complete commitment from the poet.

For a wholly serious treatment of fancy, then, we need a poem in which Wordsworth is not using it himself. This could be a poem in which he presents himself as a sympathetic outsider, or it could be the result of quite a different feeling.

> The world is too much with us; late and soon,
> Getting and spending, we lay waste our powers:
> Little we see in Nature that is ours;
> We have given our hearts away, a sordid boon!
> This Sea that bares her bosom to the moon;
> The winds that will be howling at all hours,
> And are up-gathered now like sleeping flowers;
> For this, for everything, we are out of tune;
> It moves us not.—Great God! I'd rather be
> A Pagan suckled in a creed outworn;
> So might I, standing on this pleasant lea,
> Have glimpses that would make me less forlorn;
> Have sight of Proteus rising from the sea;
> Or hear old Triton blow his wreathèd horn.
>
> (*Poetical Works*, op. cit., page 206)

Since we have not yet had an opportunity of looking at any of Wordsworth's sonnets, it is fortunate that the discussion now leads us to one of the finest and most famous of these. (It is recorded on the cassette.)

Exercise

Here are the questions I suggest we ask about it: jot down your own answers to them before reading on.

1 What, very briefly, is the point of the poem?

2 There are two ways of describing or responding to nature in this poem. What are they, and how are they contrasted?

3 What is the attitude to pagan mythology?

4 What emotion is being expressed?

Answers

1 It is a poem about man's alienation from nature, his failure to respond adequately to the beauty of the natural world. (The 'world' that is too much with us is the world of practical cares and everyday distractions—the Christian meaning, familiar from the phrase 'the world, the flesh and the devil'—and is more or less the opposite to the world of nature.)

2 The two ways of depicting and responding to nature are found in the first and second parts of the sonnet. In lines 4–7 we have Wordsworth's own description of what we are out of tune with; here nature is seen through metaphor. In the sestet, or last six lines, however, nature is seen through mythology: the sea, instead of wringing from the poet the moving and strangely complex image of baring her bosom to the moon, with its overtones of emotional and sexual surrender, is represented by the figure of Triton, the sea god, as he might appear in a mythological painting. Nature can therefore be seen direct, or symbolized by what Coleridge contemptuously called 'Godkins'.

3 The attitude to pagan mythology here is surely that it is second-best. If you are really in touch with Nature, if the world is not too much with you, then you should not need myths; but the pagan, though his creed is outworn, did have a way of responding to the natural world which was preferable to our present alienation. A few glimpses (the word suggests Wordsworth's own scepticism) of Proteus and Triton would be better than nothing.

4 The poem burns with intense passion. Try reading it aloud, emphasizing the more emotional moments. The inversion of the third line, you may then feel, is not a poetic artificiality, but the true voice of indignation, lingering heavily on 'little'. 'This Sea' can be spoken with an angry gesture, whereas 'The Sea' (incorrectly printed in your set text) would be merely neutral. The repetition in 'for this, for everything' should come out as a fierce insistence; 'Great God! I'd rather be . . . ' speaks itself; and even the last two lines do not have to be as straightforward as they might at first look, for we can read them in the tone of 'at least that would be something'.

As these remarks indicate, the poem seems to me an expression of anger. This predominant passion holds it together, lending significance to a number of tiny colloquial touches. This makes it quite different from the Poems of the Fancy. Pagan myths may be a product of fancy, but the lines in which the poem speaks its true message, the lines about the sea and the winds, are truly imaginative. It is about fancy, but it is a poem of imagination.

6 Dejection and Joy

(By PNF)

The purpose of these final sections of the Wordsworth and Coleridge units is to discuss one or two further large themes, implicit or explicit, in the work of the two poets, and to do so partly by the same method as has been used up to now, i.e., by the detailed discussion of particular poems. The vagueness of the word 'theme' is deliberate, for the attitudes of the two poets to a given question may, in certain cases, appear to be exactly opposite. However, it will still be of great significance that they addressed themselves to the same question. It is here that our minds are led out to history—to the moment of political social or cultural history to which these poets belonged; for the question will have been dictated by those historical circumstances. Let us instance one question among many: what should be the role of art and of the artist, and in what sense is art necessary to the good of the community? (Also, what *kind* of art is necessary?) This was a question that posed itself, one might almost say, for the first time at the period we are speaking of—posed itself, that is to say, as a matter of urgent and agonizing choice. (You will read more about this in Units 9–10.)

The first theme we are to discuss we have called, for want of a better title, 'Dejection and Joy'.

'Kubla Khan'

Will you now read Coleridge's 'Kubla Khan' (pp. 85–86 in the set text), with Coleridge's important foreword to it, printed in the Notes; also listen to the cassette reading?

First, a few words about the poem generally. It is often regarded as one of the high points of the 'Romantic' in poetry (using this term in a commonplace sense), and this is reasonable, for it is unforgettable and has an inexhaustible strangeness, so that a large literature of commentary has grown up round it. (Though we should remember that Coleridge himself, in his foreword, offered it as no more than 'a psychological curiosity'.)

Assuming that the poem takes hold of you, as it does with so many readers, I suggest that you ask yourself: not so much what it is 'about', in a larger sense, as what it literally 'says', and how it says it. Would you re-read it, perhaps two or three times, till you have a clear notion of how one statement in it follows on (or does not follow on) from another?

You will notice that the intensely evocative lines: 'And 'mid the tumult Kubla heard from far/Ancestral voices prophesying war!' come in pretty well unprepared-for and, more especially, seem to lead nowhere. It is, though so highly charged, a loose end. Again, the damsel with a dulcimer comes as a total surprise to us. She opens up an entirely new train of thought, though one that eventually links up indirectly with Kubla. But further, look at the lines:

> A savage place! as holy and enchanted
> As e'er beneath a waning moon was haunted
> By woman wailing for her demon-lover!

The lines are rather peculiar from a logical point of view, for one begins obediently (and enjoyably) to conjure up the picture of a woman wailing for her demon-lover; yet if one reads the lines in the most straightforward way, the woman is not to be considered as actually a part of the scene in Kubla's palace-gardens, she is merely introduced as a comparison. (The place could not have been more holy and enchanted than it is, *had* it even been inhabited by a woman wailing for her demon-lover.) Coleridge has introduced a cunning choice of options—shall we, or shall we not, regard the woman as part of the scene? is she 'real', or just a comparison? and does it matter?—and in so doing he is offering us a model of how the whole poem is being produced. It reminds us that *anything*, however extraneous, may become relevant—a very familiar situation in dreams, and here exemplified by a rhetorical device.

All in all we can afford to doubt Coleridge's own account of the origin of the poem. I don't mean that he didn't have an opium dream, or that he didn't 'compose' a long poem, or a long *something*, in the course of it; what we can doubt is that 'Kubla Khan' is a fragment from it. I say this, because it seems to me to read not like a fragment but like a complete poem.

The poem (or fragment) clearly 'hinges' upon the transition which occurs at 'A damsel with a dulcimer'. Can you observe a structural resemblance here to 'This Lime-Tree Bower'?

Discussion

Surely Coleridge is staging rather a similar process of thought? In the first part of the poem (the first two strophes) he makes an effort to evoke a scene from which he is separate and at a distance (nowhere could be more remote than 'Xanadu'; how could one begin to find one's way there?). Then in part two he realizes or asserts, with pride, that no travelling is necessary; he could build the whole palace and pleasure-grounds himself, if . . . The 'if' specifies that, in order to perform this magical feat, he requires 'delight' or joy; and the poem ostensibly speaks as if the delight were lacking—but the reader senses that it is present, a fact proved by the existence of the present poem. It is indeed a very cheerful and joyful poem in which, with that somewhat over-the-top description of the prophet-magician-bard ('Beware! Beware!/His flashing eyes, his floating hair!), Coleridge gently and amusingly mocks his own overweening poetic ambitions.

The mutual influence of Wordsworth and Coleridge

Will you now read, or re-read, Wordsworth's 'My heart leaps up' (set text, page 105), 'Ode: Intimations of Immorality' (pp. 105–10) and 'Resolution and Independence' (pp. 110–14), and Coleridge's 'Dejection: an Ode'—*this last, again, in the version in which it appears in the notes to the cassette reading.* (As Laurence Lerner has said (pp. 98–99), this is the version that Coleridge published. The earlier, much longer version is in your set text, pp. 94–104. More about this later.)

It was suggested earlier (pp. 5ff.) that, for important historical reasons, *friendship* played an especially large part in the genesis of the poems written in the Romantic period. The point is vividly illustrated in the poems we are about to discuss, which are tied together by innumerable threads of mutual influence and personal interchange. During 1801 Wordsworth wrote comparatively little, and rather naturally, considering his poverty and the fact that verse-writing tended to injure his health, he began to have doubts about his future as a poet. Then, in the spring of 1802, he began to produce a flood of poems, among them 'The Sailor's Mother', 'Alice Fell', 'The Beggars', 'To a Butterfly', 'The Immigrant Mother' and 'To the Cuckoo'. On 26 March he wrote 'My heart leaps up', and on the following day he composed the first four stanzas of his 'Ode: Intimations of Immortality'. It was a happy time for him, both in this respect and because he had become engaged to Mary Hutchinson.

His situation was in extreme contrast to that of Coleridge. Coleridge's marriage had turned out a disaster; he was in debt, was forlornly in love with Mary

Hutchinson's sister Sara, and had become dependent upon opium. For all these reasons he had been unable to write for many months; and his plight so much distressed William and Dorothy that they became quite frightened to open his letters.

On 28 March William and Dorothy went to stay with Coleridge in Keswick, and on 4 April, while they were still there, Coleridge wrote, between sunset and midnight, the long verse 'Letter' addressed to Sara, which became 'Dejection: an Ode'. While in Keswick Wordsworth had shown, or read, to Coleridge the four opening stanzas of his 'Immortality' ode, and the 'Letter' is plainly Coleridge's response to them. Stanza V of the published version is an answer to the question in lines 57–58 of the 'Immortality' ode: 'Whither is fled the visionary gleam?/Where is it now, the glory and the dream?'; and Coleridge presumably has in mind Wordsworth's 'I feel—I feel it all' (42) when he writes, 'I see them all so excellently fair,/I see, not feel, how beautiful they are!' His 'There was a time when, though my path was rough,' seems to be an echo of the first line of Wordsworth's poem; and if one wants finally to convince oneself of the conscious connection between the two poems, one may do so by referring to the 'Letter', where Wordsworth's 'My head has its coronal' is taken up by Coleridge in 'I too will crown me with a Coronal' (136).

'Dejection: an Ode'

Coleridge read his 'Letter' to William and Dorothy on a return visit to Grasmere a few weeks later, and in a letter to a friend, William Sotheby (19 July 1802), he transcribed extracts from the poem, substituting the name 'Wordsworth' for 'Sara'. We need not put down this strange action simply to discretion, for it can be argued that the poem was always in some sense addressed to Wordsworth, and indeed that his love for Sara was somehow a part of his love for Wordsworth. Even in the 'Letter' version the stress is continually on Sara as a member of the Wordsworth group and much is made of an evening, never to be forgotten, when *Sara's sister Mary* took Coleridge's head on her lap. The pattern of Coleridge's love for both Wordsworth and for Sara took the form of submission and a superstitious pride in the thought that, by eclipsing himself, he might vicariously benefit them.

Would you now re-read Laurence Lerner's discussion of 'Dejection' on pp. 98ff. Professor Lerner speaks of the abridgement of the poem as 'done clumsily'. I would disagree with him here and would suggest that the poem Coleridge published is not just an abridgement but a radically different poem, also a finer one. The issue is an interesting one, and at the end of this section I shall propose an exercise in which you compare the two poems or versions. Meanwhile will you consider stanza V and the doctrine about Joy asserted there?

At a first reading the stanza seems confusing. Music is said to *be* Joy; Joy to *be* life, and also to be the 'effluence' of Life (it can be thought of metaphorically both as a raincloud and the rain which falls from the cloud). The justification of this juggling with paradoxes comes in line 72: 'We in ourselves rejoice!' A paradox is being asserted about the very nature of human existence—that the world is created by a sort of self-reflexive process. In delighting in the world we are delighting in *ourselves* and in something that we have put there. It is a bold concept, and one that verse, with its licence to play with 'conceits', is actually more competent to express than prose.

I have spoken of the concept of reality as 'self-reflexive'. Notice now a quite different (though perhaps related) kind of self-reflexiveness. (It is one which we are constantly encountering in Coleridge, Wordsworth and Keats.) 'Dejection' is about not being able to write poems, and yet we are conscious, and the author depends upon our being conscious, that an impressive poem is here and now being written. Observe how in the later lines of stanza VII we feel the author being released from constriction into a freer and delighted eloquence. This is how one reads those lines:

> Mad Lutanist! who in this month of showers,
> Of dark-brown gardens, and of peeping flowers,
> Mak'st Devils' Yule, with worse than wintry song,
> The blossoms, buds, and timorous leaves among.

They are expansive and life-enjoying, with a return of the note sounded at the beginning of the poem ('Well! If the Bard was weather-wise', etc.), the note of an intense affection, expressed half-playfully, for the traditional English scene. Coleridge is staging a demonstration of the joyful and 'genial' poem-making power, the lack of which his poem is ostensibly lamenting.

In the same stanza the Æolian harp embodies a further comment on Coleridge's own painful situation as a poet. The harp is said now to be 'screaming' in agony, and the wind which plays upon it to 'rave' and to be 'mad'—a mad lute-player. Then, with the phrase 'Thou Actor', we are brought back to the harp, which is mocked as resembling a ham-actor or frenzied Poet. The tone is ironical, and the lines 'Hence, viper thoughts, that coil around my mind,/Reality's dark dream!' caricature a weak-minded and self-dramatizing refusal to face reality. It is the situation of stanza II repeated. The poet is not able to be stirred by the ordinary and dear features of an English spring—by the throstle's song or by 'dark-brown gardens' and 'peeping flowers'. He requires unnatural passions and excitements.

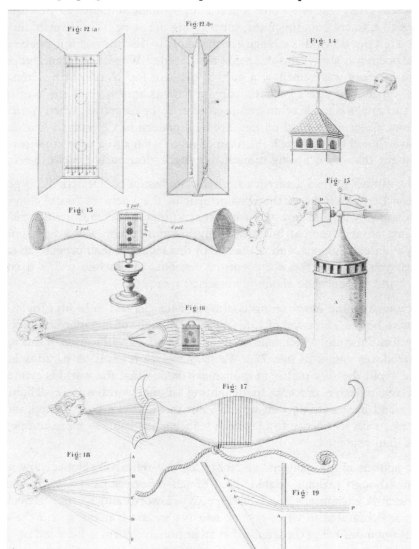

Aeolian harps, fanciful versions, Plate 4 of J.G. Kastner, The Aeolian Harp, 1856. (Reproduced by permission of the British Library Board)

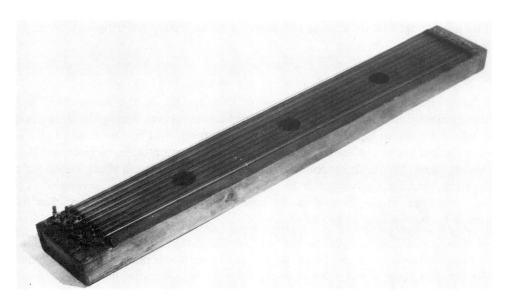

Aeolian harp. (Horniman Museum, London)

This is his weakness, as contrasted with a 'healthy' poet such as Wordsworth. (So runs the argument; but to the reader, the poise and control of the poem are saying the contrary.) Notice that the scene, musically evoked by the harp, of a lost girl on a 'lonesome wild', is very close to Wordsworth's 'Lucy Gray', but has here taken the colour of a melodramatic 'Gothick' tale.

You would not guess from the attractive blitheness of the opening 18 lines of 'Dejection' (apart from the enigmatic 'which better far were mute!') that it was going to be a melancholic poem; and what Coleridge is concerned with in this poem, it may be suggested, is giving a visible *demonstration* of the theory that the creation of poetry is impossible without Joy. (We remember a more euphoric statement of the same theme in 'Kubla Khan'.)

J.M.W. Turner, Thomson's Aeolian Harp, (*detail*), *1809. City of Manchester Art Galleries*)

Wordsworth's answer to Coleridge

Between the 3rd and the 7th of May—that is to say, a fortnight or so after hearing or reading Coleridge's 'Dejection'—Wordsworth wrote 'Resolution and Independence'. We have already discussed this poem in the present course, and shall return to it later, but a brief word is required here.

The poem might be thought at one point to be indirectly referring to Coleridge. Where?

Discussion

I have in mind stanza VI, which so exactly applies to the unpractical and impecunious Coleridge ('. . . how can He expect that others should/Build for him, sow for him, and at his call/Love him, who for himself will take no heed at all?'). Also the last couplet of stanza VII: 'We Poets in our youth begin in gladness;/But thereof come in the end despondency and madness'—a reflection which Coleridge's situation, and his analysis of it in 'Dejection', could easily have prompted. To build up your whole life and intellectual career on the expectation of 'Joy' is plainly to put yourself at great risk.

Actually it is not my purpose to suggest that Wordsworth is *alluding* to Coleridge, or that his poem is in this sense dependent upon 'Dejection'. If it is true that Wordsworth saw Coleridge as an awful warning, it is because he shared a good deal of Coleridge's outlook upon the place of 'Joy' in life and art. In his letter to Sara Hutchinson about this poem (see page 92 above) he refers to poets as 'the happiest of men', and in the Preface to *Lyrical Ballads* he speaks of the Poet as 'a man pleased with his own passions and volitions, and who rejoices more than other men in the spirit of life that is in him'.

Thus my immediate concern is merely with Wordsworth—with the nature of the fear evoked in stanzas V–VII, and with the remedy for that fear that the poem proposes. A useful hint is to connect 'Resolution and Independence' with the 'Lucy' poems, and especially 'Strange fits of passion' and 'A slumber did my spirit seal'. One way of describing what is evoked in these poems is to say that they are concerned with *hubris*—that notion of pride (or blind security) going before a fall, which figures greatly in Greek tragedy. To be in too carefree, too trustful, a state of bliss can produce a sudden reaction into superstitious fear ('Why may I not be walking straight upon disaster?'). It is this psychological phenomenon, accurately delineated in 'Strange fits of passion', and implied in the shape of 'A slumber did my spirit seal', that Wordsworth seems to be depicting again in 'Resolution and Independence'. As for the 'remedy', it runs thus. The poet finds, to his intense relief and reassurance, that his imaginative and creative powers can be aroused by such a stern and stoical human phenomenon as the aged leech-gatherer and his indomitable persistence. The fact is a conclusive psychological demonstration (or so he feels) that those imaginative powers are not just a trivial affair or a mere fair-weather friend. It is not mere *hubris* to follow the career of poet.

This was Wordsworth's answer to himself. His answer to Coleridge does not come until he writes the rest of the 'Immortality' Ode. In the lines 'To me alone there came a thought of grief:/A timely utterance gave that thought relief', the 'timely utterance' has generally been thought to refer to 'My heart leaps up', three lines from which are included as an epigraph to the Ode, and which is glancingly referred to in 'The Rainbow comes and goes' (10). Lionel Trilling, however, has argued that the 'timely utterance' was 'Resolution and Independence'. The theory seems plausible, for 'My heart leaps up' does not particularly suggest 'relief', whereas 'Resolution and Independence' undoubtedly does. (For the theory to be true, it would have to be assumed that the lines about the 'timely utterance' were a later addition to the opening stanzas, but this is feasible.)

The Ode itself has sometimes been read as being, like 'Dejection', a lament for failing poetic powers. Trilling argues convincingly against this reading (and indeed it would have been odd if Wordsworth had uttered such a lament at the very moment, early in 1802, when he was in such creative flood). According to Trilling it is a mistake to confuse the 'glory' or 'visionary' gleam referred to in the Ode

110

with poetry or the power of making poetry, and the loss of the one is in no way considered as entailing the loss of the other. According to this view it is an optimistic poem: 'It is a poem about growing; some say it is a poem about growing old, but I believe it is about growing up . . . Indeed, the Ode is so little a farewell to art, so little a dirge sung over departing powers, that it is actually the very opposite—it is a welcome of new powers, and a dedication to a new poetic subject' (Lionel Trilling, 'The Immortality Ode', in *The Liberal Imagination*).

Will you now re-read the 'Immortality' ode?

In the opening four stanzas of the Ode you will have noticed a touch of 'mental drama', in the way that a sense of loss is asserted, followed by the assertion that any grief that the loss caused has been appeased, followed by an unexpected 'But' in line 52: after all, there *has* been a loss, there is no blinking the fact. We could from this be led to expect that the whole poem should have the shape of a mental drama, but in fact what we find in the poem as a whole is something quite different: a public and celebratory statement. This is what Pindaric odes have traditionally been, and much can be inferred from the fact that Wordsworth chose this form. The latter part of the Ode may be taken as Wordsworth's considered answer to Coleridge's 'Dejection', and the answer seems to be to the effect: not that it is wrong to base your life on the expectation of Joy, but that it is a mistake to try to cling on, too long, to one sort of joy—a sort that, according to the laws of life, has to be relinquished. Let us not consider this 'answer', which sounds smug in my paraphrase (and sounds at moments not exactly smug but over-assertive even in the Ode itself), but rather the element of agreement between Coleridge and Wordsworth on the subject of Joy. Lionel Trilling, in an essay 'The Fate of Pleasure' in *Beyond Culture*, draws attention to the sentence in Wordsworth's Preface to *Lyrical Ballads* in which he speaks of 'the grand elementary principle of pleasure' and says of it that it constitutes 'the naked and native dignity of man' and the principle by which man 'knows, and feels, and lives, and moves'. It is surprising, Trilling says, that more attention has not been paid to this sentence: 'This is a statement which has great intrinsic interest, because, if we recognise that it is bold at all, we must also perceive that it is bold to the point of being shocking, for it echoes and controverts St. Paul's sentence which tells us that "we live, and move, and have our being" in God (Acts 17: 28).' He goes on to say that the sentence 'sums up a characteristic of eighteenth-century thought', and here we do not necessarily have to go along with him. But first let us quote a passage from Coleridge's Notebooks (it was printed in the posthumously published collection *Anima Poetae* in 1885) to demonstrate the closeness of his views to Wordsworth's: 'Disapprove, be *ashamed* of the thought, of its always continuing thus, but do not harshly quarrel with your present self, for all virtue subsists in and by pleasure.' Let us also refer to another fact which proves relevant, this time concerning Wordsworth. In 1805 he composed an 'Ode to Duty'. Will you please read this? (It is on pp. 120–21 of your set text.) In the Ode he says that there are those who do the work prescribed by Duty without being aware of it:

> There are who ask not if thine eye
> Be on them; who, in love and truth,
> Where no misgiving is, rely
> Upon the genial sense of youth:
> Glad Hearts! without reproach or blot
> Who do thy work, and know it not: . . .

As for himself, though, he begins to be dissatisfied with such 'unchartered freedom' and wants Duty to tell him what to do. However—correcting himself hastily—he continues: if he is to do his duty, it must be because it is what he *wants* to do. (To use Coleridge's phrase, he refuses to 'harshly quarrel with his present self'.)

Yet not the less would I throughout
Still act according to the voice
Of my own wish; and feel past doubt
That my submissiveness was choice:
Not seeking in the school of pride
For 'precepts over dignified,'
Denial and restraint I prize
No farther than they breed a second Will more wise.

Now this is an odd conception of Duty, which most people take as meaning doing what you *don't* want to do. It shows what difficulty Wordsworth had, even when he tried, in espousing orthodox views. (Even in his respectable middle age he was capable of remarking to a friend that 'he had no need of a Redeemer'.) Significantly, in the later editions of his poems, this stanza in the 'Ode to Duty' was omitted.

The duty of pleasure

I suggest, as against Trilling, that the view that 'virtue' and the 'naked and native dignity of man' subsist in pleasure is a novel one, as stated by Coleridge and Wordsworth, and not one inherited from the eighteenth century. The point may be elucidated by contrasting the word 'pleasures' with the word 'pleasure'. 'Pleasures' are things that you have or pursue; 'pleasure' or 'joy', in a Coleridgian and Wordsworthian sense, is a condition of being. When Coleridge in 'Dejection' (70) rebukes 'the sensual and the proud' he is rebuking the eighteenth century, as he and Wordsworth conceived of it. (We must remember that our idea of the eighteenth century has to a considerable degree been constructed for us by Wordsworth and Coleridge.) The eighteenth century, dominated by the aristocracy (so the thought runs), is concerned with 'having': your aim was to 'have' women; or, as an aristocrat, you were 'proud' of what you had or possessed. To 'having', Coleridge and Wordsworth oppose the claims of 'being' (a more democratic concept). Their poetry and thought is continually concerned with 'being' and states of being. You will remember how, in 'Frost at Midnight', Coleridge evokes a situation in which all intrusions from the external world are stilled or removed, so that all that is left, in this 'extreme silentness', is the poet's thoughts (in unceasing play, like the soot-film in the chimney) and his joyous sense of his own being (aptly symbolized in the joyful and dreamless sleep of the baby beside him).

This leads me to a large historical generalization: it is scarcely possible to over-estimate the effect of the French Revolution. The divide between what came before and what came after is, in a sense, absolute. If, in 1789, you were a person of intelligence and generosity, you could hardly not have had the thought that all was utterly and irreversibly altered in the world: that the past had been a terrible dream, or a lie imposed by tyrants and priests, concealing the joyful truth that the world and society were for human beings to alter to their heart's desire. It was a faith or hope dashed for the majority by the Terror and the Napoleonic counter-revolution, but the accompanying joyful sense of the limitless resources of the human *psyche* was not so easily destroyed, and it underlies the Romantic enterprise. (That Beethoven ended his last symphony, the Ninth, with a choral setting of Schiller's 'Ode to Joy' is a fact of great and obvious significance.)

The overmastering impression left on the reflective by the Revolution was that all values had been re-valued and that the names of values or virtues had been swapped round or altogether re-apportioned. Intellectual paradoxes abounded. The Revolution could be thought of as the victory of the rationalist movement known later as 'the Enlightenment'; but from another point of view it could be seen as 'Enlightenment's' last fling and expiring gesture. Goethe, who was already an adult at the time of the Revolution, illustrates the paradox vividly. For him, Newton, the hero of 'Enlightenment', was a kind of villain, typifying all that was most wrong with the eighteenth century. To break light up, by the prism, into primary colours, as Newton did, was to 'torture' it and to violate the sacred unity of Nature. The need, he told himself, was to overthrow the evil 'Bastille' of Newtonianism; thus, by a curious reversal, he lumped together the *ancien régime* and its arch-enemy 'Enlightenment'.

It is in this context of the revaluing of all things, and renaming of concepts, that Wordsworth's and Coleridge's views are to be understood. They were proposing a novel conception of 'pleasure' and 'joy', and by extension a new role for poetry. One convenient way of describing Wordsworth's project is to say that he aimed, by means of poetry, to offer new sources of joy to humanity. It would be a mistake to think that, by turning his back on political radicalism, Wordsworth turned his back on social endeavour. On the contrary, the enterprise of his 'great' period was plainly undertaken on behalf of the community at large. The fact that it entailed personal seclusion in the Lakes in no way contradicts this (and in fact he sometimes complained of the seclusion). He used himself as a specimen, and it is only in this sense that he was egocentric. He intended to be influential, and he was so in an amazing degree. Some would say too much so; for it is to a good extent owing to Wordsworth that for a century or more the British sensibility, with its infatuation with 'nature' and with 'Nature poetry', became increasingly incomprehensible to foreigners.

In studying Wordsworth and Coleridge one often finds resemblances between their ideas and those of the eighteenth century; but when one comes to explore these resemblances, they turn out to be superficial and to disguise more fundamental differences. A simple example is the resemblance between the theory about Joy propounded in 'Dejection' ('O Lady! we receive but what we give') and the influential theory of the early eighteenth-century philosopher George Berkeley, in his *New Theory of Vision* (1709). Berkeley argues that seeing is not a matter of the passive receiving of visual impressions, but rather a *reasoning* activity. (You see a man or tree as standing at a certain distance from you because of a process of reasoning, based on your prior knowledge of what size a man or a tree is likely to have.) Coleridge's theory is, as you might say, Berkeley re-applied to the human heart. (The beauty that you see is provided by yourself.) And the difference counts for more than the resemblance. Just as Coleridge and Wordsworth re-defined 'fancy' and 'imagination', so, tacitly, did they re-define 'pleasure' and 'joy'.

'Joy' is a key to much of Wordsworth's thought and career. Throughout his 'great' period he was deeply concerned with a poem which, at different stages, was called 'The Pedlar' and 'The Ruined Cottage' and which eventually appeared as Book 1 of *The Excursion*. It concerned a ruined cottage and the story of dereliction and destitution associated with its erstwhile inhabitant Margaret. The witness to Margaret's sufferings is a Wanderer or Pedlar, and this character, according to Wordsworth, is peculiarly fitted to enter into the sorrows of others because he has had no sorrows himself. It is a very odd theory, but there is no doubt that it is what Wordsworth says: being unpreoccupied by his own sorrows, '. . . He could afford to *suffer*/With those whom he saw suffer'. In the first hints of the poem, written in 1795, there is in fact no suggestion of any consolation for the sufferings of Margaret. In a 1798 version, however, the Pedlar having finished his narrative, the poet looks again at the ruined cottage and its broken walls, and

> . . . all appeared
> Colours and forms of a strange discipline,
> The trouble which they sent into my thought
> Was sweet, I looked and looked again, and to myself
> I seemed a better and a wiser man.

Other versions are tried, and finally in *The Excursion* (1850 version) we have a famous passage in which the Pedlar says that the sight of 'Those weeds, and the high spear-grass on that wall' conveyed to his mind

> So still an image of tranquillity . . .
> That what we feel of sorrow and despair
> From ruin and from change, and all the grief
> That passing shows of Being leave behind,
> Appeared an idle dream, that could maintain,
> Nowhere, dominion o'er the enlightened spirit
> Whose meditative sympathies repose
> Upon the breast of Faith.
> (*The Excursion*, Book i, lines 946–55)

He turns away and 'walks along his road in happiness'. The weeds and 'rank spear-grass', which in the earliest version had been a picture of ugliness and neglect, have by now become an image of beauty and consolation.

In the progressive transformation of 'The Ruined Cottage' we have a sort of thermometer of Wordsworth's spiritual progress. The Wordsworthian doctrine that we have a duty to be joyful is, in general, an inspiring one and comprises much of the best that he has to offer; nevertheless it always contained within it a certain streak of hardness. If one considers 'The Old Cumberland Beggar' or the sonnet 'To Toussaint L'Ouverture' in a certain light, they appear almost comically ruthless. (It doesn't matter how the old Cumberland beggar starves or freezes; it doesn't matter if Toussaint's head is (cruel joke) 'pillowed' on some dungeon's stony floor; what matters is the inspiring spectacle they offer to *us*.) This is not one's ultimate judgement on them; but it helps in perceiving the shape of Wordsworth's career. Some deep emotional dilemma was working itself out through his 'great' period, and once it had done so, the doctrine of the duty of cheerfulness became indistinguishable from a doctrine of hardness.

The two versions of Coleridge's 'Dejection'

Will you now read both versions of 'Dejection', trying to decide (1) what the main differences between the two versions consist in, (2) whether one version is to be preferred to the other (as distinct from considering them merely as different poems, each valuable in its own way), and if so, why? The following points may be helpful:

1 The largest of the many differences seems to be that the published version is essentially about the poet himself, whereas the 'Letter' version is as much concerned with Sara's feelings as with his own—about an unhappiness which a letter from him has caused her and about the supreme importance to his happiness that she should be happy.

The view of those who (like the present writer) prefer the published version is that the 'Letter' version gives one an uneasy feeling that it is more egocentric, more purely about the poet himself, than it purports to be. What most interests the poet, even as regard's Sara's state of mind and feeling, is its effect on *him* (as indeed is frankly stated at one point: 'O for my own sake I regret perforce/Whatever turns thee, Sara! from the course/Of calm Well-being . . .' (130–32)), and, according to this view, Coleridge came to realize this fact and deliberately cut out all the passages which create this uneasiness (though by doing so, he sacrificed some magnificent lines). In the published version all the allusions to the 'Lady' (which are mainly concentrated in the final stanza) emphasize not the poet's relationship to her, and their shared memories, but their difference. She is represented as all that he is not—a 'simple spirit, guided from above', as opposed to a tormented intellectual.

114

2   A less important point: various allusions in the 'Letter' version, as it stands, seem somewhat private and obscure—e.g., we are curious to know what was in the poet's hurtful letter to Sara but are not told; the reference to the 'sod-built Seat of Camomile' evidently will mean more to her than it does to us.

3   The central philosophical thought has not been quite so clearly defined in the 'Letter' version as in the published version, which makes an important change in wording, from 'We, we ourselves rejoice' to 'We in ourselves rejoice'.

4   Those who prefer the 'Letter' version might be inclined to say that the divided purposes, and the tension between these purposes, that it reveals make it a more authentic poem than the published version, where the conflict has been smoothed out and removed.

7   Figures in a landscape

(By SE)

Think back for a moment to your work on 'Tintern Abbey' and *The Prelude*. Of all the forms which nature can take, from 'the meanest flower that blows' to 'the light of setting suns', which is the one Wordsworth describes most frequently? It is landscape. Even when Wordsworth is intent on describing something as abstract as the relationship between the past and present identity of a man he will begin with a landscape.

That having been said, it must be admitted that such landscapes rarely exhibit all the characteristics expected of them. They are, for instance, rather underpopulated. Some seem inhabited exclusively by the creations of Wordsworth's own imagination, hypothetical hermits and the ghost of his former self. One could explain this absence of human life simply in terms of a blunt historical fact: in 1791 there were just over nine and a half million people in Great Britain and quite a few of those were in or drifting towards the towns, so that parts of the countryside, particularly those parts which interested Wordsworth, would be sparsely populated. A less simple-minded explanation would point to the stress Wordsworth placed on being alone with nature, on solitariness as a precondition of visionary experience. Often this instinct for solitude would express itself, as in Book I of *The Prelude*, in a series of nocturnal wanderings or in a sudden turning away from playfellows:

> Not seldom from the uproar I retired
> Into a silent bay, or sportively
> Glanced sideway, leaving the tumultuous throng . . .
> (lines 474–76)

or

> When we had given our bodies to the wind,
>   . . . then at once
> Have I, reclining back upon my heels,
> Stopp'd short; yet still the solitary Cliffs
> Wheeled by me . . .
> (lines 479–85)

Just occasionally this desire to achieve the condition of solitude forced Wordsworth not just to recollect, but also to edit, in tranquillity. The famous lyric 'I wandered lonely as a cloud' (1804) was based on an experience recorded in Dorothy's *Journal* two years earlier. The entry makes it quite clear that they *both* saw the crowd of daffodils, though in the poem it is Wordsworth alone who has the experience.

This emphasis on the absence of others, this desire to gain experience in and from isolation, should lead us to expect empty vistas and landscapes populated by the poet alone. It should also encourage us to look more closely at those poems which confound our expectations by including a significant human being in the landscape. Do poems like these, being different, represent a different attitude in Wordsworth, a moving away from experience in isolation towards experience through relationships? Or are they at one with Wordsworth's other great poetry, their approach being different but their end the same? To see how far we can answer this question I'd like to look briefly at three poems which together cover Wordsworth's most creative period.

Please read 'The Old Cumberland Beggar' (1797) and 'The Solitary Reaper' (1805), and re-read 'Resolution and Independence' (1802), in your set text, pp. 1–5, 123 and 110–14. (The second and third poems are also recorded on the cassette.)

What do these three poems have in common? Try to list one or two points before continuing.

Discussion

To be brief:

1 All three figures are alone or in some way isolated.

2 The poet observes the characters but does not really relate to them as human beings.

3 All three seem in some way, in what they are or what they do, to be part of nature.

4 Being part of nature, they seem unaware of, and untroubled by, the moral and intellectual problems which afflict the poet.

5 Though external to Wordsworth and unpersonalized (not one of them is given a name), each has an effect on the poet's consciousness.

Let's take each of these points in turn and try to illustrate them. See if you can find evidence of isolation in the poems.

Discussion

Taking 'The Old Cumberland Beggar' first:

> Surrounded by those wild unpeopled hills,
> He sat, and ate his food in solitude . . .

which suggests both his immediate social isolation and the much broader loneliness of his physical surroundings. The phrases 'solitary man' and 'solitary being' become almost a refrain through the poem, while the

> . . . vast solitude to which
> The tide of things has borne him . . .

is simultaneously an expression of the sensory isolation brought about by physical decrepitude and a description of the sparsely populated countryside through which he shuffles.

116

Wordsworth meets the Leech-gatherer in a 'lonely place' ('Resolution and Independence', lines 52 and 127), while his concluding vision is of 'the Leech-gatherer on the lonely moor'.

The first stanza of 'The Solitary Reaper' contains no fewer than four points through which isolation is hammered home.

> Behold her, *single* in the field,
> Yon *solitary* Highland lass!
> Reaping and singing *by herself*;
> Stop here, or gently pass!
> *Alone* she cuts and binds the grain . . .

Did you notice, by the way, a typical Wordsworthian technique of emphasis being used here? Her isolation is established in the first line and variations are then played upon it in lines 2 and 3, the point apparently being rounded off by the semi-colon and the invitation to the reader which follows it. Then, most unexpectedly, the point bursts through again, accentuated by an unusual word order which allows the crucial word 'Alone' to begin both a new sentence and a new line.

What about the second common feature? Can you find evidence of Wordsworth observing rather than relating to these various figures in a landscape?

Discussion

For 'The Old Cumberland Beggar' the evidence is rather negative, but no less powerful for that. At no point in the poem does Wordsworth actually talk to the man, nor is there any suggestion, although he has known him from childhood, that he has done anything but observe him and others' reaction to him. Indeed, it is this latter point which Wordsworth dwells upon in the poem: the man's social and moral function vis-à-vis the community in which he (just) subsists. It is as though the Old Cumberland Beggar were a piece of grit in the social oyster, grit which is justified because it produces the moral pearl.

If we turn now to 'Resolution and Independence', you may object to my claim that Wordsworth fails to relate to the Leech-gatherer. After all, the poet actually engages the man in a conversation which itself becomes part of the poem. Let us take a closer look at this conversation, which falls naturally into three parts. The poet initiates it at the end of stanza XII. The following two stanzas contain additional descriptive material and a further question from Wordsworth, and it is only in stanza XV that we get a report of what the old man said. But what happens as this conversation develops? Look at stanza XVI. Wordsworth's attention drifts away, the Leech-gatherer's words become unintelligible, fusing together into one continuous natural sound ('like a stream'), while the man himself becomes abstracted, dream-like, turned into a supernatural messenger with a moral and spiritual function, namely 'To give me human strength, by apt admonishment'. So the Leech-gatherer becomes re-distributed by Wordsworth's imagination, partly to nature and partly to the supernatural. This abstraction brings back 'My former thoughts . . . the fear that kills', and in order to re-anchor himself spiritually he renews his questioning. Stanza XVIII introduces the first direct speech from the Leech-gatherer, but, almost as soon as it occurs, Wordsworth drifts away again to pursue 'thoughts within myself' (Stanza XIX). There is another break at the end of Stanza XIX before the conversation is re-established and concluded in XX. By that time the Leech-gatherer has been incorporated within Wordsworth's creative imagination as a moral vision of heroic endurance. Like the Cumberland Beggar, the Leech-gatherer has become an active moral lesson rather than a person in his own right.

What of 'The Solitary Reaper'? Like 'The Old Cumberland Beggar', the evidence is negative but strong. We are invited to observe, to 'Behold', her: Wordsworth sees and listens to her but doesn't interrupt her song or, indeed, understand its language. He listens 'motionless and still' and then passes on.

These figures in a landscape are alone. The poet relates to them, if at all, in a rather odd and limited way. Why were such indirect contacts with such disconnected people so important to Wordsworth? To answer this, we must turn to the remaining three common features listed above. As they are closely related, it might be sensible to take them together while looking at each poem in turn.

'The Old Cumberland Beggar'

How does Wordsworth convey the sense of the Old Beggar being almost part of the landscape? How conscious is the old man of his effects on Wordsworth and others? Unfortunately, as Charles Lamb said, parts of this poem are 'too like a lecture', so concentrate your attention on the first 66 lines and the last section (between lines 162–97), thus skirting the over-didactic middle portion of the poem.

Discussion

Like the landscape, the Old Beggar seems to function on a different time-scale: certainly old, but ageing so slowly that in the time taken for the poet to grow up he doesn't seem to have changed at all:

> Him from my childhood have I known; and then
> He was so old, he seems not older now;

Unlike an ordinary traveller, he doesn't seem to disturb or disrupt nature:

> . . . scarcely do his feet
> Disturb the summer dust . . .

He is disconnected from all other forms of humanity by his extreme slowness of expression and movement, and by his silence:

> . . . he is so still
> In look and motion . . .

> Be his the natural silence of old age!

Being almost an extension of the landscape, the Old Cumberland Beggar seems to share the characteristics of the natural world rather than those of humanity. Like an animal, or something even more inanimate, the old man seems unconscious of himself, often of other people and certainly of the landscape of which he forms a part. He cannot even see that landscape, for he is bent down by age and sees only the earth over which he passes:

> Instead of common and habitual sight
> Of fields with rural works, of hill and dale,
> And the blue sky, one little span of earth
> Is all his prospect . . .

> . . . seeing still,
> And seldom knowing what he sees . . .

118

Did you notice, by the way, that it is a common characteristic of all three figures that they are bent over and thus inevitably out of visual contact with the landscape in which they move? Like the Beggar, the Leech-gatherer is bowed with age:

> His body was bent double, feet and head
> Coming together in life's pilgrimage . . .

Even the Highland Lass, 'o'er the sickle bending', does not see the 'Vale profound'.

Unlike the rest of humanity, the Old Cumberland Beggar is not an active agent. He has been carried into 'that vast solitude' by 'the tide of things'. He does not actively will good, rather does heaven impose that function upon him:

> The good which the benignant law of Heaven
> Has hung around him . . .

Even the act of providing food for the mountain birds is an involuntary effect of 'his palsied hand'. It is worth noting how unsentimental Wordsworth is about this man. He is neither a benevolent old gentleman nor a saintly fool; he is, as far as the poem tells us, totally unaware of the good he does. Like a rock or a river, he is intractable and unresponsive (see lines 25–43); as with them, the intellectual or moral effect he has upon others is due to their consciousness of him, not his consciousness of them. The very mindless unmovingness of the Old Cumberland Beggar transmutes him from a figure in the landscape into part of the landscape itself. As such, the moral lessons Wordsworth and others can infer from him are akin to those derivable from the rest of nature.

It is observable in certain Wordsworth poems that there are two not always completely compatible lines of argument being pursued. We might call one 'the official line' and the other 'the private voice'. The official line is often stated explicitly, almost didactically, in the poems; the private voice, which often casts a shadow over the stated official intention of the poem, leaks out through the diction or the grammar or the imagery. It happens in 'Tintern Abbey', where the official line again and again confidently asserts that the loss of that easy, animal relationship with nature is not regretted, yet at the same time a poignant sense of loss seeps through, distorting the syntax and forcing the imagery to circle round and round a past to which the poet can never return. This combination of official line and private voice creates a remarkable tension in many of the best poems, a tension which dramatizes that universal human discontinuity between what we wish to believe and what we sense to be true. Laurence Lerner has already referred to this aspect of Wordsworth's poetry in his comments on 'Resolution and Independence' (page 95 above), an appropriate example in that the gap is at its widest and most significant there, but it also occurs, less dramatically, in other poems. 'The Old Cumberland Beggar' displays a mild form of this contradiction. The official line is, as we might expect, presented most explicitly in the middle, didactic section, which begins 'But deem not this Man useless . . .' and ends at line 161. The burden of this is that no man is so debased, reduced or dehumanized that he cannot be used by nature (or God) to produce good. The Old Cumberland Beggar is the lowliest of the lowly, but he too, by following his regular begging round, can encourage good acts almost to the point of making them habitual. It is as though Wordsworth is presenting a general argument for letting beggars roam by taking the worst case and wringing value even from that. So much for the explicit official line. If we now turn to the descriptive sections of the poem which frame the sermonizing centre, we will find a distinctly different message. Take another look at the first 66 lines of the poem. How does the poet's argument for the Old Cumberland Beggar here differ from the one presented in the middle section?

Discussion

Essentially Wordsworth is saying that the Beggar doesn't so much represent the worst case as represent a totally different sort of experience. Compare, for instance, the Horseman's implied treatment of ordinary beggars ('throws . . . with a slack/ And careless hand his alms upon ground') with the way in which he approaches the Old Cumberland Beggar ('But stops,—that he may safely lodge the coin/ Within the old Man's hat; nor quits him so,/But still . . ./Watches the aged Beggar with a look/Sidelong, and half-reverted'). The distinction between beggars in general and this beggar in particular is drawn repeatedly in the first section; the

Max Beerbohm, Wordsworth in the Lake District, at Cross-Purposes. (*Reproduced from Max Beerbohm,* The Poet's Corner, *1904; Penguin, 1943*)

toll-gate keeper, the post-boy, the 'cottage curs', 'the boys and girls' all make the same point: the Beggar's nearness to nature, his alienation from the rest of humanity, his uncompromising, unconscious 'otherness', shakes people, literally 'stops them in their tracks'. In some ways, this first section seems to be arguing, it is not so much that the Beggar establishes moral habits as that his unaccommodated and unaccommodating presence doesn't allow others to follow the easy route of habit. To use a term introduced by Laurence Lerner, the Old Cumberland Beggar 'defamiliarizes' the relationship between giver and beggar.

120

'Resolution and Independence'

As this poem is discussed several times in these units, I don't want to go into it in too much detail. It will be sufficient just to identify those elements which it has in common with the other 'figures in a landscape' poems and to define its special contribution to that form. In what way, then, does the Leech-gatherer seem to be part of nature, and how does his integration with nature affect Wordsworth's reaction to him?

Discussion

As Lerner has pointed out, some of the most powerful imagery in the poem occurs in stanzas IX–XI. This imagery is concerned with three objects, each of which represents a different sort of relationship to nature. There is the Leech-gatherer himself, of course, who represents the human element in nature. Then there is the 'huge stone' with which he is compared, an inert mass which represents the most inanimate aspects of the natural world. Then finally there is the 'sea-beast', which links the other two together and stands for the middle position in nature, sentient but not conscious—the world of animals. Both the extremes modulate towards this centre ground: the man is like a huge stone, which itself is like 'a thing endued with sense'. The Leech-gatherer is thus placed in that strange and (to Wordsworth) half-attractive state of being sensitive to nature, but not self-conscious enough to sense himself apart from it.

> Such seemed this Man, not all alive nor dead,
> Nor all asleep—in his extreme old age . . .

The parallels with 'The Old Cumberland Beggar' are clear. Both men are very old, both seem half-absorbed back into the landscape, both are either motionless or move at a pace more determined by nature than man:

> Motionless as a cloud the old Man stood,
> That heareth not the loud winds when they call
> And moveth all together, if it move at all.

Clearly the Leech-gatherer hasn't been so absorbed into the 'natural silence of old age' that he cannot communicate. His speech is 'gentle' and 'courteous', but it contains nothing but a straight account of the way in which he gains his living. Indeed, it seems to be very difficult for Wordsworth to fix his attention on what the Leech-gatherer is saying: he drifts off into his imagination as the old man's words themselves become, through the imagery, absorbed into the landscape.

> But now his voice to me was like a stream . . .

Despite being detached from, indeed unaware of, the poet's spiritual crisis, the old man clearly has an effect on Wordsworth. What is the effect and how does it come about?

Discussion

It's clear, I think, that it doesn't come about because of what the Leech-gatherer tells Wordsworth, at least not directly. Although we get his account in both indirect and direct speech, it's not the verbal information that Wordsworth is concentrating on: indeed, we get it twice only because the poet was not listening to the first answer and had to repeat his question (Stanzas XIII and XVII). It is a visual image that Wordsworth is obsessed by, one which is triggered by the old Man's account but developed by the poet's own imagination. The actual figure in the landscape, the Leech-gatherer with whom Wordsworth is ostensibly having a conversation, is seen against a visionary landscape, a process which culminates in stanza XIX:

> In my mind's eye I seemed to see him pace
> About the weary moors continually,
> Wandering about alone and silently.

The interesting thing about this later version of the figure in a landscape is that it shows little of the integration of man and nature evident in the earlier imagery in the poem (stanza IX–XI) and in 'The Old Cumberland Beggar'. Apart from the one transferred epithet ('weary moors', where clearly the 'weary' refers to the Leech-gatherer's state, not the moors), there is no sense of the one's being incorporated in the other. Even this epithet introduces an alienating idea. The sense of exhaustion, of being worn out, conveyed by 'weary', does not occur in 'The Old Cumberland Beggar'; while, earlier in this poem, the sea-beast crawls out to sun itself, rather than to rest, and the movement of clouds, when it occurs, is a collective action, not the weary action of an individual element. But the most telling change is in the verb 'pace' and the adverb which qualifies it, 'continually'. Gone is the motionlessness, gone the gentle, almost imperceptible, movement of the beggar or the sea-beast, and in their place is a weary, relentless pacing. Did you notice how the wearying repetitiveness of this image is enhanced by the rhyme-scheme of the stanza? The image is placed in the second half of the stanza, where the alternating rhyme of the first three lines gives way to couplets. The couplet is a much more 'closed' form, which contains and sometimes, as here, 'traps' the meaning of a line by strong end-stops, the effect being insistent and rather claustrophobic. In this particular case the effect is rendered even more uncomfortable by the use of imperfect rhyme, a device which tends to produce a sense of frustration and unease in the reader.

You may have noticed that the stanza form throughout the poem is remarkably regular. Can you work out the rhyme scheme?

Discussion

The rhyme scheme is *ababbcc*. This, when combined with a line of five main stresses, produces the stanza known as rhyme royal. Rhyme royal has a long and distinguished history, having been used by, among others, Chaucer, Wyatt, Shakespeare and King James I. Why does Wordsworth, for what appears to be a quintessentially romantic poem, choose such a traditionally elaborate device as rhyme royal? Doesn't it tend to emphasize the 'artificial', 'closed' world of art rather than the 'open' world of nature? Yes, I think it does, and I think Wordsworth chose it for a very particular reason, a reason which should become more obvious by the end of this section.

The landscape in which Wordsworth first saw the Leech-gatherer was a product of the interaction of a real landscape with the poet's imagination, a process vividly illustrated in such poems as 'Tintern Abbey' and *The Prelude*. This second, darker vision is the product of a distracted imagination unable to anchor itself for any length of time in the real world. The result is a bleak, one might almost say existentialist, vision of alienated man against a background which can relate to him only by reflecting his own weariness.

By recalling our distinction between the 'official line' and the 'personal voice' in Wordsworth, we might reflect on the tone of stanza XX. The official line is that the poet's resolve has been strengthened by a fine example of fortitude in the shape of the Leech-gatherer:

> 'God,' said I, 'be my help and stay secure;
> I'll think of the Leech-gatherer on the lonely moor!'

Note that Wordsworth doesn't mention the Leech-gatherer separately; the moral power of the image comes from his context, 'the lonely moor'. The figure and the landscape combine to produce a beneficial effect on the poet. But what is this beneficial effect based on? We already know the nature of this vision, because it has been described in the previous stanza. The personal voice here does not so much contradict the official line as qualify it by raising a nagging and unanswered question. What is the nature of the fortitude which can be derived from such a vision? Is it the trite and selfish, 'Well, at least I'm not as badly off as the Leech-gatherer' or 'There but for the grace of God . . .'? If so, then it is both platitudinous and ineffectual, for it is notorious that those in states of depression are quite beyond the comforts provided by comparisons with those worse off, depression being an absolute rather than a relative state. The only alternative to this interpretation is that the poet sees the Leech-gatherer's state as a vivid illustration of his own condition, and the strength he derives from this comes from a stoical determination to know and face the truth, however bleak. It is a tragic view of man and his relationship with nature, particularly for someone who placed such importance on the mutually creative and recreative links between the poet and the landscape, but it is not so uncommon in Wordsworth's poetry as you might think. In his only dramatic work, a tragedy called *The Borderers* (1795–96), the hero rejects both Christian consolation and the pagan dignity of suicide, and at the end accepts a sort of death-in-life as a wanderer:

> No human ear shall ever hear me speak;
> No human dwelling ever give me food,
> Or sleep, or rest: but over waste and wild,
> In search of nothing that this earth can give,
> But expiation, will I wander on— . . .

This is not, of course, a direct and complete parallel to the poems we are looking at, but it does suggest Wordsworth's heroic ability to face the complete negation of all he believes in and make poetry out of it. The final, most effective consolation offered by 'Resolution and Independence' has little to do with the poem's concluding images but much to do with the fact that, even in the face of what might prove to be a formless and unintelligible world, the poet can create both form and meaning by writing poetry. Coleridge in 'Dejection' and Wordsworth in 'Resolution and Independence' perform that most extraordinary of all romantic tricks, poetically pulling themselves up by their own boot-straps.

The point of shaping the potentially shapeless is rammed home by Wordsworth's choice of rhyme royal. The more formal the stanza-form, the more obvious does the shaping power of the poet become.

'The Solitary Reaper'

Like 'Resolution and Independence', 'The Solitary Reaper' uses a particular stanza-form; that is, a particular number of lines bound together by a pattern of rhyme. Perhaps I should have said patterns, because there are in fact two types of stanza in this short, apparently simple poem. Can you work out the pattern of rhymes within each stanza, and then go on to see if the stanzas themselves form a larger pattern?

Discussion

There are two types of stanza: the first rhymes *abcbddee*, the second *ababccdd*. In other words, the last four lines of each stanza are exactly the same, being two couplets, but the first four lines differ in the two forms. Stanzas one and four rhyme *abcbddee*, stanzas two and three rhyme *ababccdd*. Formal devices like these are restrictive and demanding, so it is unlikely that Wordsworth adopted them for the sheer fun of it. Are there any differences between stanzas one and four and two and three which the difference in rhyme-scheme might help to articulate?

Discussion

Stanzas one and four are devoted to describing the physical circumstances of Wordsworth and the girl, while the inner two describe the possible effects and content of the song. The song, in other words, is framed, contained (but only just) by the physical circumstances which surround it both in reality and within the stanza structure of the poem. There is a slight irony here, of course, because one of the things the poem is saying is that, ultimately, the song is not contained, for at the end it is carried away by Wordsworth 'in my heart'. This final breakthrough is anticipated very early on in the poem by the very acoustics of the landscape:

> O listen! for the Vale profound
> Is overflowing with the sound.

The verb 'overflowing' is clearly doing the main job of conveying the idea of the sound flooding the immediate landscape and spreading out beyond it; but there is another device which Wordsworth is using to reinforce this auditory image. Can you spot it?

Discussion

Look at the pattern of 'o's and the dipthong 'ou' in the two lines quoted above. In both lines it's 'o . . . o . . . ou', which is an attempt to reproduce the effects of reverberating noise when the original sound gets distorted and elongated by the hills which reflect it.

Unlike the other two poems we have studied, this one is not a matter of the figure being partly reabsorbed into nature. The fusion of figure and landscape in 'The Solitary Reaper' is brought about not by a natural but a human act. The 'song', which is of course a form of art (poets often referred to their poems as songs) picked up and modified by nature, permeates it and binds the figure to her landscape.

But the effect is not purely a physical one. By the end of the poem the song 'was heard no more' and the landscape had been left behind. The 'music', however, was lodged in the poet's 'heart'. One is tempted to quote the 'Still sad music of humanity' of 'Tintern Abbey', not just because it is a reasonably good summary of the third stanza of 'The Solitary Reaper', but also because it is followed by that extraordinary sequence which ends:

> And the round ocean and the living air,
> And the blue sky, and in the mind of man . . .

The reaper's song, too, has flowed through all things in its landscape and then has plummeted down a swallow-hole into the mind of man.

In many ways 'The Solitary Reaper' presents us with the most complicated relationship of landscape, figure and poet that we have met to date. The first two poems involved essentially passive figures on whom both nature and Wordsworth's imagination worked to produce a fusion of landscape, figure and poet. In this last poem the figure has taken the initiative and the first integration of nature and man at the end of the first stanza is a product of an unconscious, effortless artistry (it 'flows'), not of the poet's more self-conscious art.

Can you hazard a guess as to the sort of song the girl is singing? It's probably traditional, certainly in a dialect or local language Wordsworth doesn't understand; it's a form which seems naturally to accompany work and its subject is either 'old, unhappy, far-off things' or 'familiar matter of to-day'. Think back to section 2 of these units.

Discussion

It is most probably a ballad. Most appropriately, Wordsworth returns to that form which had most powerfully influenced his thinking ten years before, to find an example of the power of unconscious art to dissolve man and nature into each other.

But in 'The Solitary Reaper' there is also a place for highly self-conscious—that is, Romantic—art. By the end of the poem the figure, her landscape and her song have been accommodated within Wordsworth's memory, there to be acted on in due course by his imagination and so, finally, to re-emerge as the poem we have read. We should by now have become accustomed to the idea of the Romantic poem as middle ground between the poet and nature where we can observe the process of fusion taking place; what is unusual about 'The Solitary Reaper' is that the ostensible subject of the poem is *also* the power of art to integrate. In that sense it is, of all Wordsworth's great poems, the one most preoccupied by the relationship between literature and landscape.

It is, I think, more than just a neat irony that there is a further literary complication to the story of the poem's creation, one that is not hinted at in the poem itself. Although Wordsworth did go on a tour of Scotland, and wrote many poems about it, the experience which primarily triggered 'The Solitary Reaper' was not Wordsworth's own. The poem, as he himself said, '. . . was suggested by a beautiful sentence in a MS. Tour in Scotland written by a Friend'. The friend in question was Thomas Wilkinson, who, in a work which was later published as *Tours to the British Mountains*, wrote:

> Passed a female, who was reaping alone: she sung in Erse, as she bended over her sickle; the sweetest human voice I ever heard: her strains were tenderly melancholy, and felt delicious long after they were heard no more.

It is a salutary reminder that all great literature, even Romantic poetry with its insistence on an individual experience, is a product not just of man and nature reacting together but also of the poet's awareness of literary culture and his place within it. Romantic self-consciousness applies both to nature and literature.

By way of suggesting that the literary borrowing evident in 'The Solitary Reaper' is not an isolated oddity, I would like you to read the following:

> Many of the furnaces, on the banks of the river, consume charcoal, which is manufactured on the spot; and the smoke, which is frequently seen issuing from the sides of the hills; spreading its thin veil over part of them, beautifully breaks their lines, and unites them with the sky.

Does this description, in either mood or imagery, remind you of any poem by Wordsworth that you have read in this course?

Discussion

The description comes from William Gilpin's *Tour of the Wye* (1771), a book which Mary Moorman, Wordsworth's biographer, suggests the poet had with him on the tour in 1798 during which 'Tintern Abbey' was written.

In the process of creating a figure and its landscape, Wordsworth was open to the influence of both natural objects and the views of his fellow men.

8 'Housed in a dream, at distance from the Kind'

(By GM)

The title of this section is taken from Wordsworth's poem 'Elegiac Stanzas, Suggested by a Picture of Peele Castle, in a Storm, Painted by Sir George Beaumont', written in 1806. Wordsworth saw this painting in that year during a visit to Beaumont, an old friend. The ruins of Peele Castle lay on a small island in Morecambe Bay. In 1794 the poet had spent the month of August at Rampside, Furness, with Peele Castle in plain view. The poem compares the castle, as it appeared to him then, with Beaumont's painting, each scene representing Wordsworth's deepest conviction about human life, first in 1794, then in 1806. Between these two periods, he tells us, 'A deep distress hath humanized my Soul', alluding to the death of his brother John, drowned in 1805 when the merchant ship he captained sank in a storm off Portland Bill. You will find the poem in your set text (pp. 126–27). Could you please read it now? Then consider these questions about it. What is the new conviction about life brought about by John Wordsworth's death? Is it gain, or loss, or a bit of both? Was the earlier state of mind an 'illusion', or did it involve something 'real'? What other Wordsworth poem already discussed in the units does 'Elegiac Stanzas' remind you of? Don't read further till you have made some notes on these points.

Sir George Beaumont, Peele Castle in a storm, *c. 1805. (Private collection. Photograph by courtesy of Leicestershire Museums, Art Galleries and Records Service)*

Discussion

Wordsworth's new idea about life is stated clearly in the last two verses. We can summarize on some such lines as these: 'My brother's death made me realize that the dreams of my youth cut me off from certain common experiences of human life—calamity, grief, death of those we love—for which the only medicine is "fortitude and patient cheer"; however painful this discovery, I welcome it; I am now at one with "the Kind" (i.e. humankind).' Wordsworth accepts this sombre recognition as *gain*. His soul is now 'humanized'. His earlier state was 'a fond illusion', a form of 'happiness' now seen to be pitiable, 'blind'. But was there nothing valuable in that earlier youthful state? Of Peele Castle as it appeared to him in 1794, he says:

> Ah! THEN, if mine had been the Painter's hand,
> To express what then I saw; and add the gleam,
> The light that never was, on sea or land,
> The consecration, and the Poet's dream . . .
>
> A Picture had it been of lasting ease,
> Elysian quiet, without toil or strife;
> No motion but the moving tide, a breeze,
> Or merely silent Nature's breathing life.

How do you respond to these lines? Do they not in some degree qualify the overall argument of the poem that his new condition is *wholly* gain? The second of the quoted verses surely evokes qualities we think of as peculiarly 'Words-worthian': 'silent Nature's breathing life', 'a breeze', the recurrent sign in his poetry both of that life and of the poet's creative response to it. Or in the first verse, 'the *consecration*, and the *Poet's* dream': doesn't such language work against the notion that these earlier convictions were all 'illusion'? And the famous line, 'the gleam,/The light that never was, on sea or land'—does it mean 'the light *never* was, and only my youthful delusion supposed it possible'? Or, 'never was, and how intensely I wish it could have been realized'? Don't we have to admit both possibilities? That Wordsworth himself may have been troubled by such counter-currents within the poem is suggested by his 1820 revision of these lines:

> . . . add a gleam,
> The lustre known to neither sea nor land,
> But borrowed from the youthful Poet's dream.

—a version which cuts out the more complex implication of 1806.

Another poem that 'Elegiac Stanzas' could have recalled has been discussed by Nick Furbank: the 'Immortality' Ode (see above, pp. 110ff.), an extended reflection upon the loss of 'the visionary gleam'. The Ode ends:

> Thanks to the human heart by which we live,
> Thanks to its tenderness, its joys, and fears,
> To me the meanest flower that blows can give
> Thoughts that do often lie too deep for tears.

The 'I' of the Ode's opening stanzas has become 'we', invoking, indeed celebrating, a common human condition, just as 'Elegiac Stanzas' moves from the 'I' of 1794 to the 'we' of 1806:

> Not without hope we suffer and we mourn.

It seems, then, that the new 'humanism' of 'Elegiac Stanzas', though taking sterner form, had been in gestation since at least the completion of the Ode in 1804.

You may also have recalled some lines in 'Resolution and Independence':

My whole life I have lived in pleasant thought,
As if life's business were a summer mood;
As if all needful things would come unsought
To genial faith, still rich in genial good;

The poem is not concerned with any loss of 'the visionary gleam'. But it does present Wordsworth's conception of himself as having been set apart from the common ills and dangers of life: 'solitude, pain of heart, distress, and poverty'. The figure of the leech-gatherer embodies the values necessary to dignified human survival: 'resolution and independence' can be thought of as a variant of 'fortitude and patient cheer'.

Thinking back to poems you have read in connection with these units, do you find anything surprising in Wordsworth's idea, emerging in different ways from 'Resolution and Independence', the 'Immortality' Ode, and 'Elegiac Stanzas', that in his earlier poetry he had paid too little attention to pain and loss as inescapable features of human life? Many poems in *Lyrical Ballads* address themselves exactly to these themes, surely? 'Simon Lee', 'The Last of the Flock', 'Michael', the 'Lucy' poems, the well-known lines in 'Tintern Abbey' ('hearing oftentimes/The still, sad music of humanity,/Not harsh nor grating, though of ample power/To chasten and subdue'): isn't this list of the obvious examples enough to show that Wordsworth's view of his past attitudes was—at the very least—one-sided? Hazlitt speaks of Wordsworth's 'levelling Muse', underlining the democratic spirit of such poems, the degree to which they take seriously the feelings and experiences of ordinary uneducated people. They refuse to *pity* their subjects, in the spirit of Blake's verse reminding us that 'pity' is closely, perhaps intrinsically, linked with feelings of superiority to the person pitied. We approach the people in *Lyrical Ballads* on equal terms. We learn to sympathize—that's to say, to *feel with*—the subjects of these poems, and with the difficulties and distresses which their lives entail. Did Wordsworth forget all about this aspect of his earlier writing? What criticism was he directing against himself?

Nick Furbank has already touched briefly on a remarkable line in *The Excursion,* Book I, in which Wordsworth tells us that the narrator of the harrowing tale of Margaret's life

. . . could *afford* to suffer
With those whom he saw suffer.

(The emphasis is Wordsworth's.) The narrator's sympathy with Margaret is possible only because of his detachment, his lack of any feelings about himself, the solitary wandering life which involves no personal ties of affection or duty towards anybody else. I would like to suggest that this is an important clue to the moral structure of much of Wordsworth's writing on specifically human issues.

You will remember from Laurence Lerner's and Simon Eliot's comments (see above, pp. 94 and 115ff.) the frequency in Wordsworth's poetry of an encounter between the solitary poet and another lonely wandering person. These encounters share certain characteristics. The person whom the poet meets is usually poor, old, ill or disabled in some way. Such meetings break in upon the poet's condition of meditative withdrawal. The human condition of the encountered person, though noticed, becomes less important to the poet than his thoughts about it. He sees it as pointing to the stoical dignity of the encountered person, who is then associated in a mysterious manner with Nature. The encountered person's *human value* is affirmed only by his becoming a portent, or reminder, or symbol, of the consoling and strengthening power of Nature, as a realm of transcendent values. The experience overcomes the poet's solitariness, not because of any human communication with the encountered person (he remains as solitary as before), but because he becomes for the poet the vehicle for a memorable 'communion' with Nature.

The structure of these encounters resembles that of the narrator's relationship to Margaret's experiences. There is a barrier between the poet and the signs of human 'pain of heart, distress, and poverty', signs which are, so to speak, marshalled into an overriding argument about Nature. Can we not then suggest that it is this barrier which a poem like 'Elegiac Stanzas' shows as having dissolved? Nature is no longer the beneficent theodicy in whose terms human suffering can be explained. The poet has had to come to terms with such suffering in his own life. The criticism which 'Elegiac Stanzas' directs against his earlier life is therefore not so much that he ignored human unhappiness, as that he kept it at a distance, saw it as a fate for others, a condition certainly to be meditated over and pondered, but not one that he enters into and shares.

What then of 'the dream'? 'Elegiac Stanzas' points to *this* as having constituted the barrier between the poet and 'the human'. The dream '*housed*' him. An interesting metaphor, surely? The dream gave shelter and protection, and of a specifically human kind, a house being a human construction, not something provided by Nature. What was this dream house built of? Wordsworth's encounter with the shepherd in *The Prelude*, Book VIII, gives us a lead here. It differs from other such encounters in that the shepherd is, though solitary, neither ill nor disabled. On the contrary, Wordsworth sees him as an emblem of human strength and nobility.

> Seeking the Raven's Nest, and suddenly
> Surpriz'd with vapours, or on rainy days
> When I have angled up the lonely brooks
> Mine eyes have glanced upon him, few steps off,
> In size a Giant, stalking through the fog,
> His Sheep like Greenland Bears; at other times
> When round some shady promontory turning,
> His Form hath flash'd upon me, glorified
> By the deep radiance of the setting sun:
> Or him I have descried in distant sky,
> A solitary object and sublime,
> Above all height! like an aerial Cross,
> As it is station'd on some spiry Rock
> Of the Chartreuse, for worship. Thus was Man
> Ennobled outwardly before mine eyes,
> And thus my heart at first was introduced
> To an unconscious love and reverence
> Of human nature; hence the human form
> To me was like an index of delight,
> Of grace and honour, power and worthiness.
>
> (lines 397–416)

Laurence Lerner has suggested that the expanded version of *The Prelude* (1805) is the result of Wordsworth 'philosophizing' about those experiences as a boy and young man which he recounted in the original two-book version of the poem, and that this later process of explanation and generalization, on the whole, diluted and dissipated the effect of the original. Now, whatever you have decided about this argument, it remains important to notice the intrinsic conviction and power of Wordsworth's explanatory 'philosophy': '*hence* the human form / To me was like an index of delight . . .' Here is the substance of Wordsworth's 'dream', that

Nature's purpose in these early experiences was to instruct him about the high value of human beings which, as a poet, it would be his adult task to affirm. However acquired—and we may concede that there were other cultural and educational factors at work as well—it was such convictions which directed Wordsworth's response to the events of the French Revolution, to the influential conversation of the French Republican sympathizer Beaupuy, whom Wordsworth met at Orleans in 1792, and to his belief that the Revolution was a time when

> . . . Europe was rejoiced,
> France standing on the top of golden hours,
> And human nature seeming born again.
>
> (VI: 352–54)

Why, then, does Wordsworth write, retrospectively, '*seeming*'? We may surmise from his general tone that that is not how the experience felt at the time. But after the events of the Terror, the rise of Napoleon and the conversion of French Republican defence against 'the confederated powers' of monarchical Europe into a nationalistic determination to conquer all opponents of whatever political colour, Wordsworth, like other English Republican sympathizers, qualified his early uncomplicated enthusiasm. 'Human nature', it was all too painfully clear, remained capable of acts and impulses very difficult to reconcile with the qualities

Wordsworth aged 72, portrait by Benjamin Robert Haydon, 1842. (National Portrait Gallery, London)

130

represented by the Lakeland shepherd. Wordsworth's Enlightenment faith in human goodness, given political and social embodiment in the early stages of the French Revolution, received from its later stages a very severe check. And the check had implications for his conception of his function as a poet. Did it mean that those early intimations from Nature had been faulty? As we have seen, when Wordsworth confronted the direct evidence of distress, he turned to Nature as a source of explanatory consolation. Yet the awkward question arose—had Nature instructed him misleadingly about the essential nobility of man, as the outcome of the French Revolution might very well imply? Could he be certain that, in the words of the narrator of Margaret's tale, desolation and unhappiness belonged merely to 'the *shews* of Being', not to its permanent reality? The structure of those encounters with solitary sufferers is the poetic articulation of these unresolved questions. The 'dream' that human nature was good, that its native principle was 'pleasure' (see Nick Furbank's discussion of this principle of Wordsworth's thinking, page 112 above), is set over against the observed facts of some human lives, dominated by pain rather than pleasure, lives for which human nobility could be claimed, not as a triumphant affirmation, but only as a source of dignified and stoical uncomplaint. What I have called 'the barrier' between the poet and those encountered solitaries stems from a deep-rooted hope that human life had different potentialities, for which Nature, if not contemporary society, was witness. How were these potentialities to be realized? Wordsworth had no answer—on the one hand, 'solitude, pain of heart, distress, and poverty'; on the other hand, the teachings of Nature and the conviction that this teaching had made him a being apart from others, with the special responsibilities of a poet to articulate these ideas. When, in 'Elegiac Stanzas', Wordsworth refers to the latter as 'the Poet's *dream*', he is telling us that his own personal experience of grief and loss has introduced a more radical qualification of his Enlightenment faith than he had already experienced from events in France. This qualification has such force that the ideas and convictions elaborated in *The Prelude*, standing as Wordsworth felt they did on an elaborate sub-structure of personal experience of Nature, must now be categorized as 'the Poet's *dream*'. We can perhaps now see more clearly why the poem is indeed *elegiac*, and why those stanzas still preserve a sense that the 'the gleam that never was on sea or land' represented something more than an illusion.

Coleridge, too, experienced a separation from 'the Kind'. In an early poem, 'The Eolian Harp', written shortly after his marriage, Coleridge sketches a potential hostility between the conventional Christian orthodoxy credited to his wife Sara ('Meek daughter in the family of Christ') and his own speculative and searching mind. Would you read the poem now? You will find it in your set text (pp. 16–18). The poem supposes that the breeze blowing across the strings of the harp produces seductively attractive music. How do you respond to the lines describing this music? Do they convey an impression of 'feelings' as well as of philosophical speculation?

Discussion

The philosophical speculation (lines 26–48) suggests that all living creatures resemble Æolian harps, animated by a divine breeze which is 'at once the Soul of each, and God of all'. Having entertained this idea, Coleridge then dismisses it as, from a Christian point of view, heretical. Such a notion would deny the fallen nature of man: that central Christian dogma, Original Sin. We may well suspect that by crediting this criticism to his wife, as the embodiment of true Christian theology, Coleridge is using her as something of a cat's-paw. The conflict was probably within his own thinking, and he was reluctant to explore it too deeply. Nevertheless, we do here meet a relaxed form of an opposition between 'the Kind', as represented by wife and home, and an individual speculation that sets the poet apart. How did you respond to this earlier passage?

> And that simplest lute,
> Placed length-ways in the clasping casement, hark!
> How by the desultory breeze caress'd,
> Like some coy maid half yielding to her lover,
> It pours such sweet upbraidings, as must needs
> Tempt to repeat the wrong!

Did you notice the metaphor here? The lute is a maid, and the breeze a lover tempting her to wrong. The lines that follow present, not heretical speculation, but a rhapsodic account of imaginary *pleasure*; indirect certainly, but, in the light of the opening metaphor, with evident sexual implication. So the music of the harp represents two forms of 'forbidden' searching: sexual and intellectual. With this in mind, we may reasonably think that Sara's supposed reproof was not simply directed against his meditations. (It is, after all, a curious aspect of this honeymoon poem that the 'pensive Sara' we meet in the first line, leaning affectionately on the poet's arm, is later converted into a *'daughter* in the *family* of Christ', and in the last line is hailed as a *'Maid'*.)

'The Eolian Harp' is an early exercise in the 'conversational' style Coleridge had already essayed before 1796, and which under the stimulus of his friendship and collaboration with Wordsworth he was to develop in 'This Lime-Tree Bower' and 'Frost at Midnight', discussed above (see pp. 11–12 and 51–57). Its interest here is its overall structure of an exploration into dangerous imaginary worlds which ends in a return home. What other poem of Coleridge's already discussed uses such a structure, if in a more elaborate form?

Discussion

I hope you didn't have to think long about this question. 'The Ancient Mariner' is the one I had in mind. But of course there are striking differences. The Mariner's voyage is moral and spiritual in a thoroughly committed way. His killing of the albatross brings about terrible results, both for his fellows and himself. 'The man hath penance done,' the spirits murmur with disturbing relish, 'and penance more will do.' And they are right. The Mariner manages to break the deadlock of guilt and impotent remorse imaged in the account of the charmed ship, with its load of dead and dying crewmen. But there is no return to the cheerful innocence of the poem's opening mood of adventurous exploration. The Mariner returns home, yet is it really a return?

> O Wedding-Guest! this soul hath been
> Alone on a wide wide sea:
> So lonely 'twas, that God himself
> Scarce seeméd there to be.
>
> O sweeter than the marriage-feast,
> 'Tis sweeter far to me,
> To walk together to the kirk
> With a goodly company!—

Here are all the signs of 'the Kind': marriage, communal celebration, church, family and friends. But the Mariner is a permanent stranger, doomed to travel from land to land, telling his fearful tale. We may remain uncertain about what exactly his experience *was*, to entail such calamitous results. As Brian Stone has remarked, the official moral of the poem seems painfully incommensurate with the Mariner's mysterious catastrophe. Nor can we claim that the Mariner is 'a dreamer'. Yet, to touch on an autobiographical interpretation, there is ample evidence that Coleridge (in Wordsworth's famous phrase for Sir Isaac Newton) went 'Voyaging through strange seas of Thought, alone' (*The Prelude* (1850), III: 63). However caused, an extreme alienation stands at the centre of this poem,

Coleridge aged 42, portrait by Washington Allston, 1814. (National Portrait Gallery, London)

a condition so severe as permanently to ban its victim, the Mariner, from any return to 'the Kind'. We may perhaps think of the poem as Coleridge's fictional exploration of one possible outcome to his own adventurous intellectual and moral life.

Another poem you might look at in this connection is 'France: An Ode', where Coleridge rehearses his own conversion from straightforward enthusiasm for the Revolution as a magnificent assertion of political and social 'Liberty' to bitter opposition to the France of Napoleon as the embodiment of a new tyranny. As it had for Wordsworth, England's declaration of war on France in 1793 had meant for Coleridge a painful self-division between love of country and political hope. 'Liberty', the poem concludes despairingly, cannot be found in *any* contemporary political form, but only as a spiritual presence in nature. The lovers of Liberty, runs the implication of this imagery, can find no social embodiment for their ideas: 'the Kind' will have none of them.

Later in the course, in the discussion of Keats's poetry, you will meet another example of the Romantic 'dream', as both profoundly attractive yet also threatening, in its ability to cut the poet off from satisfactory human experience. And in Shelley's *Alastor*, both the attractions and potential disaster of final alienation from 'the Kind' provide yet another variant on the theme.

Here it may be useful to end with a glimpse of a wider perspective on this element in Romantic poetry. Ernst Fischer, commenting on Romantic individualism, has written:

> One of the basic experiences of Romanticism was that of the individual emerging alien and incomplete from the ever-increasing division of labour and specialization and the consequent fragmentation of life. Under the old order, a man's rank had been a kind of intermediary in his relations with other men and with society at large. In the capitalist world the individual faced society alone, without an intermediary, as a stranger among strangers, as a single 'I' opposed to an immense 'not-I'. This situation stimulated powerful self-awareness and proud subjectivism, but also a sense of bewilderment and abandon. (*The Necessity of Art*, page 54)

The economic aspect of this explanation is rather early for our period. But the idea that Romantic individualism, a separation from 'the Kind' both chosen and enforced, was rooted in a new, if still emergent, pattern of social relationships, offers a general insight into the poems we have been considering. Such poems register a condition of solitude both liberating and alarming, both a release of power and visionary hope, and a condition of extreme loneliness with all its attendant nostalgias and self-doubt. The fact that such very different poets as Wordsworth, Coleridge, Keats and Shelley wrote important poems on this theme suggests that in contemplating it we need to search for its wider determinants in the historical movements of the period.

9   Wordsworth and Blake

(By PNF)

'Nature' is one of a certain class of words which are valuable precisely because they mean so many different things. This is quite different from being meaningless; nevertheless the word 'nature' (or 'Nature', with a capital 'N') can become meaningless, just as it can become seriously misleading, unless you take a firm decision to learn the rules and tricks of its behaviour. And never was this warning more necessary than with the literature of the Romantic period. The thing to do is to pause each time you encounter the word and ask yourself, first, which of its many meanings is being invoked: for instance, *landscape*; or *things as they are*; or *that which is not divine* (as in the phrase 'natural religion', as contradistinguished from religion based on divine revelation); or *that which is not man-made*? Secondly, you should ask yourself, is the word being employed straightforwardly, or is the writer (for whatever reason, honest or dishonest) cunningly playing upon two distinct senses of the word? (It is, as Marx points out in *German Ideology* and elsewhere, a well-known trick of those in possession of social power to try to pass off man-made institutions as part of the eternal and natural order of things.)

With this proviso, let us consider two related questions:

1   Is it true that Wordsworth made a 'religion' of Nature?

2   If so, was it a good thing?

We may begin with (2). William Blake was an admirer of Wordsworth, considering him capable of work 'in the highest degree Imaginative and equal to any Poet'; however, he was far from an uncritical admirer. He made a number of marginal comments in his copy of the 1816 edition of Wordsworth's *Poems* and of *The*

Excursion, and their main drift is that Wordsworth was actually an evil influence in so far as he worshipped Nature. He writes: 'I see in Wordsworth the Natural Man rising up against the Spiritual Man Continually, & then he is No Poet but a Heathen Philosopher at Enmity against all true Poetry or Inspiration.' Referring to Wordworth's heading, 'Influence of Natural Objects in calling forth and strengthening the Imagination in Boyhood and early Youth', he comments: 'Natural Objects always did & now do weaken, deaden & obliterate Imagination in Me. Wordsworth must know that what he Writes Valuable is Not to be found in Nature.' His comment on the last two lines of 'My heart leaps up':

> And I could wish my days to be
> Bound each to each by natural piety.

is: 'There is no such Thing as Natural Piety Because the Natural Man is at Enmity with God'. Finally, he reacts violently against two passages in Wordsworth's *The Excursion*. Here is the first (Preface, lines 63–68):

> How exquisitely the individual Mind
> (And the progressive powers perhaps no less
> Of the whole species) to the external World
> Is fitted:—and how exquisitely, too—
> Theme this but little heard of among Men—
> The external World is fitted to the Mind . . .

Blake's derisive comment is: 'You shall not bring me down to believe such fitting and fitted. I know better and please your Lordship.' And on the second passage, in which Wordsworth says that whatever sounds he is forced to hear, however anguished and sorrowful, must 'Have their authentic comment' (by 'authentic' meaning, presumably, 'fitting'), Blake remarks: 'Does this not Fit, and is it not Fitting most Exquisitely too, but to what?—not to Mind, but to the Vile Body only and to its Laws of Good and Evil and its Enmities against Mind.'

The point that most obviously emerges here is that for Blake the Imagination was to be identified with the holy and the divine and that there was an eternal war between the divine and the natural (cf. Units 2–3). For Blake, Wordsworth's errors were theological; they sprang from 'heathenism' and an idolatrous addition to the 'religion of Nature'.

Is it, then, true that Wordsworth made a 'religion of Nature'? It is at least sufficiently true, I would say, for it to be reasonable for Blake to believe so. In 'Tintern Abbey' the poet tells his sister how she will later remember that on this day they stood together on the banks of the Wye:

> . . . and that I, so long
> *A worshipper of Nature*, hither came
> Unwearied in that service: rather say
> With warmer love—oh! with far deeper zeal
> Of holier love.
> (lines 150–54)

Elsewhere in the same poem he depicts Nature as a teacher and active spiritual guide:

> . . . Nature never did betray
> The heart that loved her; 'tis her privilege,
> Through all the years of this our life, to lead
> From joy to joy: for she can so inform
> The mind that is within us, so impress

With quietness and beauty, and so feed
With lofty thoughts, that neither evil tongues,
Rash judgements, nor the sneers of selfish men,
Nor greetings where no kindness is, nor all
The dreary intercourse of daily life,
Shall e'er prevail against us, or disturb
Our cheerful faith, that all which we behold
Is full of blessings.
(lines 122–33)

The slightly New-Testament flavour of this reminds us of his later audacious remark that 'he had no need of a Redeemer': nature here seems to stand in for the Redeemer.

Finally, in the same poem again, there are the very famous lines in which he says that, in 'nature', he has felt:

A presence that disturbs me with the joy
Of elevated thoughts; a sense sublime
Of something far more deeply interfused,
Whose dwelling is the light of setting suns,
And the round ocean and the living air,
And the blue sky, and in the mind of man:
A motion and a spirit, that impels
All thinking things, all objects of all thought,
And rolls through all things.
(lines 94–102)

This is a deeply equivocal passage, which reveals more ambiguities every time you read it, and could never perhaps be reduced to a *doctrine*; but it undeniably locates the divine presence *in* Nature, as separate from it and residing or interfused within it. Hence a poet who takes a worshipping attitude towards 'nature' can very fairly be accused of idolatry. (You will understand that I am not taking sides between Blake and Wordsworth, but merely suggesting that Blake's attack on Wordsworth is not just a matter of a 'misunderstanding'.

The passages from *The Excursion* which we saw Blake criticizing were in fact probably written as early as 1798, and in that business of 'fitting' and 'fitted' one can see how strong the influence of Hartley and his Associationism still is on Wordsworth. The point is made even clearer in Book IV of *The Excursion*, where the Wanderer states the theory that the 'Forms' of Nature are capable of leading the human being *necessarily*—almost, you might say, *mechanically*—towards moral goodness:

For, the Man—
Who, in this spirit, communes with the Forms
Of nature, who with understanding heart
Both knows and loves such objects as excite
No morbid passions, no disquietude,
No vengeance, and no hatred—*needs* must feel
The joy of that pure principle of love
So deeply, that unsatisfied with aught
Less pure and exquisite, he *cannot choose*
But seek for objects of a kindred love
In fellow-natures and a kindred joy.
(lines 1207–17; italics added)

136

And again:

> —So build we up the Being that we are;
> Thus deeply drinking-in the soul of things,
> We shall be wise *perforce* . . .
> (lines 1264–66; italics added)

One can sense how alien this necessitarianism ('cannot choose', 'be wise perforce') would be to Blake and how, for him, it would smack too much of a 'Newtonian' and mechanical view of the universe.

Let us turn to a further and related difference between Blake and Wordsworth, which concerns 'the visionary'. It is illuminated by a remark of Blake's in his letter to Dr Trusler of 23 August 1799 (see the Prose Booklet): 'You certainly Mistake, when you say that the Visions of Fancy are not to be found in This World. To Me This World is all One continued Vision of Fancy or Imagination . . .' Also by these lines of verse (Butter, page 123) in a letter to his friend Thomas Butts (22 November 1802):

> . . . before my way
> A frowning Thistle implores my stay.
> What to others a trifle appears
> Fills me full of smiles or tears;
> For double the vision my Eyes do see,
> And a double vision is always with me.
> With my inward Eye 'tis an old Man grey;
> With my outward, a Thistle across my way.
> (lines 23–30)

Will you think what lines of a well-known poem of Wordsworth's lines 3–4 recall? Also, do the last two lines call to your mind another famous Wordsworth poem?

Discussion

I was thinking of the last two lines of the 'Ode: Intimations of Immortality' ('To me the meanest flower that blows can give/Thoughts that do often lie too deep for tears'). Also of the accidental, yet faintly significant, resemblance between Blake's 'old Man grey' and Wordsworth's Leech-gatherer.

Let us first look a little further into Blake's and Wordsworth's difference over 'Nature'. Part of Blake's complaint is that Wordsworth is too much hand-in-glove with Nature, instead of conducting a vigorous combat with her (or it). Perhaps he has a point. Both Simon Eliot and Graham Martin have pointed out how prone Wordsworth is to distance living and suffering human beings from himself and treat them merely as part of 'Nature' or landscape, and this raises vague ethical worries for us. You could say that Wordsworth was in a kind of *complicity* with Nature, and this may be in part what offends Blake ('I know better and please your Lordship'). Wordsworth depends upon 'Nature' as a guide and teacher. It is Nature which tells him when to create poetry and when not to. It is, in his view, only by getting into the right relationship with Nature that he is enabled to write poetry, so that in this respect Nature takes the initiative. The relationship of poet and Nature is intimate, so that when he writes in the opening of *The Prelude* (I, 41–43):

> For I, methought, while the sweet breath of Heaven
> Was blowing on my body, felt within
> A corresponding mild creative breeze,

the power to write poetry is described by a term, 'breeze', which makes it almost as much a part of Nature as the wind in the world outside.

Another major contrast emerges. Imaginative activity for Blake was in a very literal sense a matter of seeing *visions:* one might perceive a thistle in the road, and somehow superimposed on it, but entirely distinct, 'an old Man grey'. The firm distinction and separation of the two perceptions is the relationship which, in Blake's eyes, is proper between the natural and the divine. (It is not the natural which is evil; what is evil is the stooping of the human soul, which is divine, to bondage to, or complicity with, the natural.)

The lines to Thomas Butts from which we have quoted go on to a powerful climax in which Blake speaks of 'threefold' and 'fourfold' vision:

> Now I a fourfold vision see,
> And a fourfold vision is given to me;
> 'Tis fourfold in my supreme delight
> And threefold in soft Beulah's night,
> And twofold Always. May God us keep
> From single vision & Newton's sleep.
> (lines 83–88)

We need not trouble ourselves here about what precisely 'threefold' and 'fourfold' vision mean: it is a matter belonging to the more esoteric side of Blake's philosophy. The crucial concepts are 'twofold vision' (which keeps separate what, in Blake's view, must be separated) and the danger of falling into 'single vision' (the belief that what the physical eye takes in from outside constitutes 'reality').

The war against 'single vision' went along, for Blake, with his war against the doctrine that artists should work from a model. Blake himself had gone through a period in which, as an artist, he had—in his own view—been 'enslaved' to 'nature'. His final emancipation from this slavery was, for him, epoch-making. W. B. Yeats, in his essay 'William Blake and his Illustrations to the *Divine Comedy*', writes:

> . . . it was only after his return to London from Felpham in 1804 that he finally escaped from 'temptations and perturbations' which sought to destroy 'the imaginative power' . . . Blake's imagination 'weakened' and 'darkened' until a 'memory of nature and of pictures of various schools possessed his mind, instead of appropriate execution' flowing from the vision itself. But now he wrote, 'O glory, and O delight! I have entirely reduced that spectrous fiend to his station'—he had overcome the merely reasoning and sensual portion of the mind—'whose annoyance has been the ruin of my labours for the last passed twenty years of my life. . . . I speak with perfect confidence and certainty of the fact which has passed upon me. Nebuchadnezzar had seven times passed over him, I have had twenty; thank God I was not altogether a beast as he was. . . . Suddenly, on the day after visiting the Truchsessian Gallery of pictures'—this was a gallery containing pictures by Albert Dürer and by the great Florentines—'I was again enlightened with the light I enjoyed in my youth, and which has for exactly twenty years been closed from me, as by a door and by window-shutters. . . . Excuse my enthusiasm, or rather madness, for I am really drunk with intellectual vision whenever I take a pencil or graver into my hand, even as I used to be in my youth.' (pp. 118–19)

One more important point. For Blake, since a human being belonged not with 'nature' (or as he sometimes expressed it, 'the vegetable universe') but with the divine, it followed that his visions of 'the real and eternal world' took human form. (Those immensely powerful images in his illustrations to the Book of Job, of which you saw examples in Television Programme 1, are all in some sense *human* images.) The contrast with Wordsworth, whose devotion is to the forms of 'nature', in the sense of mountains and lakes and the non-human, is striking and, in this light, takes on an added significance.

Consider now the way in which Wordsworth talks about the Imagination, in his 1815 Preface (see Prose Booklet, page 26):

> In these images, the conferring, the abstracting, and the modifying powers of the Imagination, immediately and mediately acting, are all brought into conjunction. The stone is endowed with something of the power of life to approximate it to the sea-beast; and the sea-beast stripped of some of its vital qualities to assimilate it to the stone; which intermediate image is thus treated for the purpose of bringing the original image, that of the stone, to a nearer resemblance to the figure and condition of the aged Man . . .

For Wordsworth the function of the Imagination is to cause the real object, and that to which the object is compared—i.e., which is really to say, two separate *orders* of being—to blend and coalesce. The contrast with Blake's notion of Imagination, and by extension with Blake's whole outlook on life, seems—and indeed I think really is—quite a stark one. Wordsworth is preoccupied with reconciliation, compensation, accommodation, Blake with distinction and separation and the war of contraries—a vital and profitable war productive of new life-possibilities.

None the less (and here the contrast diminishes) it seems that Wordsworth, for all his advertised dependence upon Nature as guide and mentor, is ready at certain moments to cut his leading-strings and leave Nature behind. At certain high points in his verse he evokes a state in which

> . . . the light of sense
> Goes out in flashes, that have shown to us
> The invisible world . . .
> (*Prelude*, VI, 534–36).

Nature, it would seem, has no part in this state. What the poet 'sees' at such supreme moments is something (a 'glory') which is peculiar to his own soul and which is, at all events, *invisible*. (I am taking 'Goes out' as meaning 'extinguished'. It could, of course, just conceivably mean 'flashes out like a lighthouse beacon'.) His language in this connection carries a suggestion of the 'negative way', or 'vision without images', described by religious mystics. (The point is elaborated in an article 'The Via Naturaliter Negativa' by Geoffrey Hartman.) The contrast with Blake, you will observe, remains large. The most 'visionary' moments for Wordsworth are those in which he is *not* seeing anything, or seeing something for which there is no sensible or perceptible analogue: it is a far cry from Blake's 'old Man grey' or from his Tyger and Sun-flower—visions which, as we know, could be, and were, translated into line and colour.

Thus not just the word 'nature' but also the word 'Imagination' and the word 'visionary' can be seen to be very capacious ones, embracing what from one point of view can almost be seen as opposites. But, to repeat, this does not mean that they are meaningless, merely that one needs to learn their habits and potentialities.

Appendix

'The Prelude', 1799 version, First Part

(Reprinted with permission from *The Prelude, 1798–1799*, ed. Stephen Parrish, Cornell University Press/Harvester Press, Copyright © 1977 by Cornell University, pp. 43–54.)

Was it for this
That one, the fairest of all rivers, loved
To blend his murmurs with my Nurse's song,
And from his alder shades, and rocky falls,
And from his fords and shallows, sent a voice   5
That flowed along my dreams? For this didst thou
O Derwent, travelling over the green plains
Near my 'sweet birth-place,' didst thou beauteous Stream
Make ceaseless music through the night and day,
Which with its steady cadence tempering   10
Our human waywardness, composed my thoughts
To more than infant softness, giving me,
Among the fretful dwellings of mankind,
A knowledge, a dim earnest of the calm
Which Nature breathes among the fields and groves?   15
    Beloved Derwent! fairest of all Streams!
Was it for this that I, a four year's child,
A naked Boy, among thy silent pools
Made one long bathing of a summer's day?
Basked in the sun, or plunged into thy streams,   20
Alternate, all a summer's day, or coursed
Over the sandy fields, and dashed the flowers
Of yellow grunsel, or when crag and hill,
The woods and distant Skiddaw's lofty height
Were bronzed with a deep radiance, stood alone,   25
A naked Savage in the thunder shower?
    And afterwards, 'twas in a later day
Though early, when upon the mountain-slope
The frost and breath of frosty wind had snapped
The last autumnal crocus, 'twas my joy   30
To wander half the night among the cliffs
And the smooth hollows, where the woodcocks ran
Along the moonlight turf. In thought and wish,
That time, my shoulder all with springes hung,
I was a fell destroyer. Gentle Powers!   35
Who give us happiness and call it peace!
When scudding on from snare to snare I plied
My anxious visitation, hurrying on,
Still hurrying hurrying onward, how my heart
Panted; among the scattered yew-trees, and the crags   40
That looked upon me, how my bosom beat
With expectation. Sometimes strong desire,
Resistless, overpowered me, and the bird
Which was the captive of another's toils
Became my prey; and when the deed was done   45
I heard among the solitary hills
Low breathings coming after me, and sounds

Of undistinguishable motion, steps
Almost as silent as the turf they trod.
    Nor less, in spring-time, when on southern banks   50
The shining sun had from his knot of leaves
Decoyed the primrose-flower, and when the vales
And woods were warm, was I a rover then
In the high places, on the lonesome peaks,
Among the mountains and the winds. Though mean   55
And though inglorious were my views, the end
Was not ignoble. Oh, when I have hung
Above the raven's nest, by knots of grass,
Or half-inch fissures in the slipp'ry rock,
But ill sustained, and almost, as it seemed,   60
Suspended by the blast which blew amain,
Shouldering the naked crag, oh at that time,
While on the perilous ridge I hung alone,
With what strange utterance did the loud dry wind
Blow through my ears! the sky seemed not a sky   65
Of earth, and with what motion moved the clouds!
    The mind of man is fashioned and built up
Even as a train of music: I believe
That there are spirits, which, when they would form
A favored being, from his very dawn   70
Of infancy do open out the clouds
As at the touch of lightning, seeking him
With gentle visitation; quiet Powers!
Retired and seldom recognized, yet kind,
And to the very meanest not unknown;   75
With me, though rarely, [in my early days]
They communed: others too there are who use,
Yet haply aiming at the self-same end,
Severer interventions, ministry
More palpable, and of their school was I.   80
    They guided me: one evening, led by them,
I went alone into a Shepherd's boat,
A skiff that to a willow-tree was tied
Within a rocky cave, its usual home;
The moon was up, the lake was shining clear   85
Among the hoary mountains: from the shore
I pushed, and struck the oars, and struck again
In cadence, and my little Boat moved on
Just like a man who walks with stately step
Though bent on speed. It was an act of stealth   90
And troubled pleasure; not without the voice
Of mountain-echoes did my boat move on,
Leaving behind her still on either side
Small circles glittering idly in the moon
Until they melted all into one track   95
Of sparkling light. A rocky steep uprose
Above the cavern of the willow tree,
And now, as suited one who proudly rowed
With his best skill, I fixed a steady view
Upon the top of that same craggy ridge,   100
The bound of the horizon, for behind
Was nothing—but the stars and the grey sky.
—She was an elfin pinnace; twenty times
I dipped my oars into the silent lake,

And, as I rose upon the stroke, my Boat   105
Went heaving through the water, like a swan—
When from behind that rocky steep, till then
The bound of the horizon, a huge Cliff,
As if with voluntary power instinct,
Upreared its head: I struck, and struck again,   110
And, growing still in stature, the huge cliff
Rose up between me and the stars, and still
With measured motion, like a living thing,
Strode after me. With trembling hands I turned,
And through the silent water stole my way   115
Back to the cavern of the willow-tree.
There, in her mooring-place I left my bark,
And through the meadows homeward went with grave
And serious thoughts: and after I had seen
That spectacle, for many days my brain   120
Worked with a dim and undetermined sense
Of unknown modes of being: in my thoughts
There was a darkness, call it solitude
Or blank desertion; no familiar shapes
Of hourly objects, images of trees,   125
Of sea or sky, no colours of green fields:
But huge and mighty forms, that do not live
Like living men, moved slowly through my mind
By day, and were the trouble of my dreams.
  Ah! not in vain ye Beings of the hills!   130
And ye that walk the woods and open heaths
By moon or star-light, thus from my first dawn
Of childhood did ye love to intertwine
The passions that build up our human soul,
Not with the mean and vulgar works of man,   135
But with high objects, with eternal things,
With life and nature, purifying thus
The elements of feeling and of thought,
And sanctifying by such discipline
Both pain and fear, until we recognise   140
A grandeur in the beatings of the heart.
  Nor was this fellowship vouchsafed to me
With stinted kindness. In November days,
When vapours, rolling down the valleys, made
A lonely scene more lonesome, among woods   145
At noon, and 'mid the calm of summer nights
When by the margin of the trembling lake
Beneath the gloomy hills I homeward went
In solitude, such intercourse was mine.
  And in the frosty season when the sun   150
Was set, and, visible for many a mile,
The cottage windows through the twilight blazed,
I heeded not the summons: clear and loud
The village clock tolled six; I wheeled about
Proud and exulting like an untired horse   155
That cares not for its home.—All shod with steel
We hissed along the polished ice, in games
Confederate, imitative of the chace
And woodland pleasures, the resounding horn,
The pack loud bellowing, and the hunted hare.   160
So through the darkness and the cold we flew,

And not a voice was idle: with the din,
Meanwhile, the precipices rang aloud,
The leafless trees and every icy crag
Tinkled like iron, while the distant hills   165
Into the tumult sent an alien sound
Of melancholy not unnoticed while the stars,
Eastward, were sparkling clear, and in the west
The orange sky of evening died away.
  Not seldom from the uproar I retired   170
Into a silent bay, or sportively
Glanced sideway leaving the tumultuous throng
To cut across the shadow of a star
That gleamed upon the ice: and oftentimes
When we had given our bodies to the wind   175
And all the shadowy banks on either side
Came sweeping through the darkness, spinning still
The rapid line of motion, then at once
Have I, reclining back upon my heels,
Stopped short; yet still the solitary cliffs   180
Wheeled by me, even as if the earth had rolled
With visible motion her diurnal round;
Behind me did they stretch in solemn train
Feebler and feebler, and I stood and watched
Till all was tranquil as a summer sea.   185
  Ye Powers of earth! ye Genii of the springs!
And ye that have your voices in the clouds
And ye that are Familiars of the lakes
And of the standing pools, I may not think
A vulgar hope was yours when ye employed   190
Such ministry, when ye through many a year
Thus by the agency of boyish sports
On caves and trees, upon the woods and hills,
Impressed upon all forms the characters
Of danger or desire, and thus did make   195
The surface of the universal earth
With meanings of delight, of hope and fear,
Work like a sea.
                    Not uselessly employed
I might pursue this theme through every change
Of exercise and sport to which the year   200
Did summon us in its delightful round.
We were a noisy crew: the sun in heaven
Beheld not vales more beautiful than ours
Nor saw a race in happiness and joy
More worthy of the fields where they were sown.   205
I would record with no reluctant voice
Our home amusements by the warm peat fire
At evening, when with pencil, and with slate
In square divisions parcelled out, and all
With crosses and with cyphers scribbled o'er,   210
We schemed and puzzled, head opposed to head
In strife too humble to be named in verse,
Or round the naked table, snow-white deal,
Cherry or maple, sate in close array
And to the combat—Lu or Whist—led on   215
A thick-ribbed army, not as in the world
Discarded and ungratefully thrown by

Even for the very service they had wrought,
But husbanded through many a long campaign.
Oh with what echoes on the board they fell—   220
Ironic diamonds, hearts of sable hue,
Queens gleaming through their splendour's last decay,
Knaves wrapt in one assimilating gloom,
And Kings indignant at the shame incurr'd
By royal visages. Meanwhile abroad   225
The heavy rain was falling, or the frost
Raged bitterly with keen and silent tooth,
And interrupting the impassioned game
Oft from the neighbouring lake the splitting ice
While it sank down towards the water sent   230
Among the meadows and the hills its long
And frequent yellings, imitative some
Of wolves that howl along the Bothnic main.
   Nor with less willing heart would I rehearse
The woods of autumn and their hidden bowers   235
With milk-white clusters hung; the rod and line,
True symbol of the foolishness of hope,
Which with its strong enchantment led me on
By rocks and pools where never summer-star
Impressed its shadow, to forlorn cascades   240
Among the windings of the mountain-brooks;
The kite, in sultry calms from some high hill
Sent up, ascending thence till it was lost
Among the fleecy clouds, in gusty days
Launched from the lower grounds, and suddenly   245
Dash'd headlong—and rejected by the storm.
All these and more with rival claims demand
Grateful acknowledgement. It were a song
Venial, and such as if I rightly judge
I might protract unblamed; but I perceive   250
That much is overlooked, and we should ill
Attain our object if from delicate fears
Of breaking in upon the unity
Of this my argument I should omit
To speak of such effects as cannot here   255
Be regularly classed, yet tend no less
To the same point, the growth of mental power
And love of Nature's works.
                   Ere I had seen
Eight summers (and 'twas in the very week
When I was first transplanted to thy vale,   260
Beloved Hawkshead! when thy paths, thy shores
And brooks were like a dream of novelty
To my half-infant mind) I chanced to cross
One of those open fields which, shaped like ears,
Make green peninsulas on Esthwaite's lake.   265
Twilight was coming on, yet through the gloom
I saw distinctly on the opposite shore
Beneath a tree and close by the lake side
A heap of garments, as if left by one
Who there was bathing: half an hour I watched   270
And no one owned them: meanwhile the calm lake
Grew dark with all the shadows on its breast,
And now and then a leaping fish disturbed

The breathless stillness. The succeeding day
There came a company, and in their boat   275
Sounded with iron hooks and with long poles.
At length the dead man 'mid that beauteous scene
Of trees, and hills, and water, bolt upright
Rose with his ghastly face. I might advert
To numerous accidents in flood or field,   280
Quarry or moor, or 'mid the winter snows,
Distresses and disasters, tragic facts
Of rural history that impressed my mind
With images, to which in following years
Far other feelings were attached, with forms   285
That yet exist with independent life
And, like their archetypes, know no decay.
      There are in our existence spots of time
Which with distinct pre-eminence retain
A fructifying virtue, whence, depressed   290
By trivial occupations and the round
Of ordinary intercourse, our minds
(Especially the imaginative power)
Are nourished, and invisibly repaired.
Such moments chiefly seem to have their date   295
In our first childhood. I remember well
('Tis of an early season that I speak,
The twilight of rememberable life)
While I was yet an urchin, one who scarce
Could hold a bridle, with ambitious hopes   300
I mounted, and we rode towards the hills;
We were a pair of horsemen: honest James
Was with me, my encourager and guide.
We had not travelled long ere some mischance
Disjoined me from my comrade, and through fear   305
Dismounting, down the rough and stony moor
I led my horse and, stumbling on, at length
Came to a bottom where in former times
A man, the murderer of his wife, was hung
In irons; mouldered was the gibbet mast,   310
The bones were gone, the iron and the wood,
Only a long green ridge of turf remained
Whose shape was like a grave. I left the spot,
And, reascending the bare slope, I saw
A naked pool that lay beneath the hills,   315
The beacon on the summit, and more near
A girl who bore a pitcher on her head
And seemed with difficult steps to force her way
Against the blowing wind. It was in truth
An ordinary sight but I should need   320
Colours and words that are unknown to man
To paint the visionary dreariness
Which, while I looked all round for my lost guide,
Did, at that time, invest the naked pool,
The beacon on the lonely eminence,   325
The woman and her garments vexed and tossed
By the strong wind. Nor less I recollect
(Long after, though my childhood had not ceased)
Another scene which left a kindred power
Implanted in my mind.

                    One Christmas time,
The day before the holidays began,
Feverish, and tired and restless, I went forth
Into the fields, impatient for the sight
Of those three horses which should bear us home,
My Brothers and myself. There was a crag,   335
An eminence which from the meeting point
Of two highways ascending overlooked
At least a long half-mile of those two roads,
By each of which the expected steeds might come,
The choice uncertain. Thither I repaired   340
Up to the highest summit; 'twas a day
Stormy, and rough, and wild, and on the grass
I sate, half-sheltered by a naked wall;
Upon my right hand was a single sheep,
A whistling hawthorn on my left, and there,   345
Those two companions at my side, I watched
With eyes intensely straining as the mist
Gave intermitting prospects of the wood
And plain beneath. Ere I to school returned
That dreary time, ere I had been ten days   350
A dweller in my Father's house, he died,
And I and my two Brothers, orphans then,
Followed his body to the grave. The event
With all the sorrow which it brought appeared
A chastisement, and when I called to mind   355
That day so lately passed when from the crag
I looked in such anxiety of hope,
With trite reflections of morality
Yet with the deepest passion I bowed low
To God, who thus corrected my desires;   360
And afterwards the wind, and sleety rain,
And all the business of the elements,
The single sheep, and the one blasted tree,
And the bleak music of that old stone wall,
The noise of wood and water, and the mist   365
Which on the line of each of those two roads
Advanced in such indisputable shapes,
All these were spectacles and sounds to which
I often would repair, and thence would drink
As at a fountain, and I do not doubt   370
That in this later time when storm and rain
Beat on my roof at midnight, or by day
When I am in the woods, unknown to me
The workings of my spirit thence are brought.
            [Nor sedulous to trace]   375
How Nature by collateral interest
And by extrinsic passion peopled first
My mind with forms, or beautiful or grand,
And made me love them, may I well forget
How other pleasures have been mine, and joys   380
Of subtler origin, how I have felt
Not seldom, even in that tempestuous time,
Those hallowed and pure motions of the sense
Which seem in their simplicity to own
An intellectual charm, that calm delight   385
Which, if I err not, surely must belong

To those first-born affinities that fit
Our new existence to existing things
And in our dawn of being constitute
The bond of union betwixt life and joy.   390
   Yes, I remember when the changeful earth
And twice five seasons on my mind had stamped
The faces of the moving year, even then,
A Child, I held unconscious intercourse
With the eternal Beauty, drinking in   395
A pure organic pleasure from the lines
Of curling mist or from the level plain
Of waters coloured by the steady clouds.
   The sands of Westmoreland, the creeks and bays
Of Cumbria's rocky limits, they can tell   400
How when the sea threw off his evening shade
And to the Shepherd's hut beneath the crags
Did send sweet notice of the rising moon,
How I have stood to images like these
A stranger, linking with the spectacle   405
No body of associated forms
And bringing with me no peculiar sense
Of quietness or peace, yet I have stood
Even while my eye has moved o'er three long leagues
Of shining water, gathering, as it seemed,   410
Through the wide surface of that field of light
New pleasure, like a bee among the flowers.
   Thus often in those fits of vulgar joy
Which through all seasons on a child's pursuits
Are prompt attendants, 'mid that giddy bliss   415
Which like a tempest works along the blood
And is forgotten, even then I felt
Gleams like the flashing of a shield; the earth
And common face of Nature spake to me
Rememberable things: sometimes, 'tis true,   420
By quaint associations, yet not vain
Nor profitless if haply they impressed
Collateral objects and appearances,
Albeit lifeless then, and doomed to sleep
Until maturer seasons called them forth   425
To impregnate and to elevate the mind.
——And if the vulgar joy by its own weight
Wearied itself out of the memory,
The scenes which were a witness of that joy
Remained, in their substantial lineaments   430
Depicted on the brain, and to the eye
Were visible, a daily sight: and thus
By the impressive agency of fear,
By pleasure and repeated happiness,
So frequently repeated, and by force   435
Of obscure feelings representative
Of joys that were forgotten, these same scenes
So beauteous and majestic in themselves,
Though yet the day was distant, did at length
Become habitually dear, and all   440
Their hues and forms were by invisible links
Allied to the affections.

                          I began
My story early, feeling, as I fear,
The weakness of a human love for days
Disowned by memory, ere the birth of spring   445
Planting my snow-drops among winter snows.
Nor will it seem to thee, my Friend, so prompt
In sympathy, that I have lengthened out
With fond and feeble tongue a tedious tale.
Meanwhile my hope has been that I might fetch   450
Reproaches from my former years, whose power
May spur me on, in manhood now mature,
To honourable toil. Yet, should it be
That this is but an impotent desire,
That I by such inquiry am not taught   455
To understand myself, nor thou to know
With better knowledge how the heart was framed
Of him thou lovest, need I dread from thee
Harsh judgements if I am so loth to quit
Those recollected hours that have the charm   460
Of visionary things, and lovely forms
And sweet sensations that throw back our life
And make our infancy a visible scene
On which the sun is shining ?—

References

Abrams, M. H. (ed.), *English Romantic Poets: Modern Essays in Criticism*, Oxford University Press, second edn., 1975 (set book).

Beer, John, *Coleridge's Poetic Intelligence*, Macmillan, 1977.

Coleridge, Samuel Taylor, *Biographia Literaria*, 1817; ed. J. Shawcross (two vols), Oxford University Press, 1907; revised edn., 1954.

Coleridge, Samuel Taylor, *Selected Poems of Samuel Taylor Coleridge*, ed. James Reeves, Heinemann, 1959 (set book).

Ferry, David, *The Limits of Mortality: An Essay on Wordsworth's Major Poems*, Wesleyan University Press, 1959.

Fischer, Ernst, *The Necessity of Art*, 1959; trans. Anna Bostock, Penguin, 1963.

Grant, Allan, *A Preface to Coleridge*, Longman, 1972.

Harding, A. J., *Coleridge and the Idea of Love*, Oxford University Press, 1974.

Hartman, Geoffrey, 'The Via Naturaliter Negativa', in *Wordsworth: A Collection of Critical Essays*, ed. M. H. Abrams, Prentice-Hall (Twentieth Century Views), 1972.

Lockridge, Laurence S., *Coleridge the Moralist*, Cornell University Press, 1977.

Lovejoy, A. O., and Boas, George, *Primitivism and Relative Ideas in Antiquity*, Johns Hopkins University Press, 1935.

Lowes, John Livingston, *The Road to Xanadu*, 1927; Houghton Mifflin, 1955.

MacFarland, Thomas, 'The Symbiosis of Coleridge and Wordsworth', Chapter 1 in *Romanticism and the Forms of Ruin: Wordsworth, Coleridge, and Modalities of Fragmentation*, Princeton University, Press, 1981.

McMaster, Graham (ed.), *William Wordsworth: A Critical Anthology*, Penguin, 1972.

Mayo, Robert, 'The Contemporaneity of the *Lyrical Ballads*', in *Wordsworth: A Collection of Critical Essays*, ed. M. H. Abrams, Prentice-Hall (Twentieth Century Views), 1972.

Mill, John Stuart, 'Coleridge', 1840; reprinted in *Mill on Bentham and Coleridge*, with an introduction by F. R. Leavis, Chatto and Windus, 1950.

Oxford Book of Ballads, The, ed. Arthur Quiller-Couch, Oxford University Press, 1910.

Sheats, Paul D., 'The *Lyrical Ballads*', 1973; reprinted in Abrams (ed.), *English Romantic Poets: Modern Essays in Criticism* (see above).

Trilling, Lionel, 'The Fate of Pleasure', in *Beyond Culture*, 1965; Oxford University Press, 1980.

Trilling, Lionel, 'The Immortality Ode', in *The Liberal Imagination*, 1951; Oxford University Press, 1981.

Whalley, George, *The Mariner and the Albatross*, University of Toronto, 1947.

Willey, Basil, *Samuel Taylor Coleridge*, Chatto and Windus, 1972.

Wordsworth, Dorothy, *Journals of Dorothy Wordsworth*, ed. Mary Moorman, Oxford University Press, 1971.

Wordsworth, William and Dorothy, *The Letters of William and Dorothy Wordsworth*, vol. I, *The Early Years, 1787–1805*, ed. Ernest de Selincourt, Oxford University Press; revised edn. by Chester L. Shaver, 1967.

Wordsworth, William, *Poetical Works*, ed. Thomas Hutchinson, Oxford University Press, 1904; ed. Ernest de Selincourt, 1936, 1950.

Wordsworth, William, *The Prelude*, 1805 text, ed. Ernest de Selincourt, corrected edn. by Stephen Gill, Oxford University Press, 1933, 1960, 1970 (set book).

Wordsworth, William, *Selected Poems*, ed. Walford Davies, Dent (Everyman's Library), 1975 (set book).

Yeats, W. B., 'William Blake and his Illustrations to the *Divine Comedy*', 1897; in *Essays and Introductions*, Macmillan, 1961.

Further reading

Biography

Hanson, Lawrence, *The Life of Samuel Taylor Coleridge*, Allen and Unwin, 1938. An excellent biography of Coleridge's earlier years, covering his main creative period as a poet.

Moorman, Mary, *Wordsworth, a Biography*, Oxford University Press, 1957 and 1965 (two vols). The standard modern biography of Wordsworth.

Criticism

Wordsworth

Abrams M. H. (ed.), *Wordsworth: A Collection of Critical Essays*, Prentice-Hall (Twentieth Century Views), 1972. This modestly-priced paperback collection of critical essays reflects a wide variety of approaches to Wordsworth, including quite recent ones.

Ferry, David, *The Limits of Mortality: An Essay on Wordsworth's Major Poems* (see References). An advanced work by a leading Wordsworth critic.

Jones, Alun, R., and Tydeman, William, *Wordsworth's Lyrical Ballads: A Casebook*, Macmillan, 1972. A modestly-priced paperback edition of modern critical studies of *Lyrical Ballads*.

Leavis, F. R., 'Wordsworth', in *Revaluation: Tradition and Development in English Poetry*, 1936; Penguin, 1964. A perceptive and influential study of Wordsworth's sensibility and achievement as a poet.

McMaster, Graham (ed.), *William Wordsworth: A Critical Anthology* (see References). Includes early reviews and critiques.

Perkins, David, *The Quest for Permanence: The Symbolism of Wordsworth, Shelley and Keats*, Harvard University Press, 1959. An advanced comparative study.

Purkis, John, *A Preface to Wordsworth*, Longman, 1970. A useful first introduction to Wordsworth's life and works, with valuable illustrations.

Salvesen, Christopher, *The Landscape of Memory: A Study of Wordsworth's Poetry*, Edward Arnold, 1965. An extended treatment of the ideas sketched in Radio Programme 4.

Stallknecht, N. P., *Strange Seas of Thought: Studies in William Wordsworth's Philosophy of Man and Nature*, Indiana University Press, 1966. An advanced, stimulating study.

Willey, Basil, ' "Nature" in Wordsworth', in *The Eighteenth-Century Background*, Chatto and Windus, 1940. A very helpful setting of Wordsworth in his philosophical context.

Coleridge

Coburn, Kathleen (ed.), *Coleridge: A Collection of Critical Essays*, Prentice-Hall (Twentieth Century Views), 1968. Similar to the *Wordsworth* in this series, ed. Abrams, above.

Everest, Kelvin, *Coleridge's Secret Ministry: The Context of the Conversation Poems, 1795–1798*, Harvester Press, 1979. Places the 'conversation poems' in their political as well as literary context.

House, Humphry, *Coleridge*, Rupert Hart-Davis, 1953. A good brief general introduction to Coleridge, man and poet.

Jackson, J. R. de J. (ed.), *Coleridge: The Critical Heritage*, Routledge and Kegan Paul, 1970. An extensive collection of early reviews and articles on Coleridge, of great historical interest.

Lowes, John Livingston, *The Road to Xanadu* (see References). A famous piece of extended detective work on Coleridge's use of his sources in 'The Ancient Mariner' and 'Kubla Khan'.

Willey, Basil, *Samuel Taylor Coleridge* (see References). A helpful and clear account of Coleridge as thinker.

General

Abrams, M. H., *The Mirror and the Lamp*, 1953; Norton, 1958. On the Romantic attitude to creativity.

Nuttall, A. D., 'Sentiment and Sensibility', in *A Common Sky: Philosophy and the Literary Imagination*, Chatto and Windus/Sussex University Press, 1974.

A362 Romantic Poetry